A RED FAMILY

Junius, Gladys, & Barbara Scales

Mickey Friedman

with an Afterword by

Barbara Scales

and Historical Essay by

Gail Williams O'Brien

UNIVERSITY OF ILLINOIS PRESS
Urbana and Chicago

© 2009 by Mickey Friedman
All rights reserved
Manufactured in the United States of America
1 2 3 4 5 C P 5 4 3 2 1
∞ This book is printed on acid-free paper.

Library of Congress Cataloging-in-Publication Data
Friedman, Mickey.
A red family : Junius, Gladys, and Barbara Scales /
Mickey Friedman with an afterword by Barbara Scales
and historical essay by Gail Williams O'Brien.
p. cm.
Includes bibliographical references and index.
ISBN 978-0-252-03396-4 (cloth : alk. paper) —
ISBN 978-0-252-07604-6 (pbk. : alk. paper)
1. Scales, Junius Irving.
2. Scales, Gladys.
3. Scales, Barbara.
4. Communists—United States—Biography.
5. Communism—United States—History—20th century.
I. O'Brien, Gail Williams II. Title.
HX84.S4F75   2009
335.4092'273—dc22   2008032932

To Barbara's parents, and to mine.

P.62

CONTENTS

Illustrations follow page 82.

PREFACE

Mickey Friedman

This is the story of a Red family: Junius, Gladys, and Barbara Scales. "Red" in the older sense of the word. Because, before there were red and blue states, there were the Reds, the Communists.

Junius Scales was the son of one of the wealthiest families in North Carolina. He left privilege to live in a poor textile-mill village, and in 1939, on his nineteenth birthday, he joined the American Communist Party (CPUSA). One of the few publicly known Communists in the South, Junius organized textile workers, fought segregation, went underground, evaded the FBI, was indicted, arrested, unsuccessfully appealed his conviction to the Supreme Court, and went to prison.[1]

Gladys Scales came to Communism from a very different place. She was born in Brooklyn, New York. Her Jewish father was a successful small businessman who lost everything in the Depression. As her family fell apart around her and she battled her own depression, Communism offered the opportunity to imagine and work for a more caring world.

By the time their daughter Barbara was born, Junius and Gladys were under siege and anti-Communism shaped American politics. In an attempt to protect her and allow her the chance for a more normal childhood, they didn't tell Barbara that she was a "red-diaper" baby.

A Red Family is an oral history, a family's account of their rich and complicated journey in American radical politics. It's a story few Americans know, a part of our history that is rarely talked about.

Many others have tried to analyze the Communist movement in greater depth: Theodore Draper; Irving Howe and Lewis Coser; David Shannon; Nathan Glazer; and several ex-Communists, including George Charney, Joseph Starobin, and Al Richmond, have evaluated in detail the political workings of the Party.[2] In the last several decades, writing about and analyzing American Communism has become a popular pastime. I recently found a list of more than eight thousand scholarly books and articles about the Party.

A Red Family is based on interviews conducted with the Scaleses beginning in March 1971. Except for a single session with Junius when Barbara was present, the interviews were conducted individually to preserve spontaneity and to capture their separate recollections. Each session, recorded on a simple cassette machine, lasted three to four hours; Junius, Gladys, and Barbara were each interviewed three or four different times.

Let me be clear: I was not then, nor am I now, a historian. I was, and continue to be, a writer, and more recently a filmmaker and political activist. Perhaps a professional historian would have asked different questions and elicited different answers.

But I am, like Barbara, a "red-diaper" baby, so the book was very important to me for reasons I thought I knew then and, after a decade of therapy, for reasons I better understand now.

Unlike Barbara, I always knew about my father's politics. He took me to May Day parades in Union Square; I went with him to the offices of the *Daily Worker,* the newspaper of the Communist Party, where he was an editor. If I was fairly obedient, I'd come home with a photo of Jackie Robinson, the Communist Party's favorite ballplayer. It wasn't by accident that even though I grew up in the Bronx, I rooted for the Yankees' arch rivals, the Brooklyn Dodgers, the team that integrated baseball.

I couldn't escape the reality of my father's politics: from the ever-present FBI men assigned to follow him on Kingsbridge Road (and their occasional attempts to get me to talk about my dad) to our tapped telephone. There was no getting off the extraordinary tightrope I had to walk. Proud, like most sons of their fathers, I had been sworn to secrecy. I could never talk about the Party or my father's job. "Printer" was the magic answer to any question about what he did for a living.

Children aren't meant to live double lives, but I got to be good at it. Except for a first-grade slip that landed me on the wooden bench outside the principal's office, I kept the secret until college. My father, already out of the Party for four years, was called to testify before the House Un-American Activities Committee, and his appearance made it to the New York newspapers.

For me, the cold war was anything but cold; it was ferocious and unrelenting. For most Americans, my father and Communists like Junius were the enemy. All you had to do was watch an episode of "I Led Three Lives" on television—and those were the days when just about anything that made it to television was regarded as near-truth. Each new episode from 1953 to 1956 seemed more diabolical than the last. Those TV Communists were masters of deception, skilled in assassination, bomb making, and industrial sabotage. When it came to insidious treachery, those guys would give Osama bin Laden a run for his money.

Older readers might remember the movie *The Invasion of the Body Snatchers,* with its evil, alien cadre whose pods grow replacement mothers and fathers and sisters and brothers. Younger readers have their own version: the synthetic Cylons of *Battlestar Galactica.* During the cold war, the Communists were Body Snatchers and Cylons, and unlike the swarthy "Islamofascist-extremists" of today's terror nightmares, they looked like ordinary Americans. Communists could blend in undetected: they taught in local schools, worked beside you in the office or factory, served in the army, went bowling. Yet, according to the myth, what they wanted most was to take away everything Americans loved best: liberty and freedom, the right to worship God, progress and individual initiative, and the opportunity to succeed.

As you will see, Junius and Gladys were nothing like those caricatures. Nor was my father.

And so, for personal and political reasons, I wanted Americans to hear another side of the story. I wanted *A Red Family* to be something other than traditional history: a conversational book, with the sense and sound of life stories being shared—the Communist experience from the inside out.

I wanted Junius, Gladys, and Barbara to speak from the heart. I also wanted the feminine perspective. At that time, books about politics and political life primarily came from men, and we didn't often enough hear the voices of women. But most of all, I wanted and needed to make Communists real, to help a Red family make itself known to other American families. With plain talk, I hoped to bridge the political divide and move past a large backlog of ignorance and bias about the Left.

I was working full-time during the day as a file clerk for the Southern Christian Leadership Conference, and I transcribed these interviews from seven to eleven each night. Listening to the Scaleses speak over and over, making sure I got their words down accurately, helped me to absorb the material, to learn and appreciate the unique rhythms of Junius, Gladys, and Barbara.

I had hundreds of pages of transcripts. I spent hours editing, eliminating the repetition that is so common to oral storytelling, finding ways to remove the questions and enable the answers to stand on their own, to build a narrative that moved from the page to the imagination. As I came closer to shaping each of the separate stories, I began to think more about family dynamics. I knew from my own family's history during the 1950s and Mc-Carthyism that people under stress, family members besieged by powerful outside pressures and unwilling to burden others, often can't or won't confide their fears to one another.

Because the interviews were conducted separately, and because Junius, Gladys, and Barbara were often talking for the first time about some of their most difficult and complicated experiences, I began to appreciate that I knew things about each of them that they probably hadn't shared with each other. As I reread the interviews with Junius and Gladys, I understood that they had been so overwhelmed with Junius's trials and imprisonment that they hadn't had a clear idea of Barbara's experience of those times.

This only impressed upon me more the large responsibility I had taken on as the temporary custodian of their life stories. As I began to think more about their family life, I considered interweaving their stories. And while I was now re-creating another form of duplication—and overlapping time—I was doing so to reveal how the same event might be experienced in very different ways. This added new and interesting perspectives to their histories—the very form of *A Red Family* reflects that these are the intertwined strands of one family.

As you read this book, you're looking back into time times two. These are the recollections of Junius, Gladys, and Barbara in 1971 as they described events spanning more than four decades. You are reading them in a world that has changed a great deal since I finished the book in 1973. Just the smallest, perhaps most insignificant example: the book was written at a time when cut and paste meant just that. Many a time I moved typewritten segments of the book from section to section, page to page, by scotch-taping bits and pieces of paper together.

Not long after I completed the book in 1973, I found a publisher. When I informed the Scaleses, I learned that Gladys had changed her mind about publication. She didn't feel up to having her story out in the world at large, unwilling to deal with yet another round of national publicity. While I had put my heart and mind and soul into the book, I could easily imagine the public exposure the Scales family would once more face and understood why she had changed her mind.

In her interviews, Gladys was extremely open and unguarded and talked about her battle with depression with unusual frankness. And, sadly, I didn't know or appreciate then how badly her physical health was deteriorating.

It pained me to put aside a book I thought could be useful, but I moved on to other projects: teaching, community organizing, making films, and writing plays. Junius still yearned to tell his story, because in 1987, six years after Gladys's death, his autobiography was published by the University of Georgia Press.[3] I found it difficult to read. How much of my difficulty came from residual sadness and how much came from the fact that his book was so different from this one, I can't determine. *Cause at Heart* is a meticulously prepared, remarkably detailed account of Junius's journey, yet so different from the spontaneous conversations I recorded. I missed the counterpoints of Gladys and Barbara.

Junius died on August 5, 2002. Three years later, in May 2005, Barbara called me out of the blue. Gladys and Junius were both gone, and she thought the interviews were a part of history—the time had come to publish the book.

When I first thought about the prospects for this book, I wondered whether anyone under the age of thirty even knew there were such people as American Communists. But as events transpired in the last half of 2005 and through 2006, I realized that *A Red Family* is more relevant than ever.

As a Brooklyn Dodgers fan growing up in the heart of New York Yankee territory in the Bronx, I hated the machinelike precision with which the Yankees won year after year. But I was always able to transcend my baseball bias to appreciate the enormous wit and wisdom of the great Yankee catcher, Yogi Berra. Yogi best articulated one of the great underlying principles of human history: "It's déjà vu all over again!" For me, so many things seem eerily familiar.

I know, of course, that there are very big differences between Communists and Islamic radicals; yet I am struck by the common strains of the anti-Communist crusade and the War on Terror. The terrorists of Al Qaeda represent a very small percentage of the world's Muslims. But many in the Islamic world believe that the West, and the United States in particular, does not respect their culture and traditions and is predisposed for selfish reasons to intervene in their affairs.

Iraq is not Vietnam, but we seem to be making the same kinds of mistakes in Iraq as we did in Vietnam. Iraq's weapons of mass destruction have proven as illusory as the falsified 1964 North Vietnamese attack on U.S. destroyers in the Gulf of Tonkin. Confusing secular Iraq with Taliban-run Afghanistan seems as simplistic and reductionist as the domino theory, which supposedly justified the U.S. invasion of Vietnam. If you think I'm hallucinating the shadows of yesterday's cold war and McCarthyism in today's world, consider these excerpts from George W. Bush's October 6, 2005 speech about Iraq:

We're facing a radical ideology with inalterable objectives: to enslave whole nations and intimidate the world. . . . The murderous ideology of the Islamic radicals is the great challenge of our new century. Yet, in many ways, this fight resembles the struggle against communism in the last century. Like the ideology of communism, Islamic radicalism is elitist, led by a self-appointed vanguard that presumes to speak for the Muslim masses.[4]

Then add legislation like the USA Patriot Act—a contemporary version of the Smith Act—which defines "domestic terrorism" with the broadest of brushes: "[A]cts dangerous to human life that are a violation of the criminal laws of the United States or of any State" that "appear to be intended . . . to influence the policy of a government by intimidation or coercion."[5]

We need to respond forcefully and decisively to acts of terror. But once more, the government has granted itself near blanket powers to monitor legitimate political activity and even to intrude on people's right to access controversial literature.[6]

In December 2005, we learned about the extensive surreptitious eavesdropping on American citizens by the secretive National Security Administration.[7] The *New York Times* revealed that the FBI had been spying on environmental, antipoverty, and peace groups,[8] and *U.S. News and World Report* claimed that the federal government has without search warrants secretly monitored mosques, stores, and homes of Muslims in five states.[9]

This sense of a recurring, familiar danger to our civil liberties and our precious right to dissent convinces me that a new generation can learn much from *A Red Family*.

Several generations ago, American Communists became the new Salem witches. We did a disservice to them and to ourselves by insisting that their politics sprang from the breast of a foreign power rather than from the American radical vision itself. We are in danger of repeating this mistake by targeting well-meaning critics of our foreign policy.

In 1960 I began my own political life. Moved by the bravery of the young black students who refused to leave the whites-only section of the Woolworth's lunch counter in Greensboro, North Carolina, I picketed my local Woolworth's. I became a member of the Student Nonviolent Coordinating Committee and Students for a Democratic Society. In 1965, I joined thousands of others on the last leg of Martin Luther King's Selma-to-Montgomery march for voting rights. A year later, I helped organize a sit-in at City College in New York to protest the college administration's decision to release students' class standing to local draft boards.

Junius Scales and my father were both deeply wounded by their failures in the Communist movement. Profoundly depressed and discouraged, they sat on the sidelines during the civil rights and anti–Vietnam War movements. And it's clear to me that my generation's New Left suffered by not having the guidance of former Party activists like Junius. To some extent, we repeated many of their mistakes: spurred by our rage over the mindless slaughter in Vietnam, we often moved too far in front of ordinary Americans. We were often too strident and too impatient and didn't build strong enough bridges to the labor movement or transcend differences of race, class, gender, and sexual preference.

Of course, like members of the Old Left, the movements of the 1960s were under attack from the very beginning. The murder of the civil rights workers James Chaney, Andrew Goodman, and Michael Schwerner in Mississippi, the bombing of black churches, the deaths of the Black Panthers, and the assassinations of Malcolm X, Martin Luther King Jr., and Robert Kennedy made clear the price to be paid for the growing grassroots demands for social and racial justice and participatory democracy. By the beginning of the 1970s, one could not go into the streets to demand an end to American intervention in Vietnam without being greeted by police clubs, tear gas, or finally the bullets at Jackson State and Kent State.

Our responses to this violence ranged from fear to fury. Many dropped political resistance in favor of a safer, more "normal" life; some moved to the country to create alternative communities; and a tiny few chose the rage of the Weather Underground. We did much to change the country for the better: We built and sustained a decade-long opposition to the war in Vietnam; we worked hard to dismantle segregation; and while not excusing our excesses, from the deadly apathy of the 1950s we brought forth a decade of energy and enthusiasm.

And yet, a clear-eyed look at today's growing gap between rich and poor, the global ecological crisis, the pale response to the unnecessary and illegal war in Iraq, and the blatant reality of the two Americas revealed by the response to Hurricane Katrina show how far we have fallen short of our dream to transform America. Any honest witness to the stark images of black families left behind to suffer the deadly chaos of a sinking New Orleans must see how much we need to continue Junius and Gladys's commitment to confront racism.

I believe it's necessary to restore our sense of the radical tradition in American life, to consider our debt to those who've prompted us to move beyond our comfort levels and demand social progress. And for all the obvious pitfalls

of organized opposition, we suffer today for the lack of a self-conscious radical movement to renew the work and spirit of the generations of American
rebels before us, the absence of an effective, critical Left. Junius and Gladys
would have been the first to insist that any movement for social and political
change be founded upon principles of mutual respect and democratic debate
and participation. And that members be ever-vigilant that these fundamental
principles are not sacrificed for expediency or personal power.

Such a radical democratic movement points to the gaps between rhetoric
and reality, forces us to acknowledge the needs of the less powerful, and trans-
forms aspiration into action. In his dissent in the Scales decision, Supreme
Court Justice William Douglas reminded us of the profoundly American
tradition of radical action: "Belief in the principle of revolution is deep in our
traditions. The Declaration of Independence proclaims it. . . . This right of
revolution has been and is a part of the fabric of our institutions."[10] But only a
radical movement grounded in American experience and fully responsive to
its membership and the American people can fully serve these purposes.

As I look back on the political lives of Junius and Gladys Scales, I am struck
by the rigor of their self-examination and self-criticism. It is important to
remember that the Communists were always the smallest of minorities. Unlike the Bolsheviks in the Soviet Union, American Communists never held
institutional power—they never had control over Congress, the courts, or the
presidency. Theirs were the errors of the powerless, not the powerful. But such
was the power of Junius's conscience, so strict were the standards he set for
himself, that he never failed to take responsibility for his mistakes. His inability
to see the crimes of the Soviets and his failure to demand honesty, integrity,
and accountability from Party leaders haunted him until his dying day. And
perhaps because his hopes were so high and his intentions so positive, his
mistakes in the end seemed to him larger than his accomplishments.

Ironically, he was tougher on himself and his political party than most
active members of the Democratic or Republican parties, parties that wield
power over the lives, not only of the American people, but—as we have seen
in Vietnam, Central America, and now Iraq—the lives of others across the
globe. Unfortunately, their failures have far greater consequences.

For all the Communist Party's great mistakes, its membership kept alive
the desire for something better. And as the story of the Scales family shows,
the stubborn strength and urge to struggle, the sense of possibility itself, is
passed, if not from parent to child, from one generation to the next. It's not
the work of the witch but the endless urge to be free.

ACKNOWLEDGMENTS

I am grateful for the help of Katherine Jones and Anne Kofke, who began this journey with me. At various times over the years, Robert Asher at the University of Connecticut and Barbara Resnik at Simon's Rock College at Bard provided encouragement by making the unpublished manuscript available to their students.

Many thanks to Gail Williams O'Brien for her very thoughtful concluding essay.

I am indebted to Laurie Matheson of the University of Illinois Press, who answered my query letter and read my manuscript with the enthusiasm every author dreams of. She has provided me with continuing and steadfast support.

And lastly, I am proud to acknowledge Barbara Scales, who has allowed me the honor of sharing her family's story and added a powerful epilogue.

A RED FAMILY

one

Junius

Off and on for close to eighteen years I was a Communist Party leader from the South. I came from a very distinguished southern family which had been in Virginia and then North Carolina since 1623. My paternal grandfather was a big slaveholder, and my father was born in 1870. He became a lawyer, politician, and real-estate developer and was fabulously wealthy. By the time I was born in 1920, he was many times a millionaire, so I grew up pretty much in the lap of luxury. We lived in a thirty-six-room house on a lake on a marvelous wilderness estate a half-mile from anyone.

My father was fifty years old when I was born, and I was the youngest of his second family. He had raised a family earlier and, when his first wife died, had married my mother, twenty-odd years younger. I was an uncle by the time I was two.

My father had about three thousand volumes in his library and read omnivorously. He was forever buying me books. One of my favorite areas of reading, because it was his, was reading about the Civil War, and a great many of his books were slanted from the southern side. My first disagreements with him began when I was somewhere between eleven and twelve and decided that Abraham Lincoln was great. Robert E. Lee was my father's hero, and we used to have some rip-snorting arguments, although he did acknowledge Lincoln had a lot of character.

I had a somewhat lonely childhood and didn't go to public school till I was twelve. I had a tutor, an older woman who was a very able retired school-teacher. Everything about the life I lived was easygoing and unpressured. I'd sit and daydream while I was working on whatever assignment she'd give me.

My desk had pictures of all kinds of little dogs; it didn't exactly make for a disciplined intellectual approach to things. But she was quite pleasant, and we got along well.

My relationships with both my parents were very close. My father was warm and gregarious, although he was quite ill with several varieties of heart disease and substantially invalid by the time I was nine. He had to stay in bed half the time and could go upstairs only once a day.

He was a gentleman farmer and just loved to grow vegetables. Of course, the outside man had to do most of the physical work, but my father knew every plant and was a great experimenter with different varieties of vegetables. One year he went squash crazy, and we had eighteen different kinds of squash. He was also very fond of flowers. One of his favorites was narcissus (jonquils) and he had thirty-two varieties. We'd walk through the grounds between the house and the lake, quite a distance, and see whether I could tell him which of the thirty-two we saw before we got to the tiny marker in the ground. I couldn't tell you any of them now.

My father was a very good amateur forester, and he and I used to go out and prune trees. I provided the muscle power, and he would tell me what to do. I love anything in the way of trees, but I was never very much on the vegetable-garden thing.

Being the mistress of this huge house was an enormous occupation for my mother. She had a glass-enclosed conservatory with tiled floors, a huge room, twenty by forty feet, a showplace with magnificent indoor plants. Everything she touched just seemed to flourish. She made ferns do just whatever she wanted them to. Spring, summer, and fall, the garden was quite magnificent. Her rose garden was so gorgeous it used to be open to the public about two weeks a year. She got great pleasure out of that.

Her main hobby, though, was my father, and she couldn't have been more attentive and solicitous, though of course her children took up a lot of her time. She would read to me, and my aunt did, too. It seemed that everybody was reading to me, even my brother and sister—they read the funny pages to me. I learned to read when I was about four, and when I got somebody to read to me after that it was sheer fakery.

I was learning every word I would see in print and shocked my mother no end. Once, when I was about four, in a roomful of company, I tugged at her and asked, "Mom, what does k-o-t-e-x spell?" I wanted to make sure I had it down pat. Of course, in the 1920s people just didn't talk about such things, and I watched her turn beet red. She said, "Never mind, don't ask me that." I made a few choice bloopers like that.

My brother was four years older than I, and my sister five, and they teamed together while I was the annoying brat. As big brothers have a way of doing, my brother used to tear me to shreds. You couldn't manage too much conceit with a brother who had a pretty good gift of sarcasm and could knock the pretensions out of you with great ease. He could also knock the stuffing out of me. We used to fight something awful, and he used to torment me. Once, in sheer frustration, I grabbed the first thing to hand and bashed him in the head with an ice skate. It must have impressed him because he stayed away from me for a while. I think he's still a little bitter. We really didn't get friendly until he was about fifteen, when I discovered he wasn't so bad. In later life we were on much better terms.

I was so much at odds with my brother then that I made a point of not reading the books he liked best. To my great disadvantage, I was turned off to most of Sir Walter Scott, Robert Louis Stevenson, and even Shakespeare, because my brother read them with so much enthusiasm. Some of the books that influenced me most were Howard Pyle's King Arthur legends, written in pseudo–Old English, really pretty horrible books. I could tell you the whole Round Table, every knight.

Mark Twain, I suppose, was my love. We had about a thirty-two-volume set, and I don't think I missed two. If I liked a book I read it seven or eight times. I finally got over my bias against Shakespeare: my brother moved into the histories, so I read the others. And I had a fondness for poetry, which my father shared.

He was forever encouraging us to memorize poems. The longest one I can remember was that Tennyson poem "Locksley Hall," written in long rhymed couplets. Boy, if it didn't go on for pages. My father gave my brother and sister a penny a couplet. I don't think it meant a thing to them; it was just sounds and words, like the hymns you'd hear in infancy. "Gladly the cross I'd bear . . ."—and my vision of a cross-eyed teddy bear named Gladly.

I'm no great linguist, but I learned enough Italian to read Dante and enjoyed Catullus in Latin. I learned enough German to enjoy Heine and Goethe, and was fairly proficient in French. I was particularly mad about Keats and Shelley and used to memorize big chunks of Robert Burns, sort of a real aesthete in college, you know—supposedly I had read everything. Or at least I managed to give that impression to my contemporaries. It was pretty piffling when I look back on it now.

Aunt Lou, my old black nurse until I was about seven or eight, was one of the people who meant most to me. She had been born in slavery. She was twelve years old at the very end of the Civil War and remembered seeing

Johnston's section of the Confederate army as it retreated through Greensboro. She was particularly close to me. She was a family servant, I guess, till she almost went blind, and then she was sort of pensioned off.

The outdoor man, Nereus Foster, must have been close to sixty at the time and as strong as a rock. He had a beautiful face, just as black as he could be, so kind and tolerant. He had such a moral strength about him, which he'd go out of his way to impart to me. I valued his opinions immensely. He'd be working out in the woods, and I was always underfoot, waiting for the pearls of wisdom he was so generous with. I'd forget to go to dinner when I was with him.

We'd talk about everything. He couldn't read, but like many Negroes he would talk in parables, and there'd usually be a moral point to his stories. He recognized that he was dealing with a spoiled brat and, with the utmost patience, set out to set me straight. He knocked an awful lot of egocentricity out of me.

Much of my "moral sense" came from my family and, to a very great degree, from various Negro servants. I was a very unmannerly little skunk, and they taught and shaped me up—particularly the butler. I remember someone had called one morning when my mother wasn't home. I must have been about four at the time, and I went up to this lady and asked who she was and how long she was staying. Later in the day, the butler, who had observed me with great disapproval, began singing a little song as he was polishing the furniture in the dining room. I was always hanging around him, and I remember the words—"What's your name, and when are you going?"—satirizing what I had done. He didn't think that was any way for a young fellow to behave. I got the point, and oh boy, did I take it to heart.

My father, a product of Reconstruction, inherited nothing and made his own fortune. The last year he was able to practice, his law practice brought him something like $250,000.

My father was a rather patriarchal guy with an acute sense of "noblesse oblige." He was a political liberal and even a radical in matters of black education and the right to vote. From 1895 or so, he was pretty much in the center of state politics and in and out of the state senate for over thirty years.

He had made millions developing real estate—buildings, and roads, and artificial lakes—and hired an immense amount of workers. It was amazing how much of the old plantation ways hung over in the relationship of the servants to the masters in those days. I can remember going one Christmas morning with my father and the rest of the family to the house of the foreman, a black man. When we drove up, there were two hundred and fifty to three hundred workers, and an additional four or five hundred of their families—a huge gathering in front of this big farmhouse.

There was a big shout of "Christmas gift!"—a traditional Christmas greeting from slave days. I can see my father carrying two huge satchels up to the front porch, where the foreman called out the name of every man there. My father would shake hands and give each man an envelope with at least five silver dollars. That was 1925, and in those days, five dollars was a hell of a lot of money in the South. Heck, when I went to work in a textile mill in 1938 or '39, I was getting thirteen dollars a week, and that was semiskilled factory work.

This ceremony felt like a direct link to slavery: what slavery, and a more or less benign, stable sort of slave plantation, would have been like. The parents of many of these people had been slaves, some of them probably like my old nurse. This was a look into the past of the South, and I was just in time to catch it, because it was all fading away pretty fast with industrialization.

Christmas was the crown of the year for the family. My father might have been right out of Dickens, the way he loved Christmas. He was a master psychologist, making it exciting for the kids. By the first of December the beginnings of euphoria were growing in me and my brother and sister.

At Christmas there always seemed to be extra people around, and it was nothing unusual for cousins to drop in on us and visit for six weeks, six months, or even a year. The thirty-six rooms didn't go begging, and ten at the table was a small, rather intimate gathering. The emphasis was on delighting somebody with the presents you picked. And we kids were encouraged to think very carefully about what we wanted. The F. A. O. Schwarz toy catalog would arrive around the beginning of December, and I would have it memorized in three days' time.

The day before Christmas, we'd go out in the woods with a horse and wagon and cut a colossal fifteen-foot tree. The tree would be put in one corner of the drawing room, a sixty-five-by-forty-foot room with a fifteen-foot ceiling.

Christmas Eve was just hysterical joy. Everybody was nice to each other; even my brother and I didn't fight. There'd usually be a great deal of calling on friends, and the front hall would be loaded with presents coming and going. And a huge bowl of eggnog made with cream and scillions of egg and bourbon.

Part of the tradition was a huge Christmas breakfast of sausage and eggs and the usual hominy grits, fried kippers, fried apples, bacon, and waffles and pancakes. We kids could hardly eat anything, but our elders seemed to take an interminable time. When they finished, the butler, the maid, and the cook would all clear the table. Then everybody lined up, including the servants, in order of age, the older folks going in last. My father was always very gallant. He went in last no matter how old some of the women might be—he always insisted that he was older than they. I was the youngest, and I'd go first. I'd practically faint because under the tree there'd be a sea of presents: everything we'd wanted from Schwarz's catalog, and everything else we could have dreamed up would be there, just more than we could imagine.

Christmas dinner was midafternoon and just utterly unbelievable in its variety and quality. We always got the biggest turkey that could still walk on its own legs. There was a huge cured ham and scalloped oysters, sweet potato pudding with a gorgeous marshmallow topping, and six or seven vegetables. There'd be cloverleaf rolls, hot biscuits, and corn pone. Then for dessert, the inevitable mincemeat pie, ice cream with fruit topping, and with coffee, an incredibly rich fruitcake with tons of fruit and nuts in it.

Once it got dark, we put on a display of fireworks that looked like the victory celebrations in Moscow in World War II. You should have seen those Roman candles and skyrockets. And when the fireworks were over, we just about had to be carted off to bed.

We all got excited about Christmas. I still get excited. It's a marvelous holiday. There was little religious significance for us, except that the idea of peace on earth and goodwill toward men was dominant and making other people happy central. Just the loveliest time of the year.

Most of my knowledge of the world came from that immense amount of reading, and when I got to public school I must have been the most extraordinary, out-of-this-world kid to most of my teachers and fellow students. I just loved all the kids, though I'm sure I was the most naïve idiot that ever hit their social circle. I'm sure I got some of my code of social ethics out of the King Arthur stories. I was extraordinarily polite to my teachers. I'll never forget how shocked one of them was to find out that I was the main instigator of a rubber-band war. The study hall was alive with foil pellets, and the window shades disintegrated from our shots.

I lived five miles from the city. I'd go to school, and then I'd be driven home and back to the wilds. I had very few social relationships except in the summer, when kids would love to come out and swim. So most of the time I saw the kids only at school. But I wasn't really lonely. I enjoyed a certain amount of solitude.

Since my brother and sister were both attending the University of North Carolina, my father decided to give up the house. It was an enormous expense and took a minimum staff of five to keep the thirty-six rooms going. So when I was almost sixteen, we moved to Chapel Hill.

Chapel Hill was small and village-like; its sole industry, the university. For the first time in my life I lived in a community. We still had the biggest house, but I was right in the middle of things and had only a half-mile to go to school. I was enjoying a normal social life, living near kids my age and getting a big kick out of school. I enjoyed my last year immensely, and I got a little less reserved. I was showing Barbara my high-school album the other day and discovered I had been named the most dignified student, which, looking back on it, seems the most extraordinary idea anybody ever had because I was really full of hell at the time.

It was in Chapel Hill that I got my first acquaintance with radical politics, largely through a bookstore known as Abernethy's Intimate Bookshop. Or, as I used to call it, Abernasty's Illegitimate Bookstore. The store was run by a delightful, eccentric guy who in the mid-1930s published *Contempo,* quite a distinguished literary magazine. One issue would be all T. S. Eliot or Ezra Pound or Paul Green, North Carolina's own leading light. George Bernard Shaw wrote all kinds of little stuff for it. And I believe there was a whole Faulkner issue, even though Faulkner was hardly known at the time.

He published some of the first writings of some of the outstanding poets of the thirties, forties, and even fifties in a political spectrum from extreme left to right. He used to have a wooden box full of letters from Eliot, Pound, and Shaw. *Contempo* died about 1937, when most of the little mags did.

It was a marvelous bookstore, a tangled mare's nest with the most extraordinary range and number of volumes in no particular order. There were about twenty thousand volumes that you could get to and a lot more that you couldn't. I think I got to most of them. You could buy the works of Marx and Engels and all kinds of radical books, as well as just about everything else. And that bookstore was my university from the time I was in high school.

Abernethy used to run off and say, "Mind the store! I'm going someplace," and wouldn't come back for half a day. Since I was always there reading and taking a free ride on his books, he decided to make use of me. I became an employee without really knowing how it happened.

Abernethy is now a Wall Street broker and lives around the corner up on Riverside Drive, still as nutty as a fruitcake. He's past sixty, which staggers me. He always seemed infinitely older to me because he was baldheaded quite early.

Everybody knew him as Ab, but his real name was Milton A. Abernethy. He was considered a flaming radical, and not entirely without justification. He's from Hickory, North Carolina, in the mountains and came to Chapel Hill a real rip-roaring radical, so antimilitarist that he was raving at the ROTC, the Reserve Officer Training Corps. He went to State College in Raleigh, and they expelled him. So he decided the hell with them all. Not being the bashful type, he somehow got to know every literary figure of any importance in the United States, and a good many of those in England, and charmed the hell out of them with his southern talk and mercurial ways.

At one point, the Communist Party decided they were going to put a lot of money into the South and put out a paper called *The Southern Worker.* Somehow they raised money and got ahold of a huge printing press about half the size of our living room and installed it in the back of Abernethy's bookstore. It was a very secret operation. Every time *The Southern Worker* went to press, the whole town shook. Not too many issues came out before the whole project died. The printing equipment stayed, and a printer who had been head of the Socialist Party in the state moved in. He didn't own it, but nobody else did either, so he put it in order and operated a little print shop.

Abernethy's was in an old ramshackle frame building right on the main street of town, half a block from the post office. I had a favorite spot. I'd climb up a bunch of shelves to a platform about fifteen feet above the floor where there was pretty good light. I'd lie on my stomach and read by the hour, and nobody would disturb me.

You'd never know what you were going to find. One day I was wandering around and found a book that had slipped back behind something. It was James Joyce's *Chamber Music,* a collection of the first lyrics he wrote and the main portion of his poetry, and it was autographed. Ab didn't care about things like that.

There were all kinds of nooks and crannies so that if you wanted to have a big discussion, you just found yourself a corner and went to it. Some people never seemed to buy anything, and it didn't make any difference.

It was the intellectual heartbeat of the community. All of the interesting people around Chapel Hill seemed to drop in at least once a day to see what was going on. I came by one day and there was Clifford Odets, who had just come into town. I got to know him extremely well, and every time he had a play that didn't do too well, or needed to get away from it all, he'd come to Chapel Hill for a couple of weeks. Muriel Rukeyser dropped in, and Marianne Moore, Anna Louise Strong, Ralph Bates, Faulkner, W. H. Auden, and Norman Thomas. You never knew who you were going to run into at Ab's, and the most interesting students always seemed to gravitate there.

Local legend has it that when Ab opened the store, he had about fifteen Modern Library books and seven or eight Everyman books all on one shelf. And having nothing much to do, he kept very careful financial records. At the end of a month the store was completely bankrupt, so he threw his ledgers in the coal stove and had been in business ever since.

I could borrow anything I wanted to read and bring it back. Once Ab came to my room and said, "All right, I've come for inspection. I want to see how many of my books you've got. I bet you've got the whole shop here." It seems he had a customer who wanted several books I had borrowed, so he walked off with them and about five more I had already bought and paid for, then resold them to this guy. I said, "What kind of business is that?" And he said, "That's known as nationalization." So thereafter I said, "Okay, if that's the way it works, I'm glad to hear it," and every time I wanted a book I'd "nationalize" it and take it home. He always knew what I took, but we'd always play the game, and he'd say, "Junius, did you nationalize that?"

Ab would talk a lot, but most likely as not it'd be nonsense. He was very far from being a fool but played a fool half the time. He trusted everybody except his friends. He would never trust me, of course. It was also a legend that he would cheat only his friends; he was scrupulously honest with everyone else. And it was true: he'd rob you blind, in a very charming way, of course, and you'd never get mad about it.

Ab's wife was just as extraordinary. She was a delightful woman with a keen intelligence and, as we say down South, "could charm the birds off'n the bush." She was his public-relations director and took care of smoothing over his eccentricities. When he went off to war to be a soldier, she ran the bookstore so well that not only could you find things but people even paid bills.

Well, once I left high school I really didn't know what to do. It was just a matter of course in my family that you went to college. So just barely sixteen, I entered the University of North Carolina and went to something called a freshman retreat. It was the most depressing thing I ever witnessed, and I couldn't have been more alienated. The welcoming speeches sounded like a bunch of Rotarian balderdash. I was just absolutely overwhelmed and repelled by what seemed to me the pervasive ugliness of most of what was going on around me. It seemed like a sham, and going through the academic routine there seemed futile.

I was in a terrible depression. I was feeling quite suicidal and very stupidly took all my father's heart medicine. I guess it was mostly codeine, but there was a hell of a lot of it. It made me sick, and I upchucked, slept for ten hours, and that was all there was. I was very much disgusted with myself and decided I would never try that way out again. Somehow I got through my freshman year and actually began to enjoy school.

I knew that joining a fraternity would make my father happy, so I figured if I had to join, I'd join my brother's. I pledged, then stayed away as much as possible. I couldn't abide the place, especially when football season was on. I don't think there was a book in the whole fraternity house except for some yearbooks. Well, some of the hardliners there decided I wasn't taking my obligations as a pledge seriously and thought they'd lower the boom on me a little bit. The more they tried, the more I'd stay away, and they got quite upset.

One weekend they invited me around specially, plied me with booze, and got me really crocked. Somehow I had never signed the final membership papers, and they decided to get me to sign while I was looped. If I had been twice as drunk I could have seen what they were trying to do, so I got very indignant and had words with the fraternity president. We were about the same size, and he tried to shove me into a chair. "Now sign that," he says. I didn't know how to fight at all, but I let go a real movie haymaker. Well, it hit him just right, and he ended up all the way across the room with a splintering of furniture. And I got on my high horse, marched out of the place, and never came back.

Until my sophomore year I felt like I didn't have a friend in the world. I felt great kindred with authors and composers and felt I could be on speaking terms with Beethoven any old time. And I loved a lot of poets but figured I was a misfit and wished sometimes that I had been born some other time. One weekend I'd stay at home and play phonograph records, feeling all left out of it and without a girlfriend. So the next weekend I'd get some character I'd gone to school with, who was a lot of fun, and we'd go double dating and having a ball the whole weekend, floating around with some of the girls we'd known in high school. But by the time the weekend would be over I'd be so repelled by the silly ritual you had to go through to associate with girls, I'd decide the hell with it, I don't care if I never see a girl again.

I was such a lonely devil. One of the things I can remember, particularly in my freshman year, was the pervasive sexual frustration of the campus. There was some homosexuality around, but it was very much under wraps in those days and never had any appeal for me. And one of the traumas of that first year was when a Spanish instructor I admired very much tried to seduce me. I was horrified and upset.

In my sophomore year I found my first really close friend, still a really close friend today, and that made all the difference. He was from New Mexico, a couple of years older than I, and at Chapel Hill for graduate work. He had read more widely in poetry, so that was an education for me; and I knew more about music, so that was an education for him. We had a marvelous time and were inseparable.

I began to meet more and more stimulating people and met some of the northern radical students down there. The New York people were a varied lot, mostly Jewish and mostly from New York City; some were from very poor families and some from quite wealthy families. They were a real delight. They provided a little intellectual yeast because, by God, there was damned little of that among the southern students. The civil war was happening in Spain then, and we would have marvelous discussions and drink beer.

The first thing that got me involved politically early in '38 was the threat to make ROTC compulsory. That set me off like a skyrocket. I was wild with rage and wrote a scathing letter to the student newspaper. Then all my left-wing acquaintances, who never considered me "political," started paying a little more attention to me.

George Derry, a professional red-baiter and Communist-exposer, came to campus. I didn't know a thing about him, didn't know he was coming, and hardly knew he had been there. But before he came out on stage, some friends of mine were running up and down the aisles passing out a biographical leaflet generally undercutting a lot of his speech. It seems that wasn't "gentlemanly," and they got in trouble for it.

One of the guys came to me. He was from a well-known South Carolina family, and he was concerned. "These guys," he said, "are northerners and Jews, and they're going to lower the boom on them unless we can get some good solid southerners involved in this." I didn't want these guys I drank beer with and had such good discussions with to get expelled, so next thing I know I signed a letter with several others taking responsibility for the incident. There was a great hue and cry, and the student council promulgated something known as the Code of the Carolina Gentleman. The code said that anything they didn't think was gentlemanly was a violation and that violation of the code made one subject, among other things, to expulsion. We fought this pretty strongly, and I had a big confrontation with the student council. They backed off quite miserably, and the Code of the Carolina Gentleman got pretty well scrapped.

In my junior year I joined the American Student Union chapter in Chapel Hill. The ASU was a student organization formed by a merging of Communist and Socialist student organizations, and while effective, it was faction-ridden. It was perfectly obvious that there was sort of an elite in the ASU, the Communists, and I knew who they were. Although I got along fine with them, I wasn't prepared to join the Communist Party at the time. In fact, I was greatly critical of them. They seemed doctrinaire and arrogant and very narrow in their intellectual approaches to things. While I liked them as people and respected them, I didn't have the slightest intention of getting involved with them.

But a number of things came along that got me tremendously concerned with Communism. One was the civil war in Spain. It suddenly dawned on me what was going on there. Ralph Bates, the short-story writer and novelist who had been in Spain, was on a speaking tour and impressed me tremendously. As a result of his speech and talking with him, I decided I would volunteer to fight against Franco with the International Brigade. The odd thing was that this all happened about the same time I was so antimilitarist, so opposed to compulsory ROTC, and it didn't seem the least inconsistent to me. At this point, though, they were already demobilizing the brigade, so that fell through before it even got started. But the threat of fascism really hit me hard. The Communists seemed to be the consistent anti-Nazis, and that further endeared them to me.

In 1938 I attended a student-labor conference in nearby Durham, North Carolina, and for the first time in my life I sat down to a table with Negroes on a basis of complete equality. My previous acquaintance with Negroes had been as servants, and I knew no Negroes otherwise. It was a shattering experience. It seems incredible these days, but it was one of the most exciting experiences of my whole life. It just opened up a new world to me.

This meeting was also my first contact with the labor movement. I began to learn of and meet Communists, mostly northerners who were down South organizing in the trade-union movement with great difficulty and great risk. Some of them had been beaten half to death, others killed. It was a time of terrible attacks on the trade unions. And so I got an even greater respect for the Communists.

So in that junior year of mine, I discovered Negroes, the student movement, the trade-union movement, and the Communists and Socialists. At that point in my life, I suppose I had an academic career in mind. The line of least resistance was to be a professor of something, and I was oriented towards comparative literature. But it was during that summer that I got quite serious about the Party and in the course of days made up my mind to be a revolutionary.

It was always easy for me to remember how long I'd been in the Communist Party because I joined on my nineteenth birthday.

two

Gladys

I was born on September 23, 1923, on East Seventh Street in Brooklyn in a two-story house. I remember how my mother used to call across to the neighbor on the other side, "Mrs. Garfinkel, would you please throw over a loaf of bread?" They'd have conversations and pass supplies back and forth. My grandfather lived with us there, too.

My childhood really was very quiet, passive, and unhappy. I didn't have many friends, and all I can recall about my sister and brother was that they teased me all the time. I had great big brown eyes and a rather sallow complexion, and I was always told that I wasn't really a member of the family. Supposedly I had been picked up at Plum Beach, the beach where all the Italian families gathered because they couldn't afford to go to Manhattan Beach: I was a little Italian girl who happened to wander over one day from Plum Beach. They all thought that was very funny, but I was devastated.

I was afraid of so many things, I was easy to tease. I'll never forget the day, the one and only time in his life that my father had gone out hunting, and he came home with a deerskin. He kept it right under the piano. Knowing that I was a bit apprehensive about it, my dear brother and sister pulled a dilly on me. I was walking through the living room, and all of a sudden I saw the leg move. I thought it had come to life and got absolutely hysterical. There was my brother on the piano bench and my sister next to him, giggling like crazy. They say now that they teased me because I was such a cute little thing, and I was so easily teased.

My sister and I are very close now, but we haven't seen my brother in a long time. We don't have much of an extended family. When I was a little girl and my mother and father were alive, we visited them all the time.

I didn't have any friends in school until I got into third grade and had Mrs. O'Keefe. I was in the R.A., the Rapid Advancement class. For some reason, I don't know why, 'cause I always thought I was the biggest dope in the world, but Mrs. O'Keefe just loved me and thought I was wonderful. And then there was another period where I hated school until I had Mrs. Wareham, my fifth-grade teacher.

You came into the schoolyard in the morning and you lined up and went up to your classroom, and all I remember is fear: sitting in the classroom, afraid I was going to be called on, afraid I wouldn't know the answer. I don't know whether it was the teachers or me, but I just hated it. And even when I had these two teachers who I liked and who liked me, it was just, I guess, a sort of substitute-mother kind of thing.

My brother and sister read a lot, but I couldn't say I was an avid reader. It seems to me I spent most of my younger days dreaming. I kind of floated. I was just out of it. And of course that just reinforced all my feelings that I couldn't do anything.

In the first years my father struggled quite a bit. But by the time I was five or six he had made it in a real middle-class way, and we moved to Twenty-first Street. My father's business was called the Triangle Fire-Proof Door Company, and it was part of the first attempts in the building trades to fire-proof buildings. We had a very nice house on a nice street with nice trees and a nice garden, and everything was just like in the school reader, *Sally, Dick, and Jane.* We had two automobiles, and my mother learned to drive. And we had a full-time sleep-in housekeeper. But it was all within a rather limited framework; we weren't wealthy, but we were comfortable.

It was really a quite successful business until later in the Depression, and then my father was destroyed. Everything he had built up was demolished.

He went through a period of insomnia and mental depression, and at the time not many people knew about psychiatrists. He'd be sitting at the dinner table and would drop off to sleep in the middle of a mouthful of food. And I remember him walking up and down. That's when I hated my mother the most, because she was so absolutely unconscious of what was going on with him, not only unconscious but without empathy.

All she could think of was that she was being cheated; she wanted him awake for a social evening. The man couldn't sleep all night.

They sent him to Bermuda, and then Bill Brown's training camp, a health camp. They thought that what he needed was special physical fitness, that this would help his mental state. It didn't. And the only thing I was told was that he was unhappy. His depression must have lasted two or three years. It seems like an awfully long time. My Aunt Harriet, who remembers him very fondly, told me that he loved a good time and was a lot of fun. But my outstanding recollection of him has always been of a very quiet, very subdued and depressed person. I loved him dearly, but I just didn't quite know how to talk to him. It was very hard to talk to him. My sister tells me stories about how we'd sit around the dinner table, and I was always on his right. He just adored me, apparently, and always gave me some kind of a tap or touch or something. But it was quiet, always very quiet.

And then he committed suicide.

I can't say that I had any deep affection for my mother, though later in life she changed radically. I remember a very abrasive, nagging woman always fighting with my father. There was a Sunday-afternoon dinner—that was the ceremonial day, and at three o'clock we had dinner. And for some reason or other there was always some kind of a fight. And it was always started by my mother.

She was a very handsome woman, and while she gave the appearance of being strong, she was a very weak person. The only person I ever remember her giving any love to was my brother. Any attempts on my part to get affection were always cast off. She would literally push me off her lap. And I was always the kind of kid, and still am the kind of person, who was a toucher and a feeler and a lover and a kisser, and I never got that. There was nobody in my family that I ever got that kind of a response from, just the occasional touching from my father. Even to this day, it's hard for my sister—she's just now beginning to verbally express love to me—to come over and give me a kiss. I'm so temperamentally different from the rest of them. Maybe I was the little Italian kid that came over from Plum Beach.

My mother was always angry, and I think that part of it was that she was a very frustrated woman. When she was a girl, I guess around 1910, she had been offered a scholarship by Walter Damrosch. He was like the Leonard Bernstein of the early 1900s. She was extremely musical, had a beautiful voice, and was very good at the piano. But my grandfather, a very religious Jew, just knew that a good Jewish girl simply didn't go on the stage, and that's how he saw it. So the talent and intelligence she had was absolutely thwarted.

Her life until my father died was spent really doing nothing. She'd play mahjong or poker, attend luncheons, and do all the things that middle-class Flatbush ladies did. She didn't even do any volunteer work. At least some of the ladies tried their hand at that.

After my father died . . . well, she had to do something, because there was no more money coming in. In many ways she fell apart, but in many ways she pulled herself together. She had to do something with herself, and she did. She worked at a number of different jobs and was very proud of herself.

But she was still a very selfish woman. If one parent dies and the other is left with the children, particularly a young child—and I would say that ten is fairly young—some special interest should be exhibited in the child. But there never was. All she could do was take care of herself; she was just that limited emotionally. When I was fourteen or fifteen, she worked as a sales-lady in Martin's department store in Brooklyn, and she would leave money on the kitchen table for me to go down to the delicatessen to get a couple of hot dogs for supper.

Now, of course, I may be completely distorting all this. I know sometimes when I hear Barbara talking about events I lived through with her, it's like I'm a different mommy, not the mommy I think I am. I don't know, but my outstanding impression of my youth isn't very happy. I can still hear my mother nagging my father, "Dick, stay awake! Wake up! Why don't you sleep at night?"

My brother was living in a dorm at Columbia, and my sister was out of the house when my father died. She never finished college but was a very enterprising, bright young woman and was able to leave home. None of us at that time were that wild about my mother. Now, of course, my sister has all kinds of daydreams about what my mother was.

In the years after my father's death, we all had mental breakdowns. My brother's was rather extended. He graduated from law school, got married, then after about a year or so of marriage, he really started breaking down. I know my mother was very resentful that he married; he should have stayed around for a while longer and taken care of her.

Eventually my mother had to sell the house, and my mother and I moved to a one-bedroom apartment just a few blocks away. I can't even remember where I slept. I finished the eighth grade at Public School 193 and then went to James Madison High School. Periodically, my brother would come back after his marriage broke up. At times he was too ill to do anything.

My mother worked, but she was rather carefree with money. My father had left something like a ten-thousand-dollar insurance policy, and she drew from that as well as what she earned. My sister was doing quite well at the time and used to buy my clothes. We always had enough to eat, and I always had good, decent clothes. I never experienced any terrible change in living standards or any poverty. We just went from a large house to a small apartment.

I was aware, though, that there was a Depression going on. I was young and, though I never knew anybody who was really poor, I remember the strikes, the talk of unemployment, and the mood of the times. But in personal terms, all the Depression meant to me was that something terrible had happened to my father's business. And although the only difference, at first, was that we couldn't have the sleep-in help and we went down to one car, his death, I think, radicalized us all.

When I was fourteen, Bobby, a very nice boy I knew—I didn't have a crush on him or anything—came to my house one day and asked me if I'd like to join the YCL, the Young Communist League. I knew what the YCL was, and I knew something about the Communist movement because my brother and sister had been involved in politics to some extent. I had heard about Sacco and Vanzetti[1] and the Scottsboro Boys.[2] My brother used to argue about politics with my father. So when Bobby came to see me and asked if I wanted to go to a meeting, I said, "Sure." And he put it in such a way that . . . oh, it sounds so clichéd, you know: "There are people who haven't got a lot of things, and the YCL, the Communists, are trying to make things better in the world."

And this appealed to me as a way of, I don't like to use the words "helping people," but it seemed to make sense to me that maybe things could be better if a lot of people tried to do something about it. It was a terrible thing, I thought, that there were people who didn't have as much as I had, that there were people who were hungry. And I remember going to meetings thrilled at the idea that we were going to try to do something about all of that. I guess for as long as I can remember, and still it burns in me now, I just couldn't stand unfairness.

The people in the YCL were very nice and seemed to be interested in really doing things for other people. They seemed to be the brightest people in high school. I found out later that one boy, the smartest one of the whole bunch, apparently had a terrible crush on me. I could never understand why he liked me, but he used to walk me home from school every single day, and we would talk about all of the serious problems of the world.

We held street-corner meetings and had demonstrations. We were very involved in the Spanish Civil War and gave out leaflets and sold the Young Communist League newspaper. I went to every possible meeting I could, to every demonstration. I marched in May Day parades and was very active in all the election campaigns.

I was self-conscious ringing doorbells. I wasn't scared because I thought I'd get hurt or anything; I was just shy, and it took a lot of courage to ring a strange doorbell and say, "Will you vote Communist?" Many people just thought you were nuts. Nobody ever did anything nasty or ugly to me, but you could expect to be yelled at or to have a door slammed in your face.

Selling the *Daily Worker* was nothing. You'd just stand at the corner, and maybe you'd sell a couple. You might get a couple of nasty cracks, but I don't recall any hostile antagonism.

It just gave me a whole purpose for living. I mean, what fifteen-year-old thinks about whether you should live or not? But I just felt differently. I felt welcome somewhere, a part of something. It was very little a cerebral, a thought-out thing. It was much more the spontaneous feelings of wanting to do something for people. I didn't know the first thing about Marxism-Leninism when I joined the YCL. All I knew was that there were good people and bad people, and we had to do something about the bad people who were doing bad things to the good people. It was as simple as that. You were either on one side or the other.

I wasn't even aware of the Black Question at that time because there were no blacks in that part of Flatbush. I didn't know any black people. And it wasn't until I got more involved that I started meeting black people in the YCL and became much more aware. And that was a tremendous issue with me.

There was a period when the Communist Party was at its height, and all these two-bit analyses were made of people who were in the Party for "neurotic reasons." And I suppose to some extent that may have been partially true in my case, because when I got involved it was the first time I felt any kind of belonging. I didn't even feel I belonged in my own family. And even though I looked with envy at the kids who really seemed to be comfortable and talked to each other easily, I wouldn't have given up one day in the YCL for anything.

In some ways, I spent a good deal of my life on the sidelines. At meetings I was more of a listener than anything else. I didn't feel comfortable saying anything. I just didn't feel that anybody would want to hear me—I was too dumb to have anything good to say, period. All these people were so much smarter than me, what they were saying was obviously the right thing. Why did I have to add my two cents? But I was always taking on the assignments. I was a workhorse. And I don't say it with any anger: I was one of the peasants in the ranks.

A lot of our work was with the so-called mass organ, the American Student Union, which was ridiculous, because so many of the ASU kids were YCL-ers, although a lot weren't. We held ASU meetings in school. The outstanding thing that I remember as an ASU member was the trip to the national convention in Wisconsin during my junior year or senior year in high school. I don't remember too much about it except that it was a long and wonderful bus ride, and I was just thrilled to pieces that I was part of something that was really going to make everybody live a better life. And that was a damned good feeling.

And I'm convinced that even though there may have been some . . . oh, you know, neurotic needs for my desire to feel a part of this group, there was a reason this was the group I chose. Something within me responded to the things they were saying, and, as far as I was concerned then, these were the best people in the world. And as far as I'm concerned today, they were the best people in the world.

three
Junius

Joining the Party was a big step. I'd been thinking about it and reading a great deal of stuff. I can remember talking to one of the leading student Party theoreticians; we had gotten to be pretty good friends, and I argued him up a wall. After I made all of my points, I said, "I don't believe in just joining something. I think I'd rather go my own way. And that's why I'm never going to join your party," I finished.

I thought about it more and more and said to myself, "Well, if you can't go your own way and yet work within a framework, it seems like you don't have much confidence in yourself. Why shouldn't you profit from the collective experience of a party that obviously knows what it's doing? Look at the kind of people they've got in it. And they did manage a revolution in Russia. . . ." There was certainly no overwhelming feeling of allegiance. It was more or less a sense of common feeling on most issues, a rejection of liberal equivocation, and a defiance of the status quo. So I decided I had nothing to lose and joined in March.

And I was ready to leave by June. I really considered it a bit of a joke. The whole student movement seemed so full of factional nonsense and mouthing of political phraseology—pure balderdash, I thought. The Communists at school were playing at revolution: they were parlor pinks and revolutionists, and nobody did a damned thing except hang together socially and go off into sectarian groups.

Bart, the Party organizer for the state, came looking for some of the student Party and found me. He was also a southerner, from a lower-middle-class background in Georgia, and an extremely appealing guy. I was enormously impressed with him. He got me reading more things, more Marx and Lenin than I had read before, and my whole attitude on the Party changed.

Because of his southern background, Bart had been asked by the Party to go to Alabama. After the case of the Scottsboro Boys, the Birmingham area was the center of Communist efforts to organize. Tennessee Coal and Iron, a subsidiary of U.S. Steel, was there, and it was the big, heavy industry in the South. In good Stalinist fashion, the Party concentrated on heavy industry, so they concentrated on Birmingham. The city was also quite a focal point for the black movement at the time because there were so many black industrial workers in steel and coal.

So Bart went to Birmingham in 1937. It was a real medieval situation there. Bull Connor[1] was the police chief even then, and his cops damn-near killed Reds, did kill Reds. Bart, one of the leading activists, was imprisoned and put in irons which ate into his ankles and his wrists. Somehow he survived a year of this and had become fairly well known when the Party asked him to come to organize in North Carolina.

Bart was a charming, low-keyed fellow, a master of understatement, with a marvelous twinkle in his eye. He could say more with his silences than most people could with a million words. He just didn't know how to put on the airs and attitudes that were supposed to be appropriate to a Communist organizer. He wasn't much on party structure. He didn't believe in having all kinds of groups and committees and structural setups.

What he did, instead, was to go around and spend time with people in different parts of the state and try to give some direction, meaning, and orientation to whatever they were doing—try to help them affect people around them and move things forward in their own particular way.

Bart had no time for radical sloganeering that accomplished nothing and just isolated the person who was blathering it. He was an original antisectarian, and it was damned lucky for me that I met up with him. He gave me a strong distaste for leftist posturing, big revolutionary talk that didn't have anything behind it. What he valued was organization that changed things, that enabled Communists to help make people's lives better and gave a basis for building the Party on genuine achievement.

The apple of his eye was the textile organization that was going on in the state. He used to suffer for three days before he could make himself go to Chapel Hill to talk to all the students and intellectuals. He was an intellectual himself but couldn't stand the academic talk sessions. They absolutely wore him to a frazzle, and he'd go back home, and it would take him days to recover.

Bart was publicly known as a Communist. That wasn't his style, particularly, but the national leadership prodded him to conduct a campaign and run for governor. This was a way of putting the Party's program forward, so he had to go through with it, though the motions pained him no end. But he was effective just because of his influence on people and his genuine concern and interest. The people who knew him valued him tremendously and looked on him not merely as a representative of the Party but as a kind, bright, warm human being. It was all very much like the relationship of a circuit-riding minister to his faithful flock. Although he was reluctant to assume the role, he was sort of psychiatrist, problem solver, and everything else.

I'll never forget one of the first times I was visiting him. His little girl, an infant at the time, was ill, and something seemed to be wrong with the thermometer he'd brought. It registered all crazy, so he and I went down to the drugstore to see if he could change it. So he goes in explaining that it didn't work properly, and the druggist shakes it down and says, "What's wrong with it? Looks all right to me," and pops this rectal thermometer into his mouth, tucking it under his tongue. Bart took one look at this guy with a rectal thermometer in his face and tried to strike a cold, grave face but couldn't carry it off. He got a case of snickers and nearly choked to death. He had to walk out and leave the thermometer there.

No matter how much he was denounced in the papers, his neighbors just couldn't stay away from him and his wife. They were forever getting underfoot. This was his own best security, I guess, because his neighbors would be over in a flash to tell him if the FBI were prowling around.

Bart asked me if I would come to Greensboro and help him with some trade-union work the Party was involved in. I said, "Sure." He took me around and introduced me to Communist textile workers; it was then that I got acquainted with Communists other than student radicals, and it changed my whole view of what the Party was about. I decided that, though my fellow students in the Party might not know what they were talking about, this was a wonderful organization that meant business on the Negro Question and genuinely meant to create the brotherhood of man right here on earth, no malarkey about it. For quite a while I read very little theory because I was so emotionally wound up with these people: here were working people serious about the better life.

I was so absorbed by, and so attracted to, these white textile workers that every chance I got I went over and helped at the union hall. It was very romantic, really, a love affair with the whole working class, with a tremendous amount of idealization, of course, on my part. Even my language was affected; my whole speech pattern changed. I had never known a worker, never known anybody outside of servants, and that, too, was a revelation. They approached me on a very human basis and took me as I was, and not because I was a rich man's son.

So here in Greensboro was a tremendous mill village with a population of five thousand, which I had lived within five miles of most of my life, and I had never seen it—it was that well fenced-off from everything else. The only way you'd know it was there was by the factory whistle that blew at noon and at quitting time. That's how far apart you could live from working people.

There was an old leader of the Gastonia strike[2] who had been charged with the murder of Police Chief Aderholt, and some of the violence there, and had served four years in the state penitentiary. He had spent a year or two in the Soviet Union working in a textile plant and had been lionized some. He had very favorable comments about the Soviet Union. He could tell a story better than almost anyone I've ever met, and he had a million of them. I never saw the person he couldn't delight and charm. He was getting less active then because his health was going to pot, and he had a bit of trouble with alcoholism.

This summer the textile union was building toward a strike, and I just got caught up in the activities. They had no contract at the time, and conditions were ripe for a confrontation and the achievement of a contract. Bart wanted to make known the Party's presence, so we'd sit in his house and wrap little packets of literature and send it to the best textile workers we knew. I still cringe when I think of the literature we mailed out. I can almost see the pamphlets, things like chairman Earl Browder's report to the such-and-such convention of the Communist Party. Most workers couldn't make heads nor tails out of it. I can just imagine these textile workers trying to figure out what the hell all of this was about. This was something that endured throughout my entire Party career: the painful memory of how inappropriate the literature we disseminated was, how rarefied and removed from local problems. Of course, from time to time we tried to print our own material, and that was a little better, but I can groan plenty about them.

Anyway, a furious lot of activity and tremendous work went into distributing these things. I didn't get too much sleep, but I didn't need it. I was too excited. If there was anything to do, we'd stay up all night. Sometimes we'd just cover miles of territory. Bart would drive, and his wife would sit on one side of the car, and I'd sit on the other. He'd go along about twenty, thirty miles an hour, and we got so adept at bouncing these packets right up by the mailboxes. We'd drive until we ran out of literature. We'd do it in city streets and in mill villages, and if we thought the literature was appropriate, we'd go into black communities.

The Negro membership of the Party at this time was small, but it grew quite a bit later. There were mostly individual stalwarts scattered around one place or another, and they were lovely. One courageous guy was a pillar of his church—sort of a spirit crying in the wilderness. He hunted up the Communist Party and Bart because he figured it just can't go on like this. He had read in the Bible about the brotherhood of man, and he figured he had got to do something about it. He better reach out a hand and see if he couldn't talk to some of these white people. And it looked like the Communists were ones that knew what it was all about. He was just an absolutely beautiful person. And his wife was, too. His kids were shy of us, but they were very warm.

The overwhelming burden of being white in a racist society was such that you couldn't get it out of your mind for a minute. It was a constant pain in your life: meeting up with black people both intensified the contradiction of being white in a society where the blacks are the victims and intensified the feeling of anguish. But it was also a tremendous relief to reach across that chasm and talk to the oppressed people and feel at one with them, feel that you were working toward eliminating discrimination and fighting it. You had illusions, at least, that you were having some success. And these were some of the very attractive things about the movement.

Meanwhile, this was the summer of 1939, and in August came the Soviet-Nazi Non-Aggression Pact.[3] If I had been very concerned with theory, the Non-Aggression Pact would have shattered me, and if I only remained in the student movement I'm sure I would have left the Party. I would have said, "Where has all the antifascist fight gone? Here's this accommodation with the Nazis, and the Soviet radio is playing 'Deutschland uber Alles.' What kind of cynical nonsense is this?" But I knew for real. I had met wonderful Communists who I knew as people, the people at the bottom of this movement. They were absolutely true blue, and this was the Communist movement. Whatever happened on the other side of the world was probably . . . well, it didn't look good, but there must be a good reason for it. I grabbed at the first explanation that this was a stalling for time by Stalin, and that more than satisfied me.

The summer went very fast. In September I decided not to return to school and got a job drawing tax maps for Guilford County in Greensboro, where Bart lived. My brother and sister both graduated, and instead of staying in Chapel Hill, my parents decided to move back to where we had lived before.

My uncle had a much smaller, fourteen-room house and was quite worried about it, so my parents and I moved in, and I was again living five miles from Greensboro.

My pay at the time was seventy-five dollars a month, and I lived on about twenty-five of it and gave the remainder to Party activities. Seventy-five bucks wasn't bad pay for an unskilled squirt. Poor Bart was getting about ten bucks a week, he used to say, whether he needed it or not. So he decided that I better be Party treasurer. "Of course," he said, "in addition to keeping track of the funds, this means supplying them." There were damned few problems keeping track of the money because there was so little of it, and it came and went so fast.

At this point there was a textile strike going on in High Point, but I couldn't take any direct part in it. Bart didn't want it red-baited and figured our presence wouldn't be an unalloyed asset. He helped with it secondhand, through the most active Party people there, and gave a lot of useful advice.

My biggest activity back in Greensboro during that fall was organizing the American Student Union at various colleges. We had four chapters going by Christmastime. I was all over the place. Once I went to the dean of the women's college at the University of North Carolina with a number of ASU students to discuss holding a peace demonstration. He was a nice old fellow who knew my father, and in the course of the discussion, he says, "You know, Scales, I've seen you on the campus so much, I'm going to talk to the trustees and see if we can't get you some sort of a degree. Any man that puts in as much time at a girls' school as you do deserves some recognition." I think I was also dating a number of girls there at the same time I was organizing.

I had to be careful going to Bennett alone, the Negro college for women, because I'd be on the spot and so would the women if I got caught, but I could do quite well at the all-black co-ed State Agricultural and Technical College. I would usually go to Bennett with some of the guys from A&T. I'd be one white in with three or four blacks; nothing could be more conspicuous. But it's amazing what you can get away with if you just act natural and unselfconscious in the ultra-racist South. I had the upper-class training and, if I turned it on, I could be very lordly about the whole thing, and we weren't likely to be stopped by rednecks or cops.

They were such exciting days, and it's been such a long time, so my time perceptions are probably confused, but during that fall and winter it seems I was working every waking hour. The Party formed a tremendous movement of the unemployed called the Workers Alliance, and it consisted mainly of people who were on, had been on, or wanted to get on the Works Progress

Administration. The WPA was all kinds of government work projects paid for as a relief measure against the Depression. The Workers Alliance had an enormous membership nationally and was naturally quite large in some of the northern cities. But it was surprisingly large in North Carolina, and there was a very effective and influential chapter in Greensboro.

Unfortunately, one WPA project after another was being discontinued, and it was obviously on its way out. Somehow or other, although I was employed, I was elected chairman of our Greensboro Workers Alliance, probably because I knew how to chair a meeting. The Workers Alliance met at night in the largest courtroom in the courthouse where I worked. I used to get up on the judge's bench before a couple of hundred people wondering how in hell I could explain this if any of my bosses happened to see me. Well, I guess I buried the organization because, within a few months, the WPA was practically nonexistent locally.

By this time I had become state chairman of the American Student Union and had organized four of its five chapters. Bart suggested I organize an organization of the state chairmen and see if I couldn't be chairman of that. I was having a marvelous time and couldn't have been more excited.

Then, in January, my father died, and that shook me up terribly. In the last six months of his life, after I had joined the Party, I had all kinds of discussions about Marxism with him and was amazed to see how much smarter he was than I thought. Although he was upset about my joining, he figured I was going to outgrow it, and we were able to discuss all kinds of things with considerable enjoyment. We'd gotten quite close again, and I was crushed. My mother left Greensboro to visit relatives for a while, and I moved into a room in Greensboro proper.

By that time, I had gotten so involved in student work with the ASU, I returned in March to the university for one term. Bart thought it would be a good idea if I went back to finish my degree. I didn't do too much school work, though, and blew the whole quarter. I think I took incompletes in everything. But we had one of our biggest ASU activities.

The National Youth Association [NYA] had a system of grants that enabled self-help students to stay in college. It was really a kind of subsidy—enough for a guy who was marginally financed to stay in school, answering phones or working in the library. It was the only way some people could go to school, and there were between eight to ten thousand students like that in North Carolina alone. Well, there was a big move in Congress to cut off the NYA grants. I think President Roosevelt was rather neutral in the fight, and most southern congressmen were supporting the cuts, including the North Carolina delegation.

We organized a petition campaign of NYA students and involved five thousand students throughout the state. Every little jerkwater college you ever saw was involved, and in Chapel Hill we had a statewide meeting of representatives from thirty-five to forty different colleges. A great many of them were Negroes. After all, the American Student Union had big chapters in two black colleges and contacts at a dozen more. So about one-third of the 250 delegates who showed up were black. It was absolutely sensational. Nobody in the University of North Carolina administration had had the slightest idea when they gave permission for this meeting that blacks were coming. Who ever heard of an interracial meeting in Chapel Hill? It was unthinkable in 1940!

So we held it, and it went off without a ripple! The meeting was held on a weekend, and the campus was pretty much emptied out. All these black students were in the YMCA building getting sodas, and nobody there knew what the heck to do. The people working there were mostly students and too polite to refuse to serve them, so it just went off. It's amazing the things that can happen if there's no fanfare, and it's just carried off naturally. I don't doubt that if we had announced it, and made an issue of it, there would have been crosses burned and an incredible whoop-dee-doo.

We contacted five thousand National Youth Association people in fifty colleges and raised enough money to send a guy to Washington to be our lobbyist. He saw every member of the North Carolina delegation, and when the vote came, every southern congressman voted to cut out the NYA except the eleven North Carolina congressmen. To a man they voted "yes." It was a complete victory and showed what a little organizing could do. These votes were just enough to swing it, and the NYA was funded.

Unfortunately, student populations turn over so fast that we weren't able to sustain any kind of permanent structure, and within a year or so, most of those same delegates had graduated and scattered. But it was an historic occasion, not only because of this minor achievement but for the fact that this was the first interracial student meeting ever held at the University of North Carolina.

In late March I began to reorganize the student Party and recruited a lot of people. The Party grew tremendously, and so did the ASU. I was getting a pretty left-wing reputation but had a very broad range of acquaintances on campus. I was learning how to function in various organizations, how not to be too sectarian in a large group. This was the abiding disease of the New York party-office leftists: if they couldn't get everything their way, they'd say the hell with the organization. We began to learn how to behave in an organization with people who didn't agree with us 100 percent.

Somewhere in the spring, Bart asked me if I'd like to go to a national Party school. I was thrilled silly. I cooked up an excuse, got all my examinations postponed, and went early that summer. There was all kinds of secretive business. We met in Penn Station in New York City near the information desk. There were four fellows, one of us waiting at each pillar, and somebody came and picked us up one by one and put us in separate cars. We drove all over the place and then were consolidated into one car. The car took off for the north, and we went roaming up through all kinds of back roads. The school was hidden off in a farm in New England. To this day I'm not even sure where I spent those six weeks.

It was run by an American whose whole orientation was to make like a Russian Bolshevik—a more sectarian guy you'd never want to meet. He was co-leader with David McKelvey White, whose father was governor of Ohio. White, a frail, sensitive guy with a long solemn face, had been a professor of poetry at Brooklyn College and had gone to fight against Franco in Spain. He was very skinny, but had gone around Spain with about seventy-five pounds worth of fifty-caliber machine gun strapped to his back. He was a lovely fellow and counteracted some of the effect of the other guy.

The school was supposed to be for southerners; there were an equal number of blacks and whites, and people came from Louisiana, Alabama, Florida, Kentucky, North Carolina, and Texas. All but one guy was under twenty-five. We pounded away at Marxist-Leninist theory and finally had it down by the book. The central theme was the history of the Communist Party of the Soviet Union, and we read the Stalinist text that was circulated in a million copies in this country. It was a disaster. I still have the notebook filled with the notes I took. I don't look at it very often because it takes too strong a stomach to go through some of the nonsense, the mechanical applications of Marxism, and all of the dogma.

But when I got back to North Carolina I was really a "professional revolutionary" and completely committed. I had no intention of going back to college. I went to see my mother, and she was very distressed.

I went to live in the mill village in High Point and boarded with one of the families I had met with Bart. I liked them tremendously and lived with the man, his wife, and three daughters in a miserable three-room company house.

You could tell if the stars were out at night by looking through the cracks in the wall. In the wintertime, a thread would stand almost horizontal from the breezes through the cracks. There was no water inside and a cold-water faucet out back. Twenty-five feet back of the house was a little outhouse. When you got off, the seat flew up, and an automatic flush business occurred.

The entire family slept in the same bedroom. There were three double beds jammed into this one room: the mother and father were in one bed, the older daughter in one, and the two youngest daughters shared the other. The living room was mostly for ornament. It was a wasted room, because in the wintertime the only room heated was the kitchen. The kitchen was the social room, and both stoves were needed to keep it warm. And, of course, it didn't stay warm for too long because the house wasn't insulated. But that's where the whole family lived during the entire winter. And all the houses in the village were about the same.

They were a lovely family. The husband and wife were about thirteen years older than I. She was always very motherly to me, and he was like a big brother. He was quite sophisticated, a worldly sort of guy, and she was a woman of wonderful courage and drive, very strong and yet very tender. And their kids were absolutely delightful. I got a tremendous case on the older daughter. I didn't know her age at the time, and I assumed she was at least seventeen, because she sure looked it. I swear, it absolutely frightened me when, after we'd been going together pretty steady for about six months, I discovered that she was only fourteen. I was twenty at the time. Her mother told me, and I nearly died. Then she had her fifteenth birthday, and I felt a little bit better.

I even liked their dog. Through this family I got to know most of their relatives, and it was a big family on both sides. I must have stayed there for three or four months, and it was darn cold when I left. The mother didn't think I was going to survive the winter in that living room, so she switched me over to her sister's house.

Like many people's, the sister's marriage had broken up, and I lived there with her mother and son for what seemed like years. In spite of everything, I survived the first winter there. I had so many covers on the bed that if I tried to raise my feet upright I'd have broken my toes off. I had two sets of overalls: I'd work in one and sleep in the other. There'd be frost inside the house sometimes, and I'd make a mad dash for the kitchen in the morning. They kept the stove going. And the lady of the house had the most marvelous breakfasts. Country food. Sunday morning would usually be pork chops and hominy grits, eggs, and biscuits.

I got a job in the Burlington mill in walking distance of the village. I worked the night shift at Hillcrest and devoted all my days to Party activity. I just got wedded to life there. I got to know practically everyone in the village and in the plant where I worked. I just loved the people there.

Burlington was pretty hopeless for a union. They had about eighty mills, and if anyone tried to organize a Burlington mill, they just closed the mill down and transferred operations to another. They'd leave four or five hundred people out of work and desperate, and then blacklist them. You couldn't get a job anywhere. So we had no intention of organizing at Hillcrest. I just had to get a job someplace, and that was fine.

I made thirteen bucks a week, the minimum wage, thirty-two cents an hour, and had money to spare. I was in awfully good physical shape, but it was fantastically hard work. And what amazed me was that guys my age working there had faces like they were thirty-five or older. I'd find out some of them were younger than I. They were used to hard work, and they were wiry, but they absolutely couldn't take the pace.

Burlington was the most rationalized of all the mills down there. They knew how to take every last drop of energy out of you on an eight-hour shift. To survive I rationalized my job, too, and it didn't crush me. It's true I wouldn't have a dry seam in my clothes when I'd come out of the place. You'd have to take salt pills all night to keep from sweating yourself into heat prostration. It was about ninety degrees most of the time and very humid because of the rayon yarn.

These working-class guys my age would be old men by the time they made forty, if they made it, and they were just drained most of the time. The women had it even worse. A girl who started at nineteen was an old woman by twenty-nine. Usually the height of the machine was such that the women would have to sort of stoop their shoulders forward and poke their abdomens out, and the same was true in the cotton mills. The spinners had the same business: a pooched-out abdomen and slumped shoulders. It was the most frightful thing, and they all looked really old by the time they were thirty.

This place was organized by time-study experts. The speedup was incredible. One girl was twenty-five, and when I think back, she looked more like she was thirty-five. She was the star operator. She could do almost twice as much work as anybody else, their "show" operator. My God, she'd go around like she had six hands. It was just dizzying to watch her. Then one day she went stark-raving mad right at her machine, and it took five people to haul her out screaming and kicking. And she never came back. She ended up in a mental institution.

Even though I was working in another plant, I joined the cotton mill union so I could edit the monthly union paper and attend all the meetings. The chairman used to make me his parliamentarian, and I used to help smooth the meetings out. And I was always willing to do any kind of leg work.

After every union meeting on Saturday night, there'd be a big social gathering. In these days, you worked a half-day on Saturday, and that afternoon all the men in the village would go to the barbershop. This was the only bath you could take during the whole week, so we all lined up and tackled their six stall showers. They gave you a little bar of Lifebuoy soap and a towel for a quarter.

Meanwhile, back in the houses, the women moved into the kitchens. No man could go into the kitchen because all the women, from infant to grandma, would be bathing. Every house had a huge corrugated iron tub, and hot water would be heated in everything that could hold it. Everybody would use this big tub. They couldn't go dumping it out, and you couldn't give everybody a new tub of water. So you'd just add water to it, and it'd get pretty raunchy by the time the last one got their turn. But, one way or another, everybody would go to the union meeting all sweet and clean.

Saturday night was always a light dinner, and about half the village would show up at the union meeting. The meeting would begin about seven o'clock, and we'd usually try to get the business over by eight-thirty. There would be very wide participation, and if it was near strike time, there'd usually be some pretty fancy oratory, mostly delivered by women. They were much more verbal than the men, generally, and God, they were effective. I'd love to have been able to record some of those speeches.

As soon as the gavel pounded, the meeting adjourned, and a little string band would strike up, usually of union talent, with a couple of banjos, guitars, and a fiddle or two. The chairs would disappear like magic, and the whole huge hall became a dance floor. For a nominal fee, anybody could come to these marvelous dances, and we had our committee to keep things orderly and throw out the drunks.

I didn't know how to square dance worth a hoot, and some of these real tough textile women took me in hand. I swear to God, there was one woman there who was a little five-by-five but strong as an ox, and every time I'd find myself in the wrong place, she would absolutely pick me up and put me where I belonged. I had to learn in a hurry in self-defense. She'd have killed me or at least taken my arm out of the socket. I got to be a real good square dancer and used to enjoy it immensely.

I think the social part of the evening was actually more important than the meetings, because those square dances were just unforgettable, and probably did more than anything to solidify the union. Everybody from toddlers on up would take part. The old folks would sit and watch the young'uns and relive their youth, and the little squirts would be dancing with each other just so they wouldn't get trampled. The young squirts were dancing for real. The older folks up to forty or fifty were just having a marvelous time, and, of course, the teenagers were romancing like crazy. It was an extremely wholesome and delightful business. Some of my student friends from Chapel Hill would come over, and they absolutely got hooked. They'd be back every time they could.

These textile workers were about one generation, if that much, off the farm, and they had come to the city because life on the farm got tough. They had all of the country ways. One of the problems in the mill village was to try and stop people from keeping hogs in their small yards. Much of their charm and lingo was strictly farm and country. Yet they had acquired new ways, and many of them had been proletarianized by a lifetime in the mills.

The trade-union movement had really created a social revolution in the South, and I saw it in this mill village. This had been a place where the foreman reigned supreme. It was a company town with a company store and a company church. The company paid the minister, and the minister preached that the CIO [Congress of Industrial Organizations] was the antichrist. And if anybody fell afoul of the company, his credit was stopped at the company store. The company owned all the houses in the village. And if someone really fell afoul, he could be evicted from his company house. So they lived under a real reign of terror.

Well, the organizing drive was undertaken with great risk and difficulty, and a lot of people joined together and pulled a strike. The strike staggered the company, and they put on a lot of police pressure. It was a tremendously educational thing for the people there, who thought if they stayed on the good side of the foreman they would make out pretty well.

The village split down the middle on whether or not to go to church. The union people didn't want to hear the company say that the CIO was the agent of the devil, so a great many of them quit going.

The WPA at the time had some educational programs going, so the union (and the Party had considerable influence in the union) began encouraging and organizing adult-education classes on everything you can think of. People who had never finished sixth grade were enrolling and just getting the biggest joy out of it. Some learned things like typing and were able to get part-time jobs. It gave everyone a tremendous sense of self-confidence, and they were able to hold their heads up. It was a true social revolution, and most of these people became missionaries for unionism. It's true that it lost most of its momentum after a while, but at that time it was a tremendously exciting thing to participate in. The union became the social center of the whole village.

Of course, it's easy to remember the pleasant events and forget the horrors of poverty. One Saturday, I'd just gotten paid and had so much money

I didn't know what to do. I decided I'd take the three kids in the family to the movies. Well, next door was a family named Tysinger, and Ot and Mary Tysinger were probably in their late thirties and had nine children. They both worked in the mill. But Mary had been sick and hadn't been able to work, which meant that Ot's salary—he'd been working there for twenty years, since his teens, and was making fifteen dollars a week—had to support the family of eleven. The entire family was surviving on fifteen dollars a week.

When the kids, naturally excited, announced that Junius was taking them to the movies, I saw these nine Tysinger kids next door looking at me with big sad and dejected eyes. So we got hold of the Tysinger kids. I think the bus fare was a nickel each way, and the kids could get in for a dime at the movie, so I spent quite a bit. But it was the first time any of these Tysinger kids—and the oldest was twelve—had seen a movie.

So I got to see the horror of living on this kind of a wage in a textile village. The oldest Tysinger child, Carrie, was a lovely little girl, but she was skinny, and her color was bad. She had a kidney ailment, and the doctor said she should have a lot of fresh vegetables, and this and that and the other, you know, an elaborate diet, which on Ot's fifteen dollars a week was about as feasible as a snowball in hell. They ate white beans, the staple. They had biscuits sometimes, corn bread, cabbage, and fatback, but that was about it. If they had anything else, they considered it a gala occasion. And for Carrie's kidney ailment, this was not the thing.

One day, these God-awful screams came from the Tysingers' outhouse, and I ran over to find that Carrie's guts had collapsed, and she had eight inches of intestines hanging out of her. I pushed them in with the handle of a hearth broom. This was the horror this poor kid lived with. Later I heard she was married and had moved away, but it was just nip and tuck whether she would grow up or not. And I bet you anything that by the time she was thirty she was a physical wreck, if she even lived that long. You'd see kids with rickets from undernourishment, bowed legs toddling around.

What poverty and those incredible wages did to these people was horrible. And, yet, the mill owner was always putting on the dog, as we would say, flashing his money, and you'd read about all his doings, all about his family, in the society section of the *High Point Enterprise,* and here were these poor people, and it was all wrung out of them.

If anyone could doubt the existence of the class struggle, you surely couldn't while living in a mill village. It was unforgettable, especially when somebody stopped being a case and became a person. They weren't welfare cases: they were people you lived with and loved and spent your time with. It just increased my dedication and determination to do anything and everything I could to change this kind of thing.

The union grew and prospered and in the winter of '41 I was named chairman of the organizing committee of the Textile Workers' local. Actually, we had one little foothold of organized workers in a sea of unorganized workers. And seamless hosiery, men's socks and cheap women's hose, was one of the largest industries at the time. I began to collect names and contacts in various hosiery mills to see if we couldn't eventually stage a drive to organize some of those unorganized workers. I was planning to leave Hillcrest to get a job in a hosiery mill.

I was going with a girl at the time, a southern Jewish girl, a sophomore at Chapel Hill, and began courting her pretty seriously. In June of '41, the day after the invasion of the Soviet Union, we got married.

Back at Hillcrest, the company had gotten on to me and had discovered I was a union bug. The day after my wedding weekend, they fired me. I got a job in an unorganized cotton mill, and we got a two-room apartment nearby the village. It had a toilet outside in the hall, and the walls were painted a shit brindle, the most horrible color I have ever seen. But we were happy, and I was working day and night building up my contacts among seamless hosiery workers in about thirty different textile mills. I had a little file case of names on three-by-five cards, which I kept hidden in the chimney.

It was an easy walk to the Pickett Cotton Mill, but it was a killer of a job. I lasted about three months and learned to do most of the jobs there. They fired me for union activity.

Then, with elaborate phony references, I got a job at Thomas's Hosiery Mill, a long bus ride away. And, of course, working in a seamless hosiery plant made it that much easier to make contacts. There were about eighty mills in the vicinity of High Point and something like five thousand seamless hosiery workers. Anybody with twenty thousand dollars' capital could go into business and get a couple of knitting machines.

The American Federation of Hosiery Workers had been eyeing this area because it was such a wide-open shop and ripe to be organized. The wages were so terribly low and the working conditions awful. But it was tough to organize because the companies were blacklisting right and left. They soon found out that I had made contact with all the best and likeliest union people. So in the fall of '41, our union and the American Federation of Hosiery Workers decided on a joint organizing drive.

A busload of hosiery workers came in from Roanoake, Virginia, and the president and several vice presidents of the national union and a whole crew of organizers came down. We had a big meeting in the High Point union hall and officially launched the drive. I was to quit my mill job the next day and join the union payroll as an assistant chief organizer.

The meeting adjourned Sunday afternoon in early December, and as we got downstairs, somebody told us Pearl Harbor had been bombed. And that was the end of the hosiery drive because, within forty-eight hours, the government had frozen all the raw rayon and silk. By the end of the week, practically all the seamless hosiery workers were heading for Norfolk, Virginia, and Wilmington, North Carolina, to get jobs in shipbuilding and other port-related industries. It was a major exodus, and one hosiery mill after another closed down. The industry just melted away, and all my contacts and my little card file just went to pot. It didn't take me more than twenty-four hours to realize that all my organizing plans had gone down the drain, and the following day I volunteered to enlist in the army.

four

Gladys

If anything, I think that one of the problems with us at that time was that we were too selfless. To think about yourself and your own needs was almost looked down upon. It was selfish. It was disloyal to think about yourself before you thought about what was good for everybody. The young kids today have much more a feeling of themselves as individuals, and I think you have to start with that. You've got to know something about yourself before you can go anywhere.

There was no looking into yourself, no trying to deal with your inner feelings. You couldn't waste your time doing that. You had to give all your energies and your thoughts, your ideas and strength and love to everybody, to mankind. And I suppose that sort of fit in pretty well with me because I really didn't have too much love to give to myself. It was just great for me to be able to forget about myself in that sense, to give whatever I had to this more general idea.

I felt like a heroine in a way. I felt important, and I felt strong. And when I marched in the May Day parade, boy, I felt proud to be a part of that group, to be standing there, letting people know what we all thought, and what I thought. It did a lot for me.

When I was sixteen, I graduated high school and went to Brooklyn College. But that was a bust. I guess all of the seeds of my breakdown were working in me. I couldn't study. I couldn't do anything. I can't really say what led to my falling apart, but when it started, I stopped my political activity. I somehow never connected with the YCL at Brooklyn. I guess I couldn't make the transition from high school, from something I knew, people I knew, into that larger situation in Brooklyn College. I just couldn't get started there. I was in awe and felt out of place. I was frightened. I was overwhelmed. And I ran.

I had seen my brother and sister go through this, and my father and mother, too. When I was studying or reading, my mind just wouldn't stand still, stuff couldn't get into my head. One just doesn't feel as inadequate as I did at the time without knowing something was wrong. I just knew somehow that I couldn't be as dumb as I thought I was. There was a period where I didn't see a soul. I would sneak into classes and sneak into the library. I didn't want to face anything, and I didn't want to live.

I didn't talk to my mother about it. My brother was sort of the head of the family, and by that time he was a little bit all right again. He would vacillate between being kind and sympathetic, and then screaming at me, "You're stupid!" So there wasn't much stability there. My sister was out of the house and was taking care of herself. She wasn't too much help to me at the time. I didn't have anybody to talk to. I just couldn't go on living this way and finally just nagged my brother and sister to death. I told him I felt I had to get some psychiatric help, and I got to a psychiatrist. And then there was the long haul to get well.

I dropped out of school and was going to the doctor for a long time. I had a series of jobs during part of that time, before I got very ill. I always looked for the kinds of jobs where I thought I would be able to do something useful. I worked in a war plant, a United Electrical Workers union shop, the U.E., around Fourteenth Street, making dies for bullets. The die, a piece of steel about two or three inches long, was narrowed down to a short cylindrical tip. It had to be a certain size, and you had to stand there and sand it with some kind of abrasive cloth or paper, and keep measuring with your micrometer until you got it exactly right. It was assembly-line work, and I just kept doing that. It was tedious work, but again, I felt there was a purpose.

When I left home at that time the apartment situation was nothing like it was today, and my friend Norma and I found a very pleasant apartment on Seventeenth or Eighteenth Street. We picked up furniture from here and there. As we were moving in, we noticed two young men, Al and Joel, who lived in the very next apartment. Al was my first love. And, of course, the greatest thing was that both Al and I were good Communist Party members. I don't think I did very much in the Party at that time, but we talked a lot, and Al taught me a lot about politics, and music, and literature. I guess I've always been attached to teachers in some way or other.

Al was a brilliant young engineer and worked for G.E. That was a very happy period until I got sick again, and broke off completely with Al, with everybody, and went through another depressing period. I heard that after we had separated, Al married the friend of a close friend of mine, then received a call from the Russians and left his family and left the States for the Soviet Union. I don't really know the whole story, but apparently they needed his talents.

Norma and I stayed in the apartment for a while, until she went to live with Joel someplace else, and I had to give up the apartment. I would hop in and out of my sister's apartment. I think I even went back home to Avenue M, but that was ghastly—just the whole bit of being back again in Brooklyn and being so far away.

I went to work for a U.E. local in Bloomfield and found a friend there, a young girl about my age who was going through the same things as I was. We were both in therapy, and she had lost her father too. She couldn't find herself either. She was a very dear friend, and that was a rather satisfying, gratifying period of my life. Fern had a wonderful mother, and I loved them both.

For a while I had a room in Bloomfield, but Bloomfield, New Jersey, was a deadly place. So I commuted again. I lived with a succession of women—girls, really. Barbara, the woman my Barbara is named after, was married to a very old friend of the family's and divorced him. We shared an apartment in the Village. Though I never had many friends, the friendships I had were always very intense. I loved Barbara very much, and she loved me.

We lived together a year, a very happy period, and then Barbara had an appendectomy, got peritonitis, and died.

I got a job at the Central Labor Council of the CIO in Newark, New Jersey, and worked there for quite a while. But gradually I stopped everything, absolutely unable to cope. I went to visit my old family doctor in Brooklyn, the man who had taken care of my father. I was in a real fit of hysterics: I accused him of having killed my father, of letting him die. They were very dear friends of our family, and their daughter was one of my best friends, and they loved us. They called my sister, and I had to be taken away to the hospital.

I was just nuts, manic-depressive, and I guess I was manic for quite a while. They couldn't get me into Hillside, one of the best mental hospitals, so I was sent to some place up on the Hudson. There they really used the old-fashioned techniques, and I was put in a straitjacket. I was wild. You can't ever forget that feeling, being wild like that.

Then they got me into Hillside, where I got marvelous care. You know how sometimes you see a movie that's been accelerated, or hear a record that's going too fast? Well, that's the rate at which I went. I'd go around the hospital helping other patients, doing whatever I could, talking to the nurse. At first, I was in a locked building that I couldn't leave without permission. Finally, I was well enough to go to a cottage.

They started me on shock therapy. The electric shock apparently didn't work quite the way they wanted it to, so they put me on Metrazol, an older, more drastic convulsive shock therapy. You don't really feel it because you're out as soon as the shock starts. Maybe once I was aware of the convulsions. They give you a shot beforehand, and there's a table that curves up, so that when your body jumps and comes down again, it doesn't come down flat. You're tied down on both ends, restrained as much as possible, so you don't break any bones or anything. The next thing you know, you wake up in what appears like a crib. It's a hospital cot with the bars up.

You feel like you're an infant; maybe "vegetable" is a better word. You can't articulate. You're not a complete person after it. They take you back to your room, you rest and sleep again, and then gradually you come out of it. Your whole morning would be gone, but by the afternoon you were all right again. I don't know if "normal" is the word, but you were talking again.

There's a number of patients who have to go through this, and I can re-member waiting in line, waiting my turn to go in. And, of course, you're always frightened. But there's nothing to be frightened of, because there's no pain. But there was always a sense of fear. I want to tell you, though, if all mental patients could be treated the way I was treated at Hillside, it would be something. And I was most fortunate I had the private psychiatrist I had, because he got me to Hillside. Because that was a fantastic place.

I've had physical and mental pain. Physically, I haven't been too well a per-son. When they did my lung operation, they had to break ribs, and it hurt, and I was in pain, but there's no agony like that mental pain, nothing like it at all. It's a pervasive kind of pain. Occasionally, I'll wonder if my memory is poor because of the shocks, and I suppose it is. It's done, I guess, to help you forget certain things, to forget your agonies.

My brother and sister came to see me, and they were kind and loving. They knew I was sick. They never didn't love me. It's just that they never knew how to show it. And I had to be shown.

I guess my pain had to come out somewhere, and it had to come out in concentrated form. There were so many years of so much pent up inside me. Finally, I was able to get it out.

Toward the end of my stay, after four or five months of treatment and psychiatric therapy, I got pneumonia and had to be transferred to Queens General Hospital. Dr. Peck, my psychiatrist, came to see me and told me he didn't think it was necessary to go back to Hillside. And I went to live with my sister for a while.

I just knew I had to do something. I had to learn something. I just couldn't piddle around from one job to another with no skills, and I hated any kind of detail work, office work. So I decided to go back to school and went to Hunter College. I must have been about twenty-three or twenty-four. My mother had no money by then, and my sister was just barely managing to take care of herself. So I just had to take care of myself and damned well knew I had to get that degree.

For a while, I worked during the day and went to school at night. For room and board, I lived with a family on the East Side, middle-class swingers. I babysat four nights a week so they could go out. I slept on a foldaway bed in the entranceway to the apartment. Of course, I had absolutely no privacy, and they'd come home late at night and turn on the lights. I went through that for as long as I could.

Then I made day session and sought out the Party again: I'd go to meetings and attend demonstrations. The woman in charge of the employment office at school took a liking to me and got me all kinds of odd jobs. And that was the first time I ever got any pleasure out of going to school. I did well and enjoyed my course work. I still didn't have too many friends at the time and can remember eating alone at school, walking into the cafeteria unable to go over to any group. But it didn't bother me as much at the time because I was really very excited by school.

I fell in love with anthropology during my required science course. My anthro teacher encouraged me tremendously. I became an anthropology major and minored in education. I was fascinated with the history of where we came from, of different peoples, the story of mankind. Though my heart was in anthropology, I knew I had to be able to make a living. It wasn't that I was all fired up to be a teacher, but the practical side of me said you've got to be able to go out and work on something within a few years.

five

Junius

As antimilitarist as I was—I was almost a pacifist—when Pearl Harbor came and I saw the advance of fascism, I immediately figured I would defend the bad against the worst. I discussed it with the Party and my wife, and I volunteered. I spent four years in the army, and my left-wing background followed me everywhere I went.

It seemed like I was at war with the United States as well as the Nazis, because I was victimized from the second month of my enlistment until the end of the war. For the first eighteen months, I was stuck in semi–concentration camps with an overwhelming number of German citizens and Nazi cardholders who had been drafted before Pearl Harbor. Usually, the ratio would be ten to fifteen Nazis to one left-winger. At Fort Ethan Allen in Vermont, I was the post librarian for eight months and lived in the library. We had an international club of anti-Nazis: a Japanese Princeton graduate, a couple of Danes, a Jewish German refugee whose father had been a high official in the Weimar Republic, and a South German rabbi. And after hours, our "sewing circle" used to have the greatest times in the library.

After Fort Ethan Allen, I spent another six months in a little military-police camp in Connecticut. I wasn't an openly acknowledged Communist at this point, but another guy there was, and we went to see the commanding officer. He complained that he was being discriminated against because he was a Communist, and I complained that I was being discriminated against because I was a Communist sympathizer. We raised bloody hell and said we were sick of this nonsense, and we volunteered for overseas duty.

He was sent to an infantry unit, and I was sent to the Mitchel Field air force base in Long Island. I was still being watched like a hawk by army intelligence, but I became the acting top-kick of the medical detachment there, and I stayed for about eighteen months. Finally, after five different attempts, I made it overseas to Italy and spent close to a year there before the war ended.

The army, though, was a valuable experience. I worked harder than I ever did in my life trying to make the outfits I was in take shape. And I learned how to work with people of the most divergent views, backgrounds, and objectives. It was marvelous training, and I was usually in the peculiar position of having a lot of authority without the rank. Ratings were frozen, first of all, and second, army intelligence was determined that I wasn't going to get promoted if they could help it. I got used to being the acting first sergeant of a huge outfit with eighteen hundred men, and ran the damned outfit as a corporal, and got things done. It was good training not to get high and mighty with stripes on your arm. Besides, being in an army in an antifascist war is a very different thing from being in the army today, which, I gather, is a fate worse than death. Like many other Communists, I shared many rich experiences in the army in World War II.

During the war, I very much appreciated Earl Browder's efforts to broaden the Party, to dissolve it in the South and make it a less rigid Communist association. Browder was general secretary of the Party and the complete Party leader, personality cult and all. He was a very forceful guy, somewhat arrogant, but an extraordinarily able person. His whole political emphasis during the war was to unite and fight for victory over fascism above everything else. And he was looking more and more to build a broad coalition, broadening our whole approach to political change. The idea was to make the Party much less rigid in its requirements for membership, to drop the political rigidity that made everybody a real uptight Marxist-Leninist. Hopefully, radicals of any strain would feel at home in such an organization, and we could, with broad coalitions, move toward socialism.

One of my most joyful days in the army was the day that Browder was freed from prison. He was imprisoned on a passport violation, the only thing they could think to nail him with, and served close to a year. Roosevelt either pardoned him or commuted his sentence as a move toward unity in the country, and he was released somewhere in the spring of '42. I was just ecstatic.

Then, while I was still in Italy, Browder was expelled from the Party. I couldn't figure out what happened. I had really missed most of the action, and for a long time all I knew was what I read in the U.S. army newspaper, *Stars and Stripes,* and I couldn't get too much from that. People sent me a few clippings, but they were being discreet with the mail. I learned that there was a big hassle going on in the American Party and that Jacques Duclos, the French Communist Party leader, had denounced Browder as an anti-Marxist, anti-Leninist revisionist who was destroying the American Party.

This had the American Party in turmoil. Theodore Draper, in his books on the Party, goes into it quite exhaustively and with much greater detail than I could, because I'll get my sequences mixed up. But during this time, William Z. Foster came out of the woodwork and, in the most doctrinaire way, started a real Stalinist-style denunciation and demolition job on Browder, and practically everybody joined in. There was a wholesale rummaging through everybody's behavior and attitudes, which, at least in New York, was a very unsavory thing. A few honored exceptions dropped out of sight for a long period. Here was a guy who was idealized, idolized, and revered; then he was attacked and disgraced and finally dumped. I was quite upset and couldn't wait to get back and find out what was going on.

When I came back, I joined my wife in Chapel Hill and decided I'd finish my degree and go into graduate work in history under the G.I. Bill. I decided to go up to New York and reestablish ties with the Party, and see what was going on. I hunted up people and was told that Browder had been doing all kinds of bad things and that if he had gotten his way, there would no longer have been a Communist movement. It had looked and felt to me that Browder's approach would have made it possible to live like a rather normal person, to pursue our endeavors more fruitfully and productively. For me, it would have made it possible to pursue a scholarly career without feeling I was letting down the struggle or abandoning the fight.

I guess I was somewhat flabbergasted to find out I was all wrong; and I figured that this must be my bourgeois liberalism, and my bourgeois background, coming out. To my shame, I swallowed it over a period of weeks and months. And, of course, this was the beginning of one of the blackest periods in the history of the Communist Party.

Looking back, it sometimes seems like we had an almost Calvinistic sense of guilt. The true path was hard and narrow and the only path that could lead to socialism. And if you thought of leaving this example set by Lenin and Stalin, and if you welcomed this breadth, well, it just showed what an insidious middle-class makeup you had. And because of it, you were trying to take a less rocky road, one which would take you into the swamps of middle-class liberalism.

I felt terrible that even with all my dedication I had strayed so far from my true goal. And I felt terrible that I was about to be absorbed by a gray and formless liberalism which would take from the people their only true weapon and revolutionary arm, the Communist Party.

In many cases, people had been absorbed by the system, and the reality of that fact was exploited to the full by Foster and everybody else out to do Browder in. But the fact was that during the war, the Party had suddenly discovered America. Thousands of Communist veterans in the army had gotten a new feeling and understanding of the country and the people in it, and were trying to grapple with American problems.

Now remember, I came into the Party very late in the thirties, but most of those who had come in ten years earlier came into a rigid Stalinist thing. Time after time, Russian Party experience was translated and applied directly, without so much of a change in syntax, to American problems. That was the period when the Young Communist League addressed a leaflet "To the Workers and Peasants of Brownsville." This is how literally Soviet Party policy was translated from Russia to this country. There was just a pathetic lack of political realism, of any kind of realism. This might have appealed to first- and second-generation immigrants, people who'd been through the 1905 revolution in Russia, but to most New Yorkers, "Workers and Peasants of Brownsville" wasn't exactly the right approach.

In the course of the thirties, in the height and aftermath of the Depression, with the unemployment movement, in the movement to support Spain, and the struggle to build the union movement, the Communists found themselves in the mainstream of things and made sense to a lot of people. And that, in turn, made sense to Communists, and the Party was a much broader political group by the end of the thirties than it was at the beginning.

The fact that we were actually beginning to think a little for ourselves politically was unbearable to Stalin. It meant, I think, the end of his role in the worldwide Communist movement. Individual Communist parties should be used to support the Soviet Union; the hell with what went on within their countries. That was always his attitude toward the Communist parties of other countries, and it's still basically the Soviet attitude.

Well, I felt I was completely out of touch and had been for four years, really. Bart was twenty-five hundred miles away on the West Coast, and when I got "straightened out" in New York, I went along with it. It seemed like the only thing to do was to go back home and build a tight party structure. I attempted to do this, but, in retrospect, I'm happy that we generally took a rather broad political approach. And I was criticized several times for having a number of traces of "Browderism" in my approach.

With the onset of the cold war, things got tighter. I'll never forget the

Fulton, Missouri, speech of Winston Churchill,[1] the "Iron Curtain" speech which really inaugurated the cold war. That, of course, proved the validity of having dumped Browder, you see, because what illusions could you have of working with a government in a society where the government itself is leading an anti-Communist crusade? So all this tended to move us deeper and deeper into the nice little sectarian morass, where you stick to what you called "principles" but were really doctrinaire rules. The main one was that the Soviet Union can do no wrong. This was the road to disaster, and it didn't take very long. From '45, '46, when Browder was dumped, to '56, ten years' time, the Communist Party had largely shattered itself. Of course, it was under tremendous attack all the time, but there was almost no way the Communist Party could have better aided that attack than by this policy.

When I went back down home to North Carolina, the South was a very different ballgame. There was such a political vacuum in the South that the Communist movement was able to play a maximum role with minimal forces. Negroes were completely segregated, and the political situation was generally backward throughout the South. North Carolina was the enlightened part of the South, but nonetheless it was still a generation or two back of the rest of the country in economic, political, and social development. You were surrounded by such extraordinarily bad conditions.

It was during this period that a woman I knew from Harlan County wrote the famous ballad, "Which Side Are You On?" "Either," as the song goes, "you'll be a union man or a thug for J. H. Blair," the big coal operator. It was the clear choosing up of sides: you're either going to be a racist and uphold racism, or you're going to fight for Negro liberation. You'll either support the union or support an oppressive system. It was very stark, black and white, and there weren't very many grays and in-betweens.

The oppression was abysmal. In a typical cotton mill, the one in the mill village where I lived, the spinners were all women, and they were subject to physical abuse. You could get slugged by a foreman. This sort of thing took place in a lily-white industry, so you can imagine what it was like in the tobacco stemmeries, where tobacco was stripped from its stem, and where the women workers were mostly black. There, getting clouted was just commonplace. These conditions might have existed in the 1880s in the North, but it was taking place in the '30s and '40s in the South. And it accounts for why most of us southern Communists were so utterly committed.

It was so morally clear to us that trade unionism was desirable, and that anybody that stood in the way of it was either blind, vicious, or stupid. And that anybody that couldn't see the stupidity, the viciousness, and the immorality of racism fit the same categories. Of course, we figured most people were either blind or cowardly. But we felt like we were carrying a beacon light. These were self-evident things that a whole society had just bypassed. Of course, life and politics are very complicated, and we were very simplistic in a lot of ways, but in retrospect, the thing that I don't think any of us scorn or laugh at was the moral dedication and feeling we had at that time.

It's difficult to explain how absolutely isolated most whites were from blacks, and the extraordinary impact it had on me to meet on social and political terms with blacks. It just wiped out generations of conditioning. After all, my father's father was a Confederate colonel, and my father, who grew up in Reconstruction, cut his teeth in the Populist movement of the mid-nineties, a movement drowned not in blood but in absolute political expropriation. Negroes were just denied the vote when it became apparent they could gain power in the South.

My father happened to be part of the most reformist wing of the white power structure and had terrible guilt feelings about this. While he genuinely believed in good educational opportunities for blacks, it was all part of the "white man's burden." As an employer, his own policies were extraordinarily liberal, and, though he paid double the norm, it was patriarchal and patronizing. And that was about the most advanced kind of white approach you'd find. My father, of course, took a lot of flak for this and was considered very unwise for stirring up the expectations of the blacks. This was the milieu I lived in.

It's hard to remember that even the army was segregated. I remember by some snafu a black soldier was transferred to our outfit in Vermont, and I had to get two or three other guys together to stay with this guy because we were afraid he wasn't going to leave in one piece. And this was in Vermont, with no great number of southerners in the outfit. I mention little incidents like this because it's so hard to give the feel of things and very hard to do otherwise.

Even though they belonged to a Jim Crow army, the returning black veterans brought change back with them. Black soldiers had traveled all over the country, and the world, and had discovered that it wasn't all this oppressive elsewhere. They had been treated decently overseas.

After the war, there was an era of relative enlightenment. I knew a black schoolteacher with the same last name as me back in Chapel Hill. He was a very charming guy in his early twenties and had attended social gatherings at my in-laws' home not far from the center of town.

We would pick him up someplace and simply drive up the driveway to a side entrance. And if we kept the outside lights off, we didn't have to go in like we were under fire. We kept the shades drawn and could have a delightful social evening, and for a while, at least, forget the environment we were in. Without the precautions, word would have circulated among rednecks and cab drivers, and in short order people would be saying: "That house has all kinds of things going on in it. They been having niggers in socially." It would have drawn heavy attention and all kinds of subtle retaliation.

One time we had a couple of girls from New York down visiting us. We had a party of about fifteen or twenty people and had a wonderful time. It was a great talk-fest. There were two or three black people, including this teacher. One of the girls thought he was just charming and was delighted to have a chance to talk to a guy like this. The next day she was walking three or four blocks from where we lived and met up with him.

She greeted him very warmly and proceeded to walk with him down the street. Well, by the time they had walked a quarter of a block together, he said very politely, "You know, we're attracting a lot of attention, and I hate to do this, but I'm going to turn into this alley, and I'm going to run, because I don't want to get killed." And he just took off. They hadn't even shook hands or anything. But he recognized that he was in danger of his life and certainly his job. These were the facts of life in the "Athens of the South," its most enlightened community in 1946.

I remember in 1947, Bayard Rustin and two other guys, two blacks and a white, made an historic test by buying tickets and riding and sitting in the front seats of an interstate bus. A local white Presbyterian minister named Jones went to greet them when they arrived in Chapel Hill. There was such anger and violence directed toward this minister that his house was attacked. I had to organize a bunch of Communist and non-Communist veterans to stand watch, and we did guard duty. We got him and his family out of town, and occupied his house to keep it from being burned down. His assistant minister had his hair parted with a brick, and cab drivers stormed his house. This was the Chapel Hill I returned to—and it was much better than it had been before.

Well, in the spring of '46 I entered the University of North Carolina on the G.I. Bill and decided I was going to go for an academic career. The school, like most places at the time, was filled with veterans who had left-wing friends in the army and had come to school in Chapel Hill looking to participate in some sort of progressive action. They were much enlightened by their war experiences, and were determined to see that the world was a hell of a lot better place than it had been before.

With all my military and trade-union experience, I was running the Party in no time at all, and found myself a big man on campus in the veterans' organization. I was vice president of the American Veterans Committee for most of its existence. I was busily organizing Communist groups and recruiting people to the Party, and before we knew it, we had a membership of about two hundred people in Chapel Hill alone. And there were about thirty blacks in that group.

We organized the Party in terms of clubs of between five and ten people. So I wouldn't be the big wheel in everything, we developed a structure where I'd meet with a city committee which had contact with each of the clubs. Each club would have at least one member on this citywide committee, and we'd have meetings maybe once or twice a week. The bulk of the meeting would be spent discussing our activities. We would talk about, for example, how we should behave in the local chapter of the Southern Conference for Human Welfare, an organization of young southerners working for economic and social reform. We'd discuss what we had done and how effective we had been, what direction we were going, and what kind of things we wanted to push for.

Racism was on every agenda, and the movement to integrate the University of North Carolina was begun at a Party club meeting I attended in early '47. In the course of that struggle, many other people besides Communists got involved, and it was by no means solely a Communist activity. But the Party started it and pushed it, and when it seemed to falter, we were the ones who revived it again and again. We were the sparkplug, and we brought together all kinds of people, people with whom we could hardly agree, people, even, who were violently anti-Communist and often politically obnoxious. Yet the issue stayed foremost, and on our initiative, the differences were subdued.

It took five years until the first Negro was admitted into the law school, and it seems so long ago I'd almost forgotten about it, but that was something we saw through from beginning to victory. And then when the first black students came, our people tried to make life easier for them, gave them every kind of aid and assistance we could. And it all started at a Party club meeting.

It's surprising how hard we tried. There was such a dedicated attempt to change things around. Southerners, black and white, are conscience-driven, and boy, when there was something we put our hearts into, we'd take it damned seriously. And there was such an emphasis on consideration of others in the movement. I knew one guy in a Party school who could never get up in the morning: you could pick him up and stand him on his feet, and he'd collapse.

Well, someone made a political question out of it, and said that wasn't a comradely way to behave. So, by George, the next morning on five hours of sleep, one eye here, and one eye there, he gets up, staggers to his feet, into his clothes, and shows up on time. And that sort of a miracle was a common thing; when you knew you had so many meaningful things to do, the idea of frittering away time was unthinkable. That's the way I felt, and I guess you put a lot of your own personality in an organization when you're leading it.

It wasn't all meetings, though, and I guess some of the most unforgettable times were the socializing we'd do. I used to have an open house one night a week in Chapel Hill, and there'd usually be about seventy-five people there, with an informer or two in the crowd, I'm sure. But nobody quite knew who was and who wasn't in the Party, and we tried to keep it as secret as possible.

One of the funniest things that happened at one of our parties involved an old comrade friend who lived in the mountains with his wife. He was a marvelous guy, full of vigor and vim, and a committed socialist. Apparently, though, he hadn't read Lenin on the Woman Question, or Engels's *Origin of the Family*. One of the women comrades was talking to his wife, a very warm, simple person, and she says, "You know, I don't think a woman is worth her salt if she don't fix her husband hot bread for breakfast." And this absolutely staggered everybody. She'd get up every morning before sunrise and make hot biscuits for her husband.

That, of course, was symbolic of the greatest backwardness on the Woman Question. We were always concerned about the place of women in American society and read and discussed Engels and the German Communist Clara Zetkin's "On the Woman Question."[2] Lenin was a bit on the prudish side and never got very deep. But I would guess Communist husbands wash more dishes than any other husbands in the world—American Communist husbands, in any case. I don't think Soviet Communist husbands ever washed a dish.

This was an article of faith with us, and generally doing a share of the domestic chores. If somebody didn't, he was just looked at aghast, you know. We weren't able to figure out much in the way of making it a political movement, but it went pretty deep as an internal matter of lifestyle. We would always try to get more women in leadership, and by far the most outstanding leaders among the tobacco workers in Winston-Salem were women.

Of course, one of the things about my Party career was that I had very little contact with the North. I didn't have the sort of experiences the New York Communists had, experiences which probably added a healthy layer of cynicism. In the South, and in North Carolina, we had extremely close-knit and warm relationships. In the student movement everybody just loved everybody else. There were sectarian tendencies, but there was also an overriding feeling of affection and confidence in each other. We were doing something valuable and didn't get into all kinds of intra-party intrigue and hassling.

After the war, there were two main centers of Communist activity in the South: the University of Texas and the University of North Carolina. Then it fanned out from there, including, later on, the University of Florida. A lot of kids, mostly Zionist-left youth from New York, used to stop off in Chapel Hill on their way north and south. Somebody gave them my name, and I used to have them stacked up like cord wood all over my house. Carloads would come through every time there was a holiday.

During the war, the Party had inspired organizing drives in the furniture and tobacco industries, especially in Winston-Salem, the home of the R. J. Reynolds Tobacco Company. By the time I had gotten home from the war, there were something like ten to twelve thousand tobacco workers being organized in Winston-Salem, a good percentage of them black. Now this was unheard of—the same union for blacks and whites. And this same thing was going on in a large furniture plant. No one would have thought it could be done. The textile industry was all-white, so there was no question of it there, but in these industries, although the skilled jobs were mostly white, blacks and whites worked together. Here was a joint organization of black and white workers in one of the biggest corporations in the state, maybe the country. So we were really hitting where it hurt and shaking up the establishment mightily.

Meanwhile, the war had brought such prosperity to the textile union in High Point it had become like an old, comfortable, and conservative union. When I had lived there just a few years before, you'd never see a car on the street unless it was a bill collector. Now, in the spring of '46, everybody had their own car, and everybody had bought their house from the company. The company sold them for practically nothing to the people who'd been paying exorbitant rents all these years. The company had done nothing on them for twenty-five or thirty years, and they were going to need extensive repairs, so it was really no great loss.

You couldn't see through the walls anymore—they had been insulated, had paneling on the inside, rugs on the floors, and gotten new furniture. I couldn't recognize it. The same old people were there, but the kids had grown up. Kids who had been slated for the cotton mills had gotten into the army, and with the G.I. Bill were going to trade schools and to college. And the younger generation was definitely not planning to stay in the mill village. All over the South, mill villages were disappearing as company after company decided they were no longer economical.

It was an altogether transformed situation. And for the first time, the company couldn't tell you how to live and what to do. It was no paradise, but wages were now living wages. Consumer goods were just becoming available, and the villagers just reveled in it. Even though textile plants remained unorganized, my proletarians had practically become middle-class.

Tobacco, though, was a very different situation. The Party organizer for the region got called back down to Alabama, and I found myself right in the middle of things. Tobacco workers, mostly black and a great many of them black women, were being organized in Charleston, South Carolina, now a part of my district. So I was traveling like a circuit rider between Chapel Hill, Durham, Winston-Salem, and Charleston, South Carolina—going back and forth and God knows where, and all the time being a full-time student, and a married student at that. And my hands were full with all kinds of student affairs, Party and non-Party. I didn't sleep much, and it got more and more hectic.

The tobacco companies were plotting away like crazy since they were so threatened, and they got an informer who had been an organizer for the tobacco workers' union. The House Un-American Activities Committee called her to Washington, and she testified that the whole tobacco union was run by Communists, and she mentioned my name. There were banner headlines all over the state, and it created a tremendous sensation because my family was so prominent. As I recall I didn't say "yes" or "no" to her charges but affirmed my belief in a number of things and continued very much as before. Finally, the whole thing sort of blew over.

By this time, the cold war was beginning to get under way but good, and the Communist hunt was on. Some people in the American Veterans Committee started an anti-Communist drive and tore the organization to shreds. And then they blamed the Communists.

I ran across one of the leading guys in all this business some years later, and he was reminiscing. The American Veterans Committee was a very large organization, and we, as much-abused Reds, had a left faction which we could pretty much count on. And they had a right faction, so everybody made a play for the people in the center, so to speak. Well, on practically every kind of crucial vote we would win about three-fourths of the center. This guy absolutely appalled me with his accounts of all the dirty and dishonest skullduggery he had pulled. They used to stack votes, get proxies, and vote people who literally didn't exist at these meetings. And we were exemplary in our tactics.

This guy was confessing all of this to me, a typical sneaky Communist. Those guys used to have sessions at two in the morning to figure out how to obstruct the will of the Veterans Committee. This particular guy was a secretary to a senator in Washington, married with two children, and widely expected to become governor of South Carolina. But he ruined his political prospects when he ran off with a redhead.

By the summer of '47 I was getting more and more concerned with the red-baiting that was going on. I was being urged by the Party nationally and locally to come out openly as a member of the Communist Party, especially since I had been fingered by this stool pigeon. In the fall of '47, I finally decided to do it, and the Party unobtrusively put out a leaflet, and I signed it as chairman. Well, this made eight-column headlines in newspapers all across the state and put me under tremendous pressure.

By this time I had entered graduate school and was going along with graduate work in history. The reaction varied—after all, I had been there on and off for twelve years, and had gone to school with half the faculty's kids, so it was pretty hard to make all the clichés stick. I certainly wasn't a wild-eyed Russian. Everybody knew me, and I was a fairly substantial person on campus. There was general amazement, and I indicated that I had been a Communist for many years, ever since I was nineteen. It created a tremendous splash. But things went on, and I still managed to speak before the Baptist Student Union, the Presbyterian youth group, and a dozen other campus organizations.

Of course, though, it's the old history of the individual in the Communist movement: take somebody with breadth, somebody with broad connections engaged in fruitful activity for social change, and he becomes identified as a Communist, and from then on the story is declining public effectiveness and isolation. If I had not been a public Communist, I would have been infinitely more effective. But, of course, that's hindsight. What really led me to announce my membership publicly was the idea that I could, at least locally, put a crimp in some of the nonsense going around about Communists and Communism. I guess I felt that with the hysteria and absurdity of the cold war, instead of the anti-Communists having a nameless, formless target, which included anything they didn't like, I would stand up and give it a concrete and creditable shape. I thought I could make that contribution because I was highly regarded and considered a top graduate student. I would answer them in this way.

My first marriage pretty much fell apart by the fall of '48. I don't think she was temperamentally suited to the kind of pressure that was beginning to descend with the cold war and the increase in anti-Communism. Then, when I became a known Communist, the pressure and publicity were tremendous and the strain constant.

The fact was that "Communist" was about the dirtiest word in the book, and her husband was a Communist. You lose your anonymity, and you're conspicuous as hell twenty-four hours a day. Anything and everything you do is observed. People you don't know, know who you are. And people you don't know are looking at you all the time. You're never completely at ease.

It was a hell of a strain, and then, too, the marriage was a casualty of the war. When you go away at twenty-one and come back almost four years later, at that stage of your life it's a long hiatus. Things really never went right again.

There were continual physical threats, so we moved into a house in Carrboro, a mill-village-like suburb of Chapel Hill. Our neighbors were very backward people, and while they were cordial and polite, they were aghast that real, live Communists were around. My first wife was rather placid and sweet and gentle, and it tore her all up to feel the constant pressure. There was no end to the threats and publicity. I don't remember whether a cross was burned in the yard while we were still married or not, but the isolation from the community was increasing.

And of course, there was the tendency for friends to get more ingrown. When you're isolated politically, you turn to your closest friends and try to hold each other's hand, and she had that tendency pretty strongly. It wasn't easy being married to the only public Communist in the South. It wasn't easy at all.

I tried to take it in stride. It'll squash you if you don't. You're front-page news every time you open your yap, and you have to live with it. You can't give a damn what anybody says about you; you've got to get a hard shell. I don't think my former wife realized the repercussions when she agreed with my decision to declare myself publicly. I don't think she knew as well as I did what it would mean, and how hard it would be to function, what a burden of responsibility it puts on you.

We in the Party grew increasingly isolated, and the process repeated itself time and time again. We would discover a wonderful individual who was left-oriented and get him into the Communist movement. And in a matter of months or sometimes years, our main achievement would have been to have radicalized him and isolated him to the point where he could hardly live in his community anymore. No matter how broad his ties nor how much respect there was for him, we'd end up with a guy isolated and politically useless. And it happened because we frequently pushed him into positions that were not viable in the environment in which he lived and worked—in his union, for example.

We met some wonderful black guys in Durham, North Carolina, members of the old and reactionary American Federation of Labor Tobacco Union, and spent a lot of time with them. We loved them dearly and knew their families. They were the rank-and-file leaders in the shop, the guys everybody went to and looked to—the real leaders, not the union bureaucrats. They were incorruptible, and they didn't kiss the foreman's behind. And yet, because we followed the party line on trade unions, we managed to get their necks stuck out so far that people were scared to talk to them, much less come to them for leadership. And we managed to get them isolated because they trusted and, I think you could say, loved us.

Their strength was very precarious, and instead of obliquely pushing, we put them in constant battle with their conservative leadership. The union leadership was playing footsy with the company, and a struggle based on the real needs of the workers, a movement on any specific issue in the plant, could have led to a gradual transformation of the union. But it was much easier to distribute leaflets late at night denouncing the leadership.

It's fine to denounce them, but what's the alternative? Who do you go to? Many workers took this as an attack on their own union, and it put our guys on the spot. Ultimately, the union hacks were able to pinpoint them. It was just another example of an approach used in every field: the push for extreme, way-out positions.

It was a policy, I think, that was unconcerned with any long-range objective. It was based on the belief that there were only a handful of really good people, and you ought to get them into the movement. Of course, it was utterly disastrous, and as much as we loved each other in the movement, people became less and less able to function in their own surroundings. As the pressure grew, it got worse and worse, and finally, we could hardly talk to anybody except each other. We had lost our union base, our mass base, so to speak. Not that they were that vast, but there were ten thousand workers organized in Winston-Salem, and thousands of furniture workers and tobacco workers in eastern North Carolina and Charleston, South Carolina.

Electrical workers in Tennessee were organized almost entirely by Party people both on and off the union payroll. The union still survives, and certainly working conditions were transformed, but the people that organized them were out and, along with them, much of the heart and soul of unionism. Four or five years after organizing these workers, I doubt if most of them would even dare to go to a union meeting.

In some cases the union was lost: R. J. Reynolds is still an open shop. Still, it'll never be anything like the hell it was. The foreman used to walk among the Negro women smacking them or patting their behinds. But this extraordinary union, with its extraordinary leadership, just went down the drain, defeated by a narrow margin in the Labor Board elections in '49.

Remember, this was an integrated union, more black than white. But being so very sensitive on the Negro Question—we were so glad to have Negroes organized—we leaned over backwards until the company began to terrorize the white workers who had gone along with the union and supported the blacks. It was considered "white chauvinism" for a white man or woman to argue with a black man or woman in the Party leadership. And, more and more, the national black leadership of the Party imposed a line of political thought on the situation.

They would come down and meet with the union leaders and fan sectarian feeling. They tended to take an extreme line on white workers. "If they've got any guts," they would say, "let them stand up and fight," ignoring the fact that for a white worker to just belong to a predominantly black union at that time was an act of great courage in the South. And many of the black workers had immense respect for the white workers who would go along with them even a little way.

The proportions at Reynolds were maybe sixty-forty black to white, and the company was smart. They divided and chipped away at the white workers until it became mainly a black union. The effect of the Party's policy was to damn the whites. "It's the blacks who are the real heroes," the Party leaders insisted. So they were; but objectively, by not supporting the whites, we just lost our chance for an alliance between blacks and whites, the only way we could possibly win. Then the company put in labor-saving technological devices and eliminated thousands of black workers in the stemmeries by putting in machinery. The company was systematically taking black jobs and giving them to whites, making various departments all-white. They just reversed themselves and shifted the ratio of workers back to 75 percent white to 25 percent black. Any chance at black-white unity was pretty much shot.

On top of this, the company did a tremendous job of red-baiting the union. And we did just about everything to aid them. If the Italian Communists led a steel strike in Italy, don't think Local 22 of the Food and Tobacco Workers Union in Winston-Salem didn't have to send a resolution supporting the strike. Every time somebody with a brass-hat brain in New York decided we ought to get more support for this or that international cause, they'd call on this huge local, Local 22, to come along and pass a resolution of support. And each and every resolution would be loudly announced in the local press: "Local 22 Supports a Communist Cause!"

The first black city councilman in the South, a middle-class minister, was elected in Winston-Salem out of a Communist initiative. So, with nice working-class sectarianism, the union leaders decided, "This guy is a minister, he's part of the bourgeoisie." And so he became the main enemy there for a while. Pretty soon you've got the black community split: a black working-class community pitted against the considerable black middle-class community.

The National Association for the Advancement of Colored People, the NAACP, would even be attacked by this union leadership. Finally, you had a whittled-down union standing in splendid isolation—isolated from the rest of the trade-union movement in the state and isolated in its own community.

More and more, the Left was cutting its own throat, eliminating possible allies and going it alone. And an inability to compromise, an inability to modify tactics, became what we considered "a principled position." I used to hate the sound of those words, "a principled position," because that meant you had to denounce some guy who was perfectly fine on a particular issue but disagreed with you on something much less immediate and more abstract. We set standards for political purity that were unable to be met both within the Party and for people we worked with outside.

In 1948, although it produced tremendous activity, the Progressive Party was a real disaster for us. We got all kinds of people who had been active in the Democratic Party into the Progressive Party, where they were subject to all kinds of attack and lost much of their influence.

But to be fair, even though we made plenty of mistakes, we did prestigious things on the Negro Question. And this is one area where I'm less inclined to denigrate our achievements. There's no question we raised the conscious-ness of the entire white South on the Negro Question. We roused their con-science to a considerable degree, and conducted practical-defense fights with the most far-reaching effects among liberal, intellectual, and church groups throughout the state.

Even though the tendency was to consider the NAACP a very reactionary organization because of their anti-Communism slant, and to bait them, my pet approach was to try to put them in a position where they would have to come to the defense of people we couldn't defend half as well.

We had a case where a black guy, Mack Ingram, a father of eight, was charged with the rape of a white woman down in Caswell County. I discovered the case by accident when I read two lines about it in the Greensboro paper. Caswell County is a real Deep South county in North Carolina, and about the last time it had made the news was during the twenties, when they lynched four Negroes from trees on the courthouse lawn. It was that sort of place. The pros-ecutor admitted that Mack Ingram was no closer than seventy-five feet from the "victim" but charged he had leered at her. It sounded awfully peculiar.

I got ahold of Louis Austin, the very courageous Negro editor of the *Caro-lina Times,* and asked him if he knew anything about it. He had missed the story but knew somebody he could call down there. So we left his office, went to a payphone, and called a Negro businessman he knew there. And this guy says, "Man, that thing stinks to heaven."

Well, I got somebody to drive me there, and Louis's friend put me on the floor of his panel truck because he couldn't be seen riding with a white man. I had a Negro comrade with me who could take photographs. I interviewed Mack Ingram, and we took pictures of him and his family; and then I went on foot and interviewed white neighbors. I got a tremendous in-depth story. It turned out that this girl had what in the South we called "round heels"—she had a very bad reputation and needed an excuse to have the abortion she wanted.

We turned the story over to Louis Austin, who gave me some kind of pseudonym for a byline and published the whole thing with all of the pictures. He used the whole front page, and it created a sensation. I phoned in the story and sent the pictures up to a black reporter at the *New York Post*. He rewrote it and journalized it up a bit and it appeared in the *Post* and made a national splash. As soon as the article appeared, I called on the governor to declare martial law in Caswell County. When a man could be charged with, and convicted of, rape while the prosecution and the complaining witness admitted he never got closer than seventy-five feet, there was no law and order.

Well, this created a scandal, and I was being denounced all over the place. The governor couldn't say much except that he was going to investigate it. Little Caswell County was besieged by the State Department, and diplomats and foreign secretaries of a dozen foreign nations were calling for information.

As part of the same statement, I called on the NAACP to defend Mack Ingram. The NAACP denounced the hell out of me, too, but because it was just so monstrous, they had to take the case. The next thing you know, Mack Ingram had good lawyers, and the Party didn't have to do another thing about it.

Around this time, I finished all my graduate course work at the university, but I couldn't get permission for my dissertation subject. I wanted to do something like you're trying to do, go out while some of the survivors of the old Socialist movement in North Carolina were still alive and interview them. But the people in charge were scared to agree to it. Some of them later testified for me at my trials, but they didn't seem to have the guts to go along with my dissertation. I guess they figured the university trustees would be riding herd on them.

By early '49, I had become head of the Party and was the district organizer. Like Bart before me, I was going around not just North and South Carolina now but to Virginia, Tennessee, and even Mississippi. And I was keeping in touch with even single individuals, trying to give them perspective and keep them from being exposed.

six

Gladys

One day, my friend Bobby said, "Come on, Gladys, let's go up to Camp Unity for a weekend. Let's see what it's like." He was looking for a girl, and I suppose I was looking for a boy. The second night we were there, this young man and woman came to our table. They didn't say a word to each other, and I thought for sure they were married. He was awfully cute. She got up and left, and it was obvious then that he had nothing to do with her. Bobby started talking to him. And we just sort of became interested in each other immediately. It was a very fast courtship.

Junie had been separated from his first wife for about a year or so and had been a hunk of misery. The Party people down South were just like a family, and one couple in particular just insisted that he get away. He was working too hard, looked tired, and had no girl. The circles were rather limited, and everybody was coupled up. So they packed him off to Camp Unity. And that's where I met him.

It was a weekend in July, and we went to the Paul Robeson concert in Peekskill. Junie and Bobby and a couple of other people and I drove there together. The crowd was great, but we were surrounded by hostility, and Robeson had a bodyguard around him. It was a rousing meeting; there were speeches, and then Robeson sang, and it was wonderful. As we all got in our cars to go home, word slowly got back that all the windows should be raised. And there was this line of people standing there, shouting and throwing rocks while the state police stood by. It was pretty rough. And, although nothing happened to our particular car, others were pretty banged up. When we got back to Camp Unity, we got word that a group of guys didn't get out. So Junie and a group of men went back and got them back.

We spent the rest of the weekend together, and then he came to New York City, and we spent every moment together. He had already started talking about marriage.

After he returned to North Carolina, we wrote constantly. He wanted me to come down Christmastime to meet his family and friends, and wanted all his friends and comrades to meet me. And, of course, I was scared stiff because I knew his family wasn't really waiting with open arms for me.

I was still really quite shaky and unsure of myself. I had discussed with my psychiatrist whether I was ready to leave him, and although he never met Junie, he said yes. But it takes a long time for you to internalize all of this, for all the health that you've gained over those years to really become a part of you. Junie knew my whole story and was just wonderful.

My first introduction to the Communist Party of North Carolina was Junie's dear friends, Bernie and Bea Friedland. Bea, a wonderfully compulsive kind of nut, though never having met me before, just started running up and down the Raleigh station platform and found me. And she pulled me along until I saw Junie. On the trip back to Carrboro, Bea, who has always been a rather nonconformist thinker, made some derogatory comment about all of the big photos of Stalin in the May Day parade. And everybody laughed. I thought this was absolutely blasphemous, and I remember my first very judgmental reaction: "Very bourgeois woman . . . humph, humph."

Bernie was the district organizer, and he was from New York City. And, of course, you couldn't help but be tremendously impressed with Bernie. Even though he was a Stalinist dictator, he's a love, and his outstanding quality was that of a humanist, somebody who cared for people. I just loved him from the moment I met him, and to this day, they are our dearest friends.

We went to our little house in Carrboro, and I guess I expected some kind of log cabin because Junie kept saying, "Now you know it's a very simple little house, not fancy, and there's not too much to it." But I remember being tremendously impressed with it. It was a mill house, and this was the middle of winter, so it was cold enough. There were oil heaters in each room, and the inside was cozy. Coming from the odd rented rooms I had lived in recently, this looked just like heaven. I was with Junie, and we were in this little house, someday my home, and I was just very happy. There was a small wood-burning stove to heat water and cook on, and it was very romantic.

The next morning, we got on the bus to Greensboro to meet the family. I was terrified, but Junie, as usual, was calm. We were met at the bus station by his brother Arch, a dark rendition of Junie with that same kind of sweetness about him, only without that strength you immediately feel in Junie's presence. He's a very kind person.

We pulled up to this perfectly beautiful house . . . this was no middle-class bit. This was upper-class, and it wasn't even the big house that Junie had grown up in. There was nothing ostentatious about it; everything was elegant but simple. There were gorgeous Oriental rugs on the floor, gracious furniture, and rooms and rooms and rooms: a dining room, living room, sun porch. It was just so spacious.

I was introduced to the family, and Mrs. Scales could not have been sweeter. She had a penetrating smile. I'm sure she sensed my nervousness, and despite any objection she may have had to our relationship, she was a sweet, lovely lady.

This was the big day, Christmas day, and we had eggnog, and gifts were given out. And then we went into this sit-down dinner, the whole blooming bloody bunch of us, and I never saw so many forks and knives, spoons, and glasses, and napkins and plates upon plates, and it was just like in an upper-class *Better Homes and Gardens*. I was petrified. I didn't know which fork to use for what, which spoon to use when, and which glass to drink wine out of. So I just sat there very quietly and followed Junie, doing everything he did.

Their cook, Agie, who had been with them for many years, came out and served the dinner. She was lovely and obviously adored Junie. The general love and warmth of feeling toward Junie was unmistakable. There was no question that he was his mother's favorite; and Aunt Lucy, even though violently disagreeing with him, loved him. Arch, of course, respected him, and his sister Mary Leigh was certainly attached to him . . . perhaps more from a sense of family duty and obligation than real warmth of feeling. But, then, she doesn't show very much.

There was just this very restrained, refined, high-type air about everything. There was laughing and joking, but it was a quiet kind of laughing with everything at a quieter, lower level than I had been used to. I mean, when my mother and father had parties, my father got whopping drunk. There was noise. I was used to fun noise. But there was no noise here: it was just very elegant.

After dinner, people retired and did things quietly on their own. Mrs. Scales came in, and though I don't remember the conversation, I remember she tried very hard to make me feel comfortable. She heartily disapproved of this relationship, I knew. I was Jewish, and I was from New York, and, she later wrote Junie, the difference was just too great. It just could not be a happy marriage: and what if there were any children?

I respected and loved Mrs. Scales. She was a wonderful woman. I don't know whether I could say she ever loved me, but I know that she did wind up respecting me.

The rest of the week was spent meeting all of Junie's Party friends. I was just fantastically impressed with these people, and with how much they genuinely loved Junie and teased him, teased us, tremendously happy that he had found somebody he loved and would settle down with.

I was immediately accepted and felt very happy about the prospect of being married to Junie, moving down there and being a part of this Party group. And again having a purpose in life.

I left North Carolina and went back to the city until February and finished the term at Hunter. Junie came up, and we spent a week together and got married. My friends and family gave us a party, and then we went back down to North Carolina.

And then the real thing: that cold little cabin, a coal fire, finding it difficult at times but never questioning the kind of life we were living. I simply aspired to be where I was, with whom I was with, and among the people I was with.

We were more like an extended family in some ways than a political group. There was a concern for one another's well-being, and the feeling went all the way from politics to the personal: Are you getting along all right? How's your health? Do you have any problems? A non-living-together type of commune, in which everybody cared for everybody else, and where the children in the group were like the children of everyone. And, by God, this small group really did care about one another in a way I never saw before.

Many of us had been pushed out by families because we had taken this particular political position. Everybody has a need for family, for the closeness of other human beings. They don't have to be blood families. Even the hard, sophisticated, and cynical New Yorkers who were a part of that group have always said there never was a group like it. And whenever there's a regathering of the clan, it's just with the same warmth and love that's always existed; it's a bond among us which will last for as long as we live. And we all still have this mutual concern for one another's children.

The first decision we made was that I should go back to school and get my B.A. And within a few months, I was pregnant with Barbara. We were deliriously happy, even though we hadn't planned it, and Junie's mother said we were absolutely crazy out of our minds. Junie got a raise from twenty-five dollars a week to forty. I continued school through April and was walking around the campus big, fat, and pregnant.

I was part of a Party group, and we had discussions, trying to raise issues in the student community, continuing the fight for black students. But whatever I could do politically was limited because I was Junie's wife. He was so well known that my presence would immediately bring attention to anybody

I was with. We worked rather quietly at that time, though there were some brave souls who sold *Daily Workers* at plant gates, but after a while, even that was stopped.

By the time I got there, everything was kind of underground, a more secret type of work. I hesitate to use those words because they do have pejorative connotations. But the government destroyed people's lives, destroyed their careers, and we were forced to work this way. And it's the people who made us behave that way who should be criticized, not us.

Some of our critics at the time said that we were a bunch of neurotics who enjoyed this secrecy kind of thing, but it wasn't fun and games for us to have had to work in this way. We all would have much preferred to work openly and honestly among the American people, like any other political group.

One of the first things I did was to work with an integrated group that ran a night school in the black area of Chapel Hill. I helped teach black people who wanted to learn how to read and write, or to improve their English.

The black issue was a big topic of discussion. There was the question of the separateness of the black nation. And always the question of expunging racism from one's self, the whole question of criticism and self-criticism. Believe me, we spent a lot of time doing that.

We couldn't become too much involved in anything else, really. You look inward much more, and although there were all kinds of prohibitions against psychiatrists and psychiatry, what it came out as was almost a kind of group therapy.

There were study groups in Marxism-Leninism, and people were involved in organizational work, the attempt to organize R. J. Reynolds. But I was in more of the student community.

My main impression is of time spent in small groups, discussing how to make ourselves better people so we could fight better and be more principled. I suppose in a way it was a little crazy because we really tore ourselves apart, examined one another's insides to see if we were good or bad, an almost constant soul-searching. The worst thing was that, because of the fear of saying the wrong thing, we were not completely honest. As much as we tried to look into ourselves to root out the bad and reinforce the good, there was a lack of candor. There was a frame of reference, you know: we knew what we were supposed to be and how we were supposed to think and accepted those limitations on our thinking.

There's no question about it: we were in mental straitjackets. Some people started trying to wriggle out earlier than others, but some of us never even questioned it. We just stayed firmly planted there. Never for a moment did we question that we were doing anything but the right thing, nor were we anywhere but in the right party. Nor did we question the orders that came down, and indeed they were orders. And although there were explanations and discussions, and always a time to question, that was really more form than content. Most people accepted what came. It was democratic centralism, and the question is, How democratic can democratic centralism really be?

In a way I felt like a noncelebrated celebrity. Part of it may have been my being so self-conscious about things. But the only people I knew on campus were the Party members. And in town, I never had a sense of being part of the community, and I think that feeling of participating in the larger community, the American community, is quite important. It's one thing to have your own ideas at variance with established ideas, but it's another thing to be looked upon as a leper when you're walking through town.

Now, of course, this is all in retrospect, because at the time I wasn't afraid. I would say, "Well it's their problem if they misunderstand us, if they can't see what we're trying to do. They're narrow, and they're prejudiced. It's all their fault." I guess part of that is a youthful kind of romanticism, and, like today's youngsters, it's in the blood of the young person. I was proud of Junie, proud of what he was doing, and proud to be a part of it. I never feared for my safety, though I feared for him sometimes when he was out on the road.

Barbara was still an infant when the Party ordered Junie to leave home. I think I said, "Don't they know you have a six-month-old baby?" And Junie convinced me that this was the thing to do.

Things got really hot, and the national leadership had to assume that anybody in a position of leadership was going to be arrested. Now, in the South, Junie was the only open Communist and a native southerner, the son who turned against his class: the perfect person to be arrested. So without any real knowledge of whether or not there was a warrant out for him, he, like many others, went underground. The government was never open in their legal behavior. We just had to live with the assumption that they were going to get him someday. In fact, Junie's first wooings included the warning that he was probably going to be arrested someday.

I couldn't live in Carrboro with Barbara by myself and work, too. So with very little reluctance, my mother broke up her apartment in New York and came down South to live with us.

The FBI made no attempt to hide their surveillance. Most of the time I was being watched constantly: two neighbors, in particular, gave their homes to FBI agents. Then there was an FBI agent within the Party, Ralph Clontz, the biggest joke of all: a cigar-smoking, great big pad–carrying, obvious FBI agent. Occasionally, somebody would say, "Do you think Ralph Clontz is an FBI agent?" And Hank, the district organizer, or Junie would kind of laugh and say, "How could he be? He's so obviously an agent that he couldn't possibly be one."

Clontz came over to see me often, out of so-called comradely concern. Everything about him was utterly repulsive and false; even his laugh was wrong. As time went on, we really became more and more cautious in front of him. And yet for some reason—why, I'll never know—we played his games.

It didn't make that much difference because, really and truly, the FBI-agent business is so ridiculous. In my experience, there was never anything that we did or said that any of us would ever unsay or be ashamed of; in no way was what we were saying antithetical to the best interests of the United States. I don't know what went on in other places. I don't know about any actual connections with the Soviet Union or any of that jazz. But I know that the people I worked with, and talked with, and met with were interested in only one thing—and that was to make this a better world. And that's why it never concerned us all that much what Ralph Clontz heard, because all we talked about was how to make this a better world. The FBI knew perfectly well what we were doing and what we were thinking and what we were talking about. . . . Did we believe in socialism? Of course we believed in socialism. That's why we were in the Communist Party: we believed eventually in communism. So what was the big thing Clontz was finding out?

Now, of course, one of the reasons he was there was to help build a government case against Junie. Obviously Junie had been tabbed for prosecution.

Then there was the surveillance. And it meant that I had to live a horribly isolated life. Everything was cut off. People couldn't come to the house, and I couldn't go visiting unless it was carefully prearranged. If I went to see anyone I had to take all kinds of circuitous routes. Junie's former in-laws, who lived in Chapel Hill, treated me as a third daughter and were really the only ones who came around. Poppy, Junie's former father-in-law, would come over on weekends to take us for a ride, and that was a really big deal for all of us. They loved the baby and were deeply concerned about us. They were the mainstay of my social life.

My mother was a good egg. She didn't quite understand what was going on but loved Junie and adored that baby. Barbara brought her more happiness in her later years than anything else could possibly have. She never questioned anything and always believed that we were really trying to help people. She became an entirely different person, quieter. . . . Do you know

Sholom Aleichem's story about the guy who's worked hard all his life, and when he finally gets to heaven they ask him what he wants? And he says, "I just want a roll and butter." That's what she was like. As long as you treated her kindly, and she could be near that baby, that's all she cared about. I don't think I could have come through that period without her.

Junie's mother was outraged by the FBI. He went to see her a couple of times while he was underground. One time when they were getting ready to leave the house, a car came and parked nearby, and Junie said, "That's the FBI." Mrs. Scales said, "I don't believe it. Let's go and see if they follow us." They started out, and sure enough, the FBI followed them. I think that truly enraged her; it just offended her basic sense of decency. And she couldn't believe that they would do this to her son. She was an anti-Communist, but she didn't think Communists should be thrown in jail and persecuted.

A couple of times they came to my door and announced they were from the FBI and wanted to talk to me. Of course, the only pleasure I had was slamming the door in their faces.

I had a job as a window trimmer for Lerner's department store in nearby Durham, though I don't know how the FBI allowed me to get it. I even got it under my own name. It was a pleasant job with a certain amount of fun and creativity to it. So I went to work and came home to my baby: I played with her, bathed her, fed her, sang to her, and told her stories. She was a huge part of my life at that time.

It's hard to tell how conscious she was of Junie's not being around. I don't know. I never asked her about it, really. She never asked for "Daddy," never cried for him. But again, she has this Scales quality . . . you don't really know what goes on inside. By the time she was one or two, she certainly knew that there wasn't a father around all the time. There was a little girl born at exactly the same time who lived right across the street whose daddy was always home. Barbara was a bright little girl, so I'm sure she must have been aware of it to some extent. But I never heard a peep out of her about it. She just accepted it, on the surface, at least. What went on underneath I'll never know . . . and whether she remembers it I don't know. And, yet, when she was with him, she certainly knew who he was, and loved him, and played with him. I haven't ever really thought about how she accepted that situation.

Those times we had together, we had to compress emotions that are usually played out over long periods. But there were wonderful times; there was never any complaining or whining or bitching from any of us. And there were the funny things that happened, like the time there was no bed for the baby, and we put her to bed in the motel dresser drawer. But somehow or other, Barbara always accommodated herself to it, no matter what we did with her. She always lived with it.

I hated being separated from Junie: we have always been a very close couple, and even when we read, we like to sit next to each other. But when you feel like you're fighting for a cause, you just believe it's the right thing to do. I was being loyal and good to my husband, loyal to my party, and I was uncomplaining. And I had to do it also for my child, so that the world could be a better place for her. So even though I was very lonely, I was not devastated. It started to get more difficult towards the end, particularly when our visits were cut down, and as the months became years. But having that baby made a great deal of difference.

At one point there was a story in the local papers about Junie, and I came to work in Durham the next morning, and everybody knew who I was. Somebody in Lerner's top management must have been a fairly decent guy because there was never a question of my being fired.

There was nothing unpleasant, really, although the other workers were cool. A couple of them wouldn't talk to me, and that was rather uncomfortable. But the boss was the same. He was a garrulous, open kind of a guy, and all he cared about was that the store made money. I was very good: I had just gotten a five-dollar raise—fantastic for Lerner's. They usually only gave half that. So he said I could stay as long as there was no decline in revenue.

Nobody really enjoys the feeling of being rejected by another human being. And it's much more difficult to take that kind of rejection when you're alone. It's different when you're marching in a May Day parade and people boo you—you're there with your comrades, protected by your community. I had no community at that time, and that was a rather unpleasant situation.

Each day, after I got off the bus in Durham, I walked a certain way to work. If anybody had a message for me they could stop me on the way. Lo and behold, one day there's Junie. I get into a car, and he tells me that the latest word is that we're only supposed to see each other twice a year. It was just unbelievable. We were down to once a month, and now it was to be twice a year. I finally put my foot down, and I said absolutely no. I said, "You better go back and tell them that I'm not about to do that." And that was the only time I really rebelled against an order.

I suppose because of what happened to me and my father, I just felt very strongly that this baby should have her father, and this father his baby. It was just a terrible thing for both of them that they had to be separated. Even as a baby you could see that she was so much like him: she looked like him and was just as bright as she could be.

She was born with a maturity, a poise, that in my younger life I certainly never had. There was nothing that seemed to floor her or daunt her, nothing she wouldn't tackle or try, from climbing out of the crib, running around, to riding a bicycle. This poise, the reserve, and more cerebral quality was the Scales temperament. On my side, we're much more emotional, and I don't say any less bright, but it's different. She may have started looking a little more like me in some ways, and I think some of her qualities can be identified with me, but, to this day, she is essentially her father's child.

Finally, the night came when Barbara and my mother and I were to leave North Carolina to come meet Junie in New York. We thought that we had really planned carefully. There were no signs of packing. The few things we had, we packed in suitcases hidden under the bed. Bill, a friend, was to pick us up at eleven-twenty-five at night so we could make a one-in-the-morning train from Raleigh to New York. Bill came in and got us. We pulled out the suitcases, and I carried the baby. We got in the car and, sure-shooting, out comes an FBI car from the neighbors' house. Bill drove around, backtracking all over the place. We thought we got rid of them, but we probably didn't. We got to Raleigh and made the train, and apparently there was no surveillance. Who the hell knows? They might have known where we were going all the time. But that's one midnight ride I'll never forget.

Of course, we left a house full of things. But Junie's mother and his former mother-in-law came to the house the next day or so and packed everything. Here's a woman who had been waited on by servants all her life, and she neatly packed everything and took the valuables to the attic of her house and either sold or gave away the furnishings. She was a woman who could literally cope with any situation. She could attend the queen's ball, or clean out her son's house after his wife and baby fled in the middle of the night because of FBI harassment.

seven

Junius

Gladys and I were married in February 1950 and lived in Carrboro. My neighbors across the street and about two city blocks away had FBI agents living in their houses. There they'd be with binoculars watching everybody that came to the house. I used cabs a lot because I didn't want to get too many people's cars involved. We'd drive off, and before the cab could get two blocks, there'd be three or four carloads of FBI agents behind it. We'd drive around like a funeral procession. Often the cab drivers were in on it with the FBI. But friends would come in spite of the harassment. It made them mad, but we were friends, and they didn't want to be intimidated.

Gladys was a New Yorker and a Brooklyn émigré, and I warned her before the marriage, "I'm probably going to go to jail." In 1950 it didn't take any vast imagination to see that the way things were going I'd be in trouble. I was the only open Communist in the South at that point, and they sort of concentrated their fire on me.

Up till then, the FBI had been inhibiting me considerably, but I figured the most they could do was arrest me. The Ku Klux Klan threatened me. One Sunday afternoon, this long, low truck with a bunch of guys with shotguns kept driving around and around the house at three or four miles an hour for about forty-five minutes. I guess I was scared because I took my shotgun and cleaning equipment and went out and sat on my front porch. I sat there and cleaned my shotgun, and they left. Later they burned a cross on my lawn.

In April of '51, our child Barbara was born. Then, in July, I got orders from the Party up in New York and the southern director of the Party, who particularly tended to panic, that we should all go underground. And so we made ourselves very hard to find.

I had to leave home before my daughter was even six months old and, as the surveillance gradually intensified, had to stay away for longer and longer periods. FBI agents swarmed around me so that I couldn't go to see anybody without putting the finger on them.

Somewhere in the fall of '51 I started living with friends, mostly not Party people, in different cities. I'd come home sometimes and spend a few days, but gradually that got to be too difficult. It was just as difficult to leave again.

So Gladys would take Barbara in a wicker basket and leave with the help of friends, switching from car to car, and I'd meet them on weekends. Sometimes we'd stay at a friend's place. One of our favorite stunts, to make sure we weren't being followed, was to go lickety-splitting down a highway and stop at a motel. We'd sign in for the weekend while a friend drove the car on down the road. Somebody would come pick us up Monday.

The FBI had their hands full because we thought up more and more stunts. And you know, they're not very smart. They're just too rigid. The only way they were able to keep tabs on us was with stool pigeons. When they tried to do it themselves, you could outwit them every time.

I remember once I hopped into a friend's car, and we knew perfectly well the FBI were following, so we drove like a bat out of hell. My friend got about a good block or so ahead of them and was turning around a corner. Just as they rounded the corner, they saw him slamming the car door on my side. I was on the floor of the car, but they just assumed that I had gotten out. And as we drove off, he could see them in the mirror hopping out of their car and swarming all over somebody's house, convinced I was there. I bet they were camped out half the night there, trying to figure out where the hell I was.

Meanwhile, we were having a nice conversation while I was sitting on the floor of his car. He drove around for a while and then went home. The agents were sitting there at his place. He went in and left me on the floor. And they never thought to come look. Five minutes later they gave up and drove away, and I got out and went back inside the house. Meanwhile, my friend went to get everyone I needed to see, and over the next two days or so I had a chance to talk to everybody.

I once visited my mother outside of Greensboro in my uncle's home, and the FBI just terrorized her. They kept tabs on the house all night long. They had a system: one car would get on the road on one side of the house and sit there for five minutes. Then they'd pull on by with a soft little toot on the horn, sweeping their searchlights over the yard until another car would take their place. And this went on every five minutes all night long, as long as they thought I was around.

The next morning after breakfast I said to her, "Well, this is nonsense, but I'll have to give them credit for spoiling a visit." So I went out the back of the house, went across a corn field and to a road where a county bus line operated. I hopped the bus, rode through Greensboro, and hitchhiked to Durham. The FBI were hysterical. Apparently they caught all manner of hell for losing me and were terribly upset about it.

But, of course, this was a miserable way of living, and I couldn't really see Barbara. Also, I had gotten to be a big responsibility to the non-Party people I stayed with—I was putting too much pressure on them and just couldn't stand doing it. I don't recall any of them that reacted openly to the pressure or asked me not to come, but I was afraid of making life too tough for them. I felt I had an obligation not to put them on the spot. So I had to narrow down the number of people I stayed with and relied more and more on public transportation. I became a master of bus and train schedules and an expert hitchhiker. I ranged over an area of a few thousand miles: north of Virginia in one direction to northern Mississippi in the other. From Charleston, South Carolina, to Memphis, Tennessee, and from Roanoake, Virginia, to Atlanta, Georgia.

I would visit people for two and three days at a time, trying mostly to restore morale—back to being a little bit like a psychiatrist and circuit-riding minister. We were all so close that invariably I'd have personal problems pushed on me. My policy was trying to keep people from getting into these narrow, boxed-in positions where they would be standing so damn far in front of everybody else and drawing all the fire, you know. I tried to get them to stay a little bit protected and to encourage what we considered healthy trends. And it certainly worked out better in the South than anywhere else.

Occasionally I'd go up to New York for meetings. They thought they were experts in "security," and they were really crazy on cloak-and-dagger malarkey. There was this elaborate plan set up two months before for a meeting I was going to attend up there. I was instructed to dress in such and such a way with a bow tie. So I presumed I was going to meet someone I didn't know.

Well, I got to New York the night before and probably hadn't slept for thirty-six hours. I never wore bow ties, so first of all I had to spend two bucks of my scarce money on a cruddy bow tie, which made me feel like a fool, and I was told to have some kind of flower in my buttonhole. I was supposed to be carrying the latest edition of *Life* magazine and had to wear a hat. I never wore a hat, so I had to buy one. I got the cheapest one I could find, but I think I had to spend seven bucks for it, which nearly bankrupted me.

Then I discovered that the latest issue of *Life* wasn't going to be on the newsstands until three o'clock in the afternoon, and I had to be up around 181st Street at four-fifteen. So I waited madly till the stack of *Life* magazines came off the truck, grabbed one, rushed for the subway, and dashed up to 181st Street. I was supposed to stand on a particular corner a few blocks from the bridge. The plan was, somebody would come up and say, "Could you tell me which way is the George Washington Bridge?" And I'd say, "Yes, I'm going there myself. I'll show you." I got there with five minutes to spare, absolutely gasping for breath. I had the *Life* magazine, I'm decked out just right with the bow tie, and I'm standing there waiting for anybody at all, trying to be as unself-conscious as possible. A car drives up with three people I've worked with for years, and they yell, "Hey, Junius, come on for Christ's sake, we're late!"

This was security, New York style. But the absurd thing was that the FBI had so many agents infiltrating the Party that we could win all these little battles and still lose the war. Because if they couldn't find me for weeks on end, they eventually had enough agents and informants to find out where I was going. And they could get on my track again by watching the places they figured I was most likely to go. It was very amusing to outwit them, but it was also very deceptive, because they had the apparatus and the stool pigeons and the overall clout to keep you pretty much contained.

While the idea was to make it harder for them to keep tabs on us, and that seemed to make practical sense to a lot of us, politically it was a disaster. It was almost impossible to function the way we were accustomed. Here's a group that goes underground; well, then, people assume you've obviously got plenty to hide, that you're up to some kind of plotting and conspiracy. And nine people out of ten would assume that.

First of all, I couldn't make enough contact with anybody to keep on top of things. At least before going underground I would visit with people in one city for a while, and I'd have a real good feeling that I'd been helpful. I felt I was able to get them into a broader method of work. But I was beginning to feel that it wasn't worth all the effort and expense, that I was a liability rather than an asset.

I lived on an incredibly small budget during this time. I had to look respectable, so I had a fairly expensive suit, one of the first suits you didn't have to press. You could wash it if you had to and let it drip dry. And I had a couple of the early, expensive drip-dry shirts. If you were in a hurry, you could wash them, then roll them up in a bath towel. They'd be a little damp, but you could wear them again in an hour. I could live out of my briefcase for four or five weeks by washing my underwear, my shirts, and ties, and my suit even, if it was necessary. I had to wear a clean shirt all the time. I had to keep up appearances all I could, because half of my presentation was to look as prosperous as possible—or, if nothing else, at least look like a fairly successful salesman.

It was costly and, though I lived like a Spartan at the time, our sources of income were limited. I began to feel that the best thing I could do would be to get a job someplace under a phony name and take time off. In fact, I proposed that to the Party, and that was another source of friction, because this threatened the position of some of the Party brass. You get used to a Party job as a full-timer. You get a meal ticket—it's what they called a "pie card" in the trade-union movement—and you get the attitudes to go along with it, and then develop political positions to support it.

The longest I can recall being away from the family was more than two months. My God, I didn't know what my little kid looked like. That was the roughest. And it got more difficult. One nightmarish time we were to meet in Durham, and the FBI got on Gladys's tail. We just never met up that time. It was terribly frustrating. And we had to wait longer and longer between meetings. Sometimes she would come to New York, and we'd have to have everything worked out weeks and weeks before.

We couldn't work this stuff out on the phone. I have assumed that every phone I've lived near since I was nineteen is tapped. Also that my mail was opened, which it was. So telephones were used sparingly, and if we did talk, it was in prearranged gobbledy-gook. When I'd see her, we would work out plans for the next time. We never wrote it down, but we never forgot either. And if plans had to be changed I'd get word to her through second or third parties. I got awfully good at that, and we always had alternate plans, and we never had a mixup.

But, as I say, for all this business you pay a big toll. And meanwhile, they had informers in the group. Much more important than that, though, was the fact that you were getting increasingly isolated from people and organizations and what was going on in the nation. Our ability to move and influence people was constantly declining.

I didn't get tired, but I did get discouraged about the outlook for the time to come. But we had these feelings that we were holding the fort almost alone. Senator McCarthy was pounding at the gates. Who else was going to stop him? We were so intensely outraged by McCarthyism that we were able to keep our internal differences from blowing sky-high. When there's that much pressure on you, you can't exactly argue among yourselves too much, or discuss problems rationally, and figure out what you're doing and where the hell you're going. All you see is the outrageousness and injustice of the latest attack, and you close ranks, delay the thinking and the discussions of what's wrong with what you're doing. And if anybody had said that the Soviet Party was wrong, that would have been blasphemous.

Over time, we had less to do, less contact with people outside the Party. We became increasingly involved in intra-party activism. You're looking inward all the time, grow in on yourself, and that's when you have all these questions of ideological difference. And what I look back on with the most shame is that there'd be times in discussions with some of my friends in the South when I'd absolutely run out of gas. Their positions, their criticisms, sounded right, you know, and I couldn't go riding roughshod over them. These people were very dear to me. And I simply couldn't answer them. They were in much more contact with reality than I was.

In 1953, or thereabouts, we had so little influence in the unions it was pathetic. We still had contact in several different textile mills in the Durham area, though, and were putting out a paper directed mainly at Erwin Mills. There was a big local union there, and the paper was tremendously popular with the rank-and-file workers. We were in contact with people who worked there, and although they were extremely cautious, they met regularly with our people. They'd bring back news of what was going on in the union and what was bothering the workers, and we'd come out with this stuff. The paper was very well edited and written, and we'd always double-check with our sources of information to make sure we didn't pull any bloopers.

We had learned a little something along the way, and our paper was directed mainly against the practices of the company and only secondarily lambasted the union leadership—and only when they were engaged in sellouts of sorts. So it was an extremely popular paper and could be found in every latrine in Irwin Mills, and was read and passed around surreptitiously. It was the talk of the whole mill area, and there were big discussions every time an issue came out.

Of course, copies of this paper would get to New York, and the southern and national trade-union brass would see it. They decided it was oriented too much on local issues and not ideological enough. We listened carefully and decided we had been shortsighted. And I went back to explain that our paper wasn't ideological enough. Very promptly, my buddies handed me my head. But, you know, I gave them an awful hard time. Finally, they just practically knocked my brains out and embarrassed me even more by quoting me back to myself. That was really the straw that broke the camel's back.

And from that time on, I began to be ambiguous in my relationship to my Party superiors. It seemed to me that I was in constant wrangles and disagreements with the two top guys in the southern committee. They were loyal and quite rigid Fosterites. We could hardly agree on the time of day.

Finally, things got to be impossible for Gladys, and we worked out a sneaky departure from North Carolina, and she and Barbara and my mother-in-law all took off for New York. We got an apartment in the Bronx.

Gladys's mother was invaluable. She had come to live with us when I started "undergrounding," and she did all the babysitting whenever Gladys had to go somewhere. Gladys bore up incredibly well. She had gone to the University of North Carolina in Chapel Hill while still living down there, and got her B.A. in education the semester after Barbara was born. And it was quite a joy to have them in the Bronx. I just had to make like a traveling salesman, making long trips, operating out of New York under another name. I still spent most of my time in the South. But when I'd come to New York, I'd live at home. I was on one of these trips when I got arrested.

Up till then, there was no warrant out for me. They got an indictment and a warrant on the afternoon of my arrest. They knew through their informers I was coming to Memphis, and they knew where to get me. But they were doing their damnedest to trap me coming in at the railroad or bus station so they wouldn't have to reveal the fact that they had informers. They had set up a fantastic ring around the city. I learned about this because a guy I knew had a roommate who had a superficial resemblance to me. Well, he'd been away and was coming back to Memphis on the bus the very afternoon they were looking for me.

So, as he gets off the bus, three guys grab him, slap handcuffs on his wrists, and announce, "We got you, Scales, don't struggle!" Pistols drawn, they hauled him into the men's room, gave him an awful shaking down, tore into his clothes, pulled out all of his identification, and went through all his luggage. One of them was running around, keeping everybody else out of the men's room. And then came big apologies. They'd gotten the wrong man.

The guy who had made the arrangements for my trip had informed only four people that I was coming. I had traveled by train, then took a bus from Cincinnati to Memphis. Even the driver had spotted me. So, about ten or twelve miles out of Memphis, I hopped off the bus. There was a city trolley line that ran out by the highway to some rural areas, and I rode it into the city until we converged with another trolley line. I took that to another city bus that went through Overton Park, a big park in the middle of Memphis. It was quite densely wooded, and I hopped off, and I walked through. There were any number of ways that I could have left the park, so if anybody was going to follow me, they would somehow have to show themselves. So I walked through the park until dark and went to a convenient movie theater to wait around.

The couple I was going to stay with were going to meet me at a particular street corner about eight o'clock. I knew the fat was in the fire when somebody got on the bus about a block before the corner. And he just looked like an FBI agent. He sat back behind me, and I rode a block past where I was going to get off. He signaled somehow or other, and I saw a car following the bus. I got off, and cars kept going by, so I just took a whole bunch of papers I didn't want found on me, and tore them in little bitty bits. I put them in a street sewer just as a thunder storm came up. A flood of rain started, and I got soaking wet.

Then I thought, what the hell, since I'm surrounded, I might as well go to the rendezvous anyway and see what happens. So I did, and about four carloads of FBI agents piled out with pistols. By that time I knew what was going to happen, and I was very calm about the whole thing. Much calmer than they were, anyway.

It turned out that the couple, both factory workers, panicked somewhere along the line and became informers. I think they got paid rather well. So the FBI knew exactly where I was headed.

They radioed Washington, and J. Edgar Hoover made a splash about it, you know, that they apprehended this dangerous character. And, the next day, there was a big to-do in Memphis. The funniest thing is that after I was arraigned, close to midnight, I called George Charney, a friend of mine in New York, and one of the second bunch of Communists who were convicted. He had won his case on appeal, so he was at home and the only guy I could figure to call. He and Elizabeth Gurley Flynn were about the only two public Communists who could be reached. I finally got George at about one-thirty in the morning, waking him from a sound sleep, and he tells the operator it must be a mistake: he doesn't know anybody in Tennessee.

Finally I told the operator, "Tell him this is Junius Scales, and I've just been arrested." "Oh, Junius," he asks, "what's going on?" So I said, "What's going on? I'm arrested under the membership clause of the Smith Act. What do you think I ought to do?" Well, by this time it got funny as hell, and we were laughing away with these six or seven FBI agents sitting all around. I said, "I guess I'll be needing a lawyer," and he said he'd take care of everything. Then I said, "You got any profound advice to give me before I hang up?" And he says, "Well, just sit tight"—about the most superfluous advice I've ever gotten.

eight

Gladys

If I thought the Carrboro house was a castle, the little three-and-a-half-room apartment that we had on Anderson Avenue in the Bronx was absolutely palatial. There was hot and cold running water and heat all the time. And we were together. Barbara was three now, and we had been separated from Junie for almost two and a half years. Of course, we were still living underground and had to be very careful. We couldn't see our friends and my family.

Barbara and Grandma slept in the bedroom, and Junie and I had a pullout bed in the living room. And we lived a very quiet life. Junie worked full-time for the Party, and he was always taking forays out to go back down South. You can't get a normal job and then suddenly take a week off to go down and organize in the South. And, under another name, I got a job as a comparison shopper for Macy's.

What I always did when he was away was to turn on the radio, and I heard the news that morning that he had been arrested. I went in and told my mother, and, of course, having that baby was always the thing that made us keep calm. My thoughts in any time of emergency always go back to Bernie, and I think I may have gotten in touch with him. He was such a big shot in the New York State Party by then, and I knew he would tell me what to do. I knew I had to do something—I knew I had to get Junie some defense. Eventually, I was in John Abt's law office, and he was great.

I couldn't see Junie in Tennessee where he was arrested, but my mother took care of Barbara, and I did go to see him when he was moved to the jail in Winston-Salem. I'm sure one of the reasons Barbara maintained whatever stability and sanity she had is because my mother was the constant figure in her life. If I had to run here to prison, or there to a trial, my mother was always there. And the couple of times I was gone for longer periods, there were other very dear friends with whom I left her.

At the time, we were still in the Party, and there was still a purpose to all of this. I was frightened, and I didn't know where it all might end, but I felt this was part of the deal. This was a part of his being a member of the Communist Party. Of course, his bail was ridiculous: it was one hundred thousand dollars.

I was in touch with his mother, and it was very painful for her. She tried to help us out as much as she could. The idea was to try and get somebody other than a New York lawyer. So if I could, my job now was to find him a lawyer who wouldn't be too much out of tune with Greensboro and a Greensboro jury. We finally wound up with an excellent lawyer from Washington, D.C., David Rein.

I was down there during the first trial, and that was hard. I think I even stayed with his mother. There was some legal reason he was freed, and then there came the whole period of waiting to see whether there was going to be a second trial. Being a perennial optimist, I always said, "No, no, there won't be a second trial. . . ." And, of course, there was a second trial. I get the two trials mixed up and sometimes don't know which trial I'm remembering. I suppose that's a case where not having memory has nothing to do with electric shock or anything other than sheer trauma. Those years were just ghastly; they were horrible years.

Mrs. Scales went to court every day, and Aunt Lucy and Mary Leigh, and John whenever he could. Junie made Archibald stay away because he worked for the government. I want to tell you, that family was something. And I sat right behind Junie, as close to him as I could.

It was just a completely unbelievable experience. The people who were testifying against him were stool pigeons, and they weren't talking about my husband or about the party to which I belonged. According to them, we were wild revolutionaries, and the school we attended taught murder. That was something I remember so clearly, because there was one guy at that Party school we attended who had been in the army. One night, everybody was sitting around a table, and the guys just started talking about their army experiences, and this guy was telling a story about how he was taught in the army to kill a man with a pencil, simply taking the pencil and shoving it in the jugular.

Of course, there was an undercover agent at this school, Charlie Childs. He was our great southern white working-class guy, the guy we were so proud of. So he's paraded out at the trial as, I must say, a surprise witness, and he tells this story about how murder was taught at the Party's school. That's the kind of thing that went on up there on the witness stand. It was just one lie after another. Except for one thing that George Clontz said, something to the effect that, "and Junius Scales said that he hoped his daughter would grow up under socialism."

It was unbelievable. You had to pinch yourself. You had to wonder why people didn't stand up and scream, "What's going on here?" That's why the Kafka novel, *The Trial,* is so great, because it's the story of all political trials, whether in the Soviet Union, the United States, China, Israel, wherever. Junie was declared guilty, of course.

By then we had two marvelous lawyers, McNeil Smith, a southerner, and Telford Taylor, and they worked together as a beautiful team. They finally got the bail down to some reasonable figure, and I think his mother paid a good deal of it. And then, again, the whole process of appeals.

We moved to 448 Central Park West, and Junie and I still didn't have a bedroom. It wasn't until my poor mother died that we finally had our own bedroom. It was a fairly nice three-room apartment, and by then there was no question of hiding identities or anything like that, so we saw all our old friends again. It was a pleasant apartment, and we had Central Park to go to with Barbara. At least Junie was around and, even though it was nerve-wracking, we were all together. For Junie, it was just a series of getting a job and getting fired, getting another job and getting fired.

I went back to Lerner's as a window trimmer and then made the big leap to Ohrbach's. I was doing very well there, and had just gotten a five-dollar raise, when I was called into the personnel department and told that my services were no longer required. It was obvious that the FBI had been there. I decided somehow or other I was going to teach. Yeshiva University was offering a master's in education for a very low fee, and they made arrangements for you to earn two thousand dollars a year while you were a student.

Somehow or other, we managed to exist on whatever money he and I were able to make, and we waited from one appeal to the next. The next court up turned us down, and there was the wait for the Supreme Court. And then you're always carried along with the hope that the best thing will happen. Except for Junie; Junie was always sure he was going to jail.

The actual breaking period, when we left the Party, was almost meaningless to me. He was still looked upon as a Party member, and we were so involved in this fight to keep him out of jail. My activity was practically the same as when I was still in the Party, trying to get lawyers and raise money. And it wasn't until later that the rude awakening came, and I knew what it meant not to be in the Party, and knew what kind of people were left.

Most of our close friends had either already broken or were breaking at the same time as us. There are a couple of people who are still in and are, to some extent, friends of ours, and to whom it made no difference that we left. They kept seeing us and calling us, particularly when Junie was in trouble. But our closest friends all seemed to be doing the same thing. George Charney was the one who stayed in the longest, and he stayed because he really thought he could do something about democratizing the Party. When he saw it was hopeless, he got out also.

Some of our friends had started the march out even before the 1956 Khrushchev report documenting the brutality of Stalin. The handwriting was obviously on the wall, particularly for some of the people who were involved in the cultural area—the edicts were getting stronger and stronger about what they could and couldn't write about.

Leaving the Party is still a very painful topic. . . . We laugh over some of the stories; we cry over some. But so many lives were ruined. So many people who could have made such very fine contributions to this society didn't do it, and couldn't do it. By the time they came to their senses, many of them couldn't recoup whatever abilities they had, or whatever beginnings they had made before they became full-time Party people. It was horrible. Yet one can't blame that entirely on the Party. It was the stupidity of the government. Had the government encouraged political freedom—although I don't know where in the hell you're going to find a government like that—there would have been many more opportunities for people to recoup and produce, to do something for society.

Many people were very bitter. They were hurting. Junie is one of the few people who isn't bitter. He was distraught and destroyed and upset, particularly because as a leader in the Party, he was personally responsible for changing the course of so many lives. This was something, I think, that upset him more than anything else. There's a kind of defeated or defeatist quality to "bitter." He was miserable, but he wasn't bitter.

The Party knew they had talented people and used their talents, yet many stupid things were done with people. One was a period of "industrial concentration," where intellectuals and students were taken out of school and put into factory work. They were going to organize the workers. First of all, they stuck out like sore thumbs. You can't take an intellectual and put blue jeans on him and make him look like a worker. The workers didn't particularly trust him. They weren't really at ease and neglected their own talents. It was just like putting a square peg into a round hole.

Junie was misused and, I might say, used by the Party because he was a white aristocratic southerner. He was never meant to be a chairman of the Party. I mean, he was a wonderful leader. People loved him, but that was just not his role. If the Party had had any brains, they would never have pulled him out of school to have him work full-time.

Here was a man who was obviously an intellect, a scholar who could have been a Communist professor or intellectual. But no, they saw a beautiful opportunity here to have an indigenous leader of the southern Party, and that's all they saw. Some of his greatest talents are working with people, and people loved him. He was probably less a political leader and much more a friend and confidante, a real helping person. I don't know whether he thinks so or not, but a great political leader he was not. . . .

It's hard to make generalizations about the effect the break had on the children. It had different effects on different children. Some children were hurt by it. I don't mean that they were knowingly hurt, or that they were aware of what was going on politically. I think they were hurt by the fact that their own needs were not fulfilled by parents who were too involved in the Party. But there was no question that people felt that what was best for the greater good was best for everybody. And therefore, in the long run, children were going to benefit from it. And that was the most fallacious kind of thinking.

The children reacted in any number of ways. Some reacted negatively to their parents, became emotionally disturbed. Or they went the other way, and couldn't care less about the Left and socialism. And then there were some who so actively turned against the Party and what it stood for, that everything they did was just antithetical to what their parents believed. They acted for their own personal and material gain, concerned for themselves above all.

There were other children who did fairly well, and still others who became dedicated Communists. And some of them just decided they weren't going to take part in this life at all and went off. There were children like Barbara, who though she was political, was never interested in becoming a Communist because she had read and heard about the Party.

I think to some extent she was also hurt by the whole progression of events. I can't really put my finger on just how. Again, not having her father around in her younger life was a terrible loss. Once she had her daddy back from prison, he was really a very involved father.

And just because people left the Communist Party didn't mean they necessarily left behind the ideals they joined the Party for. Those ideals and ideas were still the same. Many of us, I think almost all of us, still believe that there has to be some form of socialism, but how the heck you ever get there, and what you do with it once you have it, we don't know. But the basic ideology of people didn't change.

Now, you know, we're all anti-Soviet. And many people don't believe any longer in many of the tenets of Marxism, simply because they've looked into it more carefully, and realized in today's world they're obsolete. Well, how could a philosopher writing in the time he did look forward to this kind of technological society we have today? But the basic humanistic, idealistic things that we all believed in remain, and consequently there's no change in our morals and our standards. These things remain the same for our children.

There were other changes: some people withdrew completely, and some people found other ways to participate in groups. Some found a new way to pursue their ideals in service professions: psychology, social work, and teaching. There were people who immediately hooked up with the New York City Reform Democrats or with the War Resisters League. Some people just read and talked but withdrew from any kind of activity. George Charney is a very interesting example of somebody who has, in his own unique way, continued the good fight by reading and writing.

Then there were some people who, for whatever reasons, could not do anything. Junie feels he really can't actively participate in anything. Whether he's right or wrong, he just feels that bringing his name into any kind of activity can only hurt it. And that's one of the reasons he doesn't become particularly active in his union—some people don't care what kind of Communist he is: anti-, ex-, pro-, or what. The word "Communist" is enough. So there were some people who were absolutely stymied and couldn't do anything. And Junie continued to have hard times finding jobs. Whenever he'd get one, the FBI would knock him right off it. And it was financially difficult.

Meanwhile, all through this period, there was the waiting. You just can't live with something like this every single second. So sometimes, in the course of daily events, we'd almost forget that he was facing jail. But Sunday nights and Mondays you never forgot, because Monday was the day the Supreme Court handed down its decisions.

We talked about it a great deal, anticipating what would happen and what we would have to do. And I'm sure in his own way, Junie was trying to prepare me for the reality of it. But you just can't. And, of course, we never told

Barbara until it actually happened because we were playing it for broke. We felt that she was too young to live under the pressure of such a burden for so long a time. We felt that if the decision went against us, then that would be the time we would have to tell her. So it was just sort of wait and hope. And you play the numbers game, and you look over the Court, keeping count, going over and over the justices, trying to figure out who'll vote how.

I couldn't believe it was going to happen. And Junie kept saying, "Yes, it's going to happen." Here was a guy who had left the Party and was being punished for being in the Party. Even being punished for being in a political party is a horrible, stupid thing, but that he had left the Party was too much. It was sheer lunacy. I couldn't understand why people on the radio and television weren't screaming about the idiocy of this situation. It was a nightmare.

It was a Monday morning in June, and I was in a car driving home from somewhere and had the radio on. I heard the news. I don't know how I ever got home, but I got there about four o'clock in the afternoon, and Junie was on the phone talking to lawyers and the newspapers. Junie, of course, was extremely strong. He's a very dignified person, and he was not about to give an inch in any way. He was going to take it and hate them for it—not even hate. What could he do? There was nothing he could do about it. And he was the strong one.

Junie had gone to school to pick Barbara up. Then we had to tell her about it, and we had to tell her fast before she heard it on the radio or from anyone else. It was very hard. We sat on this couch . . . I can't even remember the words we used. I guess Junie did most of the talking. And he told her. . . . I don't think it even sunk in. It was just such a shocking thing. She kept talking about her poor daddy, her poor daddy who was going to prison, and she didn't think about herself. She understood what was happening, but she didn't know what it meant in terms of herself, or how she would be feeling, really. And I didn't either.

He had to have several medical operations, and so it was a while before he had to surrender. He went in on October 2. We spent a great deal of that summer with my sister, who had a place near Tanglewood in the Berkshires in Massachusetts. Barbara was magnificent, and I don't even think she cried at that time.

It's very painful to think about. I don't ever think about it, really. This is the first time I've talked about it in such a long time.

Junius in Carrboro, North Carolina, newlywed, ca. 1950. This is the house where Junius and Gladys lived when they were wed and where Barbara was born. Eventually, Gladys's mother moved there to help with raising Barbara. The FBI paid the neighbor for news of who came and went, and the Ku Klux Klan burned crosses in the yard. The house now bears a plaque, placed by the North Carolina American Civil Liberties Union in 2002, identifying it as the house where Junius Scales lived. (Barbara Scales collection)

Gladys in Carrboro, North Carolina, newlywed, ca. 1950. (Barbara Scales collection)

Junius, baby Barbara, and Gladys, 1951. (Barbara Scales collection)

Junius, Barbara, and Gladys, ca. 1953. During most of the period from 1951 to 1954, Junius was underground, and the family was separated. In 1954, the family moved in the dead of night to New York to live under an assumed name. In this photo, Junius was either underground or just recently arrested and released on bail. (Barbara Scales collection)

Barbara, 1954. (Barbara Scales collection)

Gladys, portrait as a young woman. This photo probably dates from the early 1940s, about seven years before she met Junius. (Barbara Scales collection)

Gladys, ca. 1959, thirty-seven years old. This photo was taken at the home of Gladys's brother, Howard Meyer, at Rockville Center, Long Island. The Scales family, with grandmother Minnie Meyer, went regularly to visit Howard's family on Sundays from about 1959 to 1963. Howard, a lawyer with a special interest in civil liberties, was very helpful to Junius and Gladys in considering the legal matters that framed their lives. (Barbara Scales collection)

Barbara and Gladys, ca. 1962. Gladys's special concerns about Barbara's happiness and well-being were an ongoing preoccupation. This photo probably dates from Barbara's early adolescence, a period during which Gladys sought particularly to help the young girl understand her father's imprisonment and then the later reintegration of the family. (Barbara Scales collection)

Barbara, ca. 1967, sixteen years old. Richard Nickson took this photo at his home in Englewood, New Jersey. Barbara had spent the day in Central Park with friends and then had joined the family for an evening with the Nicksons at their large family home and gardens. (Courtesy of the Nickson family)

This photo of Gladys with a student and a volunteer parent seems to date from the 1970s and would have been taken in her office in Hartsdale, New York, where she coordinated a reading program for Greenburgh School District 8. The program involved family and community in tutoring children with reading difficulties. (Barbara Scales collection)

Gladys, portrait, 1980. The impact of the cortisone treatment for lymphoma tells in the puffiness in Gladys's face. Her natural optimism was in evidence even during this last summer at Peaceable Hill. (Barbara Scales collection)

This somber photo, taken by a stone wall at Peaceable Hill just months before Gladys's death in 1980, displays her physical deterioration as well as the stoic courage of Junius, her constant companion and aide. They lived her illness with no illusions, counting every day, no matter how difficult, as good fortune. (Barbara Scales collection)

Junius in Richard Nickson's study, cutting and pasting the *Cause at Heart* manuscript in the pre-computer age, ca. 1979. The Nicksons lived in a huge New York loft with floor-to-ceiling bookcases and ample reading and work space. Junius would often come from work at the *New York Times,* where he finished at about 10:00 AM, and spend the day working with Richard. In addition to working on the book together, the two would often listen to music, particularly to opera, and discuss recent literary publications and current political issues. Over the sixty-five years of their friendship, a delight in each other's companionship was sustained around common interests and with unflagging wit and good humor. (Photo by Lia Nickson. Courtesy of the Nickson family)

Junius and Richard Nickson, ca. 1979, working on an early draft of *Cause at Heart*. Junius worked for years, sifting through documents, letters, and memos and reading histories of the period covered in his memoirs. After writing a draft of a chapter, which could take weeks or months, he would then spend a day at Richard's. They would read through the text, often aloud, looking for "clunkers" in form or content. They tried to make certain that the story was honest, consistent with published facts, and true to their memories. They gave great attention to the language of the book, assuring that it clearly communicated the ideas and experience it recounted. (Photo by Lia Nickson. Courtesy of the Nickson family)

Junius, ca. 1987, visiting his parents' home in Chapel Hill, North Carolina. This was the home where Junius and his parents lived after the sale of the family's Hamilton Lakes Estate, while Junius attended the University of North Carolina. His father, Alfred Moore Scales, lived his last years in this house. (Barbara Scales collection)

nine

Junius

I was arrested in November of '54, and I guess I was in jail, first in Memphis, and then in Winston-Salem for a couple of months. They set a one-hundred-thousand-dollar bail, and it took between six weeks and two months to get that reduced. There's always a very disturbed atmosphere in jail, and the penitentiary is a bit more relaxed. A week in jail is like a month in the penitentiary. I managed to get out just in time for Christmas.

The Smith Act, under which I was arrested, was passed in 1940, and it had two clauses. One was the conspiracy clause: the conspiracy not to *overthrow* the government but to *teach* or *advocate* the violent overthrow of the government. And the other was a membership clause. The membership clause, which was much more drastic and carried much heavier penalties, forbade membership in an organization that advocated the overthrow of the government. I never considered that the Party did that—and still don't.

I mean, there's plenty of leeway for counter views, but my position, which I took in public repeatedly, was that if the Communist Party couldn't win a majority to support its position then we deserved political oblivion. Of course, I did feel that if anybody was going to overthrow the constitutional guarantees of this country, we had a right to fight back. The violent overthrow of the government just seemed like an absolute absurdity.

For a while I became a professional defendant. I spent half my time trying to get my defense organized and trying to raise money for all of the expenses. I spoke at this and that and the other so-called broad affairs, which were all Party-arranged. The Emergency Civil Liberties Committee was going to help me, for example. Oh, they were going to be such a big help. And it turned out they wanted me to organize affairs through my contacts, and they'd take half the money. And it would be called a "broad" affair because the ECLC would sponsor it instead of the Party defense organization.

I had to keep going back to North Carolina for pretrial motions. Getting a lawyer was a major undertaking. David Rein, one of the few lawyers who had the guts to defend the Party and other left-wingers, came down and handled the trial marvelously well.

During the trial, in the spring of '55, the government named a lot of names, which made life pretty difficult for a lot of my friends. To follow it up, later in the year they had the House Committee on Un-American Activities come down to North Carolina. So after my conviction, during the appellant stage, I was trying to organize a defense of the Party in North Carolina, getting lawyers for the people there and knocking myself out. This time, the idea of getting much if any mass work done went more or less by the board. We had become a small defense organization.

This was a miserable business, you know, but there were a few spots of encouragement. And it took place back at the textile mills in the Durham area. There was a guy who had been working in a textile mill who was named as a Communist in my first trial. He had his master's degree and was halfway towards his doctorate when he had begun to work in this mill and had been successful in reorganizing it—so successful that when the company fired him, the workers walked out on strike, and the entire mill was closed down for nearly a week. The only way they got them back to work was with a top-level sellout from the national office of the Textile Workers Union.

In spite of all the difficulties, some people were so resourceful and so persistent that they were able to make mass ties and function. But, generally, as soon as the word went out that you were a Communist, you were dead. Which, if you think about it, pretty well knocks the organization in the head. In spite of acts of great personal courage, people would end up isolated and ineffectual and sometimes damned lucky if they could make a living and survive.

So I was living in the Bronx, making forty-two dollars and fifty cents a week as a Party organizer, the highest pay I ever got. Gladys had a series of jobs: she was a comparison shopper at Macy's and a window trimmer at Ohrbach's. She got to be a fashion coordinator at Ohrbach's, but that job was too good, so the FBI got her fired.

Once the first trial was over, the appeal business began, and there was the preparation of the appeal briefs. The Party wanted me to get a well-known national figure as a lawyer, and so I had to travel the country trying to find one and raise money. In fact, Francis Biddle, the former U.S. attorney general under Roosevelt, got me in touch with Telford Taylor, one of the prosecutors of the Nazis at Nuremberg, who agreed to be my lawyer for my Supreme Court appeal and my second trial.

Life was pretty miserable. I had gotten various jobs along the way, but as soon as I'd get a few paychecks, the FBI would find me and get me fired. I was tried in '55, and the appeal was finally argued in '56 before the Supreme Court. The Supreme Court reversed the conviction and sent it back to the district court on a technicality, assuming, I guess, that that was the end of it. But the Department of Justice figured, where else could they get a district court or a circuit court as reactionary as the Fourth Circuit in the South? So they dropped nearly all their other cases around the country and concentrated on mine.

My confidence in the Party steadily declined. I had never had very close ties with most of the top Party leaders. After my arrest, I was pretty much lionized. And while before '56 I knew there was plenty wrong with the Party, after I was arrested I got to know most of the functionaries. I got to see a lot of what was going on in the top Party circles up close, and I was quite horrified.

There was great cynicism and bureaucratic behavior. I began to meet with the national committee and the top southern leadership, and it seemed we just couldn't agree on anything. Relations became increasingly bitter, and I began to have very serious differences with the national committeeman in overall charge of Party work in the South. Actually, I disagreed with two guys, both black, and that put me in an awkward spot. Our differences were increasing with the years: more and more I felt that this sectarian business, and the whole policy of being underground, was just stupid. They would say, "You can't function if you don't." Function schmunction!

At that point, you know, it probably would have been much better for all concerned if most of the Party structure hadn't existed. Because, in a way, the government used us where they weren't able to use stool pigeons—and they used me to finger everybody. Well, the FBI probably knew nearly everybody anyway, but if all those people had functioned in their own environments, using their own wits and their natural instincts, they would probably have done better than following an isolated and disoriented Party bureaucracy.

Then came the Khrushchev bombshell, his Twentieth Soviet Party Congress revelations about Stalin, and this seemed to blow everything wide open in the Party. I gradually identified in the internal fracas with the John Gates group, the editor of the *Daily Worker*. I figured the only thing to do was to reorganize the Party from stem to stern, chuck Marxism-Leninism as a rigid theory and reexamine every aspect of it.

Maybe we could do something if we worked really effectively, and perhaps we'd deserve a footnote in history somewhere. But I felt we had been way off the deep end on every practical question.

When the Hungarian Revolution came along, the Party response was, "American imperialism has infiltrated Hungary and inspired this whole thing, and the Red Army had to go in to clean it up." The Party toed the line with the Soviet invasion of Hungary. And from thirty-five years of training, so many people fell in line.

I think I almost killed the Party chairman, William Z. Foster, with apoplexy the week fighting was raging in the streets of Hungary. I said that if I were in Budapest I'd be with the workers throwing Molotov cocktails at the Red Army tanks. To Foster, this was the absolute end—there could be no more outrageous statement.

Most of us just threw up our hands. And by that time there was so much disillusionment, such bitterness and resentment against the high-handed and undemocratic mess-up which flourished in that underground situation. There had been absolute discipline, everybody was a little dictator, and there was no semblance of democracy in the Party.

Of course, this big discussion over the Khrushchev speech and Hungary was the most democratic thing which had happened in years. For a few months we had lived with the hope that we could get the bulk of the Communist Party, the people dearest to us, and take it down another road. Maybe do something like the SDS, the Students for a Democratic Society, tried to do a generation later—try to throw out all the doctrinal baggage and start from scratch. Try to think about what makes sense, try to have an open mind, and a searching approach, while participating in progressive politics as much as we could, in as many different areas as we could.

I had gotten a Christmas job at Saks Fifth Avenue in '56. Saks had their annual sale, which lasts until New Year's, and then you're out. Apparently, I was a very successful salesman of boys' furnishing, so they decided to make me a junior executive and give me a well-paying job in boys' suits, commission and all. But as soon as the FBI heard about it, they got me fired.

This just happened to be the weekend of the National Party Convention in February 1957. I hadn't planned to go because I had had it by then. But the people in North Carolina, on my final trip down there as Party leader, had urged me to go and at least holler for them. Since I had just been fired and didn't have a job to tie me down, I went.

By this time, the division and the hatred inside the Party was just so thick you could cut it with a knife. We boiled for three or four days of, for me, utter futility and pain. Foster was vicious as a snake, and he was much more contained than others.

I wish I hadn't gone to the convention. Our differences of opinion were so great, and we just had such contempt for the people who wanted to stay in this ingrown infected bubble, that there was just no possibility of working with these people anymore.

Because we all felt so deeply about our politics, I'd say some of us still thought we were basically on the right track into '56. I'm probably speaking of the bulk of the Communist Party at that time. In the three-year period—'56, '57, '58—about 60 or 65 percent of the Party dropped out. Most of my close friends did.

As I was walking out of the convention with two friends, one of them says, "Well, there goes twenty-five years shot to hell," and the other guy says, "twenty-eight years shot to hell." I only had eighteen. But I don't really think it was all shot to hell.

There was strong pressure to stay in. Some of the guys still in told me, "You can't leave. Your case is still pending, and you know the Party won't support you." I said that I didn't give a damn what the Party did. The Party had made me hire a lawyer at a tremendous fee which I couldn't begin to raise, and I had refused to do it until they promised to financially back it. Sure enough, after I left, they refused to pay the fee.

I think the essential conflict was with those who wanted what already existed: a nice comfortable—maybe not so comfortable—but a tight, rigid organization that followed the Soviet line and mainly got its influence as the American franchise of Soviet Party thinking. I suppose you could trace it back to the idea of a violent and conspiratorial revolution, a dogmatic Leninist-type organization. The whole concept of a little bunch like this making a revolution that's going to change a great country with as many currents as this was utterly absurd and abhorrent to a lot of us. And I, and a lot of others, rejected that entirely.

We believed that we could have a very positive effect on the direction of the country as long as we were riding along and floating with the mainstream of what was going on in the country. We quit when it became perfectly obvious to us that long habit and an atrophy of thought and feeling made it impossible to revitalize the American Party.

The rupture was so complete and wide that we looked back in amazement to see how far back this split had existed, and in how many different ways.

We had over the years absorbed the whole radical movement and fractured the Left. For many years you could hardly function as an independent radical.

And by the fifties and the cold war, when McCarthyism was riding at its peak, the Left and liberals were fragmented. Half the liberals were so exasperated by years of dealing with the Communist Party that their anti-Communism was incapacitating them. And anybody who wasn't anti-Communist was suspect among liberals. The whole liberal movement was in disarray.

After the convention, I got a job in a restaurant. There was this left-winger who owned three or four restaurants. He was probably a millionaire, you know, one of those left-wingers always wanting the workers to charge the barricades. Nobody's so revolutionary as a really wealthy Communist. Anyway, he had mostly former Party functionaries as his restaurant managers. So I got a job in one of them. The manager there sort of worked on the theory that the worst thing in the world was a boss, and since circumstances forced him to become one, he was going to live up to the tradition. He was a real bastard. And there's nothing like a Communist boss. I stood it as long as I could, until I developed varicose veins and had to get out of that kind of work. At least the job had the advantage that the FBI couldn't get me fired.

Then, for about forty-eight hours, I had a job teaching in a Yeshiva. The FBI got wind of that particular job because a friend discussed it over my tapped telephone. I was very amused by the guy who had to unhire me. He had filled my name in ink in nice little squares all over his schedule, a square for each of the different things I would be teaching during the day. I often wonder what he did with that schedule.

Finally, in 1957, I got a job as a copyholder reading printed material for a proofreader in a printing plant. I gave some cock and bull story and had prepared an incredible resume. I had it down pat and got the job at sixty dollars a week to start for a five-and-a-half-day week. So I started to work in this proof room, and the desks were all crowded together. I'm reading away, and I look twenty inches away from me, and who do I see but an old Party functionary, Phil Bart, who I'd known for twenty years. He's also a copyholder, and he later became national organizational secretary of the Party.

I had just dropped out of the Party after the February convention. But in the following December of '57, the government reactivated my case. I told them at the printing plant that I had an unavoidable personal matter to attend to. I was prepared to quit but they said to forget about it and to come back when I got things straightened out. I was gone about five or six weeks.

I started my second trial in February '58. I had two lawyers: Telford Taylor and a local lawyer, MacNeil Smith, probably the best trial lawyer in North Carolina and a member of the state's most prestigious firm. And they did a hell of a job. It was quite remarkable to watch as Telford Taylor and Mac Smith, just in passing, put on a better defense of the Party than anybody had done at the other trials. Meanwhile, I couldn't get a nickel from the Party. And, in fact, every effort we made to raise money for legal expenses was deliberately undercut by the Party. They were knifing me in the back at every turn.

If anything, the second trial was more frustrating than the first. It had absolutely nothing to do with my life, my political activities, or anything else. It was simply unbelievable. I hadn't read Kafka's *The Trial* at that point, but that book is an understatement of the feelings I had during both my trials.

The government's case lasted about two and a half weeks, and it was a full two weeks before anybody who took the stand had even seen me before. They were all testifying about this "violent" organization to which I readily admitted I belonged. I heard all about John Lautner and the dozens of professional informers. It was like puerile science fiction. In a courthouse four blocks from where I was born, I was found guilty by a jury of my fellow townspeople and was sentenced by a judge (reputed to be a slum landlord) to six years in prison.

I came back to New York and returned to work at the same printing plant. The wages improved a bit, and I worked there until 1960, when the union chairman asked me if I'd like to take a proofreading test. I didn't know anything about printing, but I boned up for about six weeks and cooked up a record of having worked in print shops as a kid. I took the test and passed it and was put on a waiting list. About six months later, in June, a job opened up, and I went and blundered my way through a couple of weeks. I somehow passed the grade there and got my union card, and while on the job I gradually learned to be a proofreader. I came back to my first place of work as a proofreader: local boy made good. And I was working there when the Supreme Court conked me five to four on my appeal.

Felix Frankfurter, who was at the end of his rope and pretty much at the nadir of his liberalism, was the swing vote and made it five to four against me. Of course, he retired, and a few months later I was sitting in the clink with the almost certain knowledge that if the case had come before the Supreme Court just a little later I'd have the vote six-three in my favor. But that was the Smith Act.

Of course, the Supreme Court decision was front-page news, and the FBI promptly moved to get me expelled from the union. The chairman of the International Typographers Union had just about twelve days left to his term and was just about to be replaced. So the FBI visited this old character and said that I was still a Communist and demanded that he take away my union card. According to union rules, I had only one more day to go before my union status was official, one more day when nobody could question my credentials. So this old jackal, a lame duck president, announced that he was going to take action to remove my union card. He claimed that when I had applied for membership I was actually a Communist. So I hit him in the mail with photostats of North Carolina papers with eight-column headlines showing in '57 that I had left the Party, and we offered uncontested testimony from my trial.

Melvin Wulf, who worked in the New York office of the American Civil Liberties Union, knocked that in the head. He was courting a lovely girl whom he planned to marry, and they had planned a big weekend together. I spoiled his whole weekend because he stayed in town and got ahold of every labor leader he could reach, and on Monday morning my jackass president was deluged with phone calls. So I kept my union card.

And while I was in the clink, a whole bunch of people got together to raise money to pay my union dues. I found out later that Party people, people out of the Party, Trotskyites, Socialists, the damnedest collection of people contributed very substantial sums to pay those monthly dues. One of the guys would go around every month and collect it—a very moving thing for me to know while in prison.

I mentioned Phil Bart, the Communist who had sat a few desks away from me when I was a copyholder. We had worked at this place for some months. He was quite disgruntled and unhappy about the Party, although he never left. He was sort of an old Party warhorse, you know. This was everything to him, and he was pushing sixty-one and just psychologically incapable of leaving the Party. So he worked as a copyholder for a while and then went back on the Party payroll on a full-time basis.

Well, a few days before I was to go into the penitentiary, he called and said he knew I had left the Party and knew my feelings but he just wanted to meet me to say goodbye. We had worked together and had been friendly for many years, and I had built him a hi-fi set. I said sure, I'd meet him, and we met at Times Square. We went into Hector's Cafeteria and had some coffee, and for about twenty minutes or so reminisced about people we'd worked with, and people in the Party, and that was it. We shook hands, and he wished me well.

The last legal action before I went to prison took place a couple of weeks later in Alexandria, Virginia, where the trial judge resided. With a forlorn hope, we entered a motion for reduction of sentence. My lawyer made an eloquent plea, and the government presented one thing: a report from two FBI agents that I, Junius Scales, did meet one Philip Bart at Times Square and go to Hector's Cafeteria and there did have a cup of coffee, et cetera. And they presented an affidavit that Philip Bart was currently the national organization secretary of the Communist Party, USA, and they submitted that I still maintained my secret connections to the Party. Even though during the trial itself they had conceded that I was no longer a member of the Party, they decided this was the best way to counter the move for a reduction of the sentence. I got a temporary stay of sentence to have my gall bladder removed, and then it was off to jail.

ten

Barbara

I've been raised in a different way, raised with different principles than most people in this country. And because of that—even before I knew what it was to speak out—for some reason I've always felt that I've had something to say to the people of the United States, that I know something they don't know. I've been in contact with people who live by principles which enable them to survive, I think, in a much healthier, more productive, and much more gratifying way than most people of their background.

And I've always wanted to know what really happened, what they went through, where their principles come from, and what it's all about, because I think there's something there that's very important.

In the last couple of years, I've been at the age of consciousness, and able to talk to people instead of just being a kid, hanging around. And now that I've talked to my parents' friends, I realize more and more that, although many of them are bitter, and many of them are very sorry and sad about their lives, at least they have a kind of vitality, with principles and morality. They pay a special kind of attention to the world. They don't use words like these, but whatever the words are, it's a different way of living in this country, an almost separate kind of culture. And I come from that, different even from people I know in the movement today.

I was born in Durham, North Carolina, and anything I know about that time is completely reconstructed. For a long time all I could recall was a picture of me on a tricycle at about two and a half. Then, gradually, in the last few years more of the story of my early life became clear to me. My mother told me that the night the Rosenbergs were killed as spies I was in a little basket on the porch, and she heard the news on the radio. My father was underground at that time, and she came running out, very, very frightened, because at that time anybody who was a Communist, and certainly my father, a known Communist being pursued, was very threatened. She was not just terribly troubled, and very sorry about the Rosenbergs, and bitter, but very frightened. And it had been a nightmare of hers for the three years before.

There were stories about me playing with the girl across the street. Vicki was my age, and I'd always thought, you know, nice Vicki, nice policeman, neighbor policeman. Then we moved from there when I was three.

Last summer, I decided I was tired of not knowing anything at all about what had happened there. So I hitched down to Chapel Hill with a friend, and we were traveling together and exploring. We met all sorts of people and went looking for Abernethy's Intimate Bookshop, which just wasn't there anymore.

I decided to go and try to find the house that we lived in. I figured it must be something so far-out and different from anything anybody growing up in a big city must have been exposed to. So I called my parents and told them I was in North Carolina. And they were . . . well, kind of upset and anxious. They had left there with not very good feelings about the town and the state. But I asked them what the number of the house was, and where it was, and set out for a look.

Sure enough, during the past fifteen years the numbers had changed, and I walked up and down Carr Street until I saw an old man sitting on a front porch. I walked over to him and asked if by any chance he knew where the house had been eighteen years ago. And he thought for a minute. And I said, "It was the home of Junius Scales." He said, "Scales? Junius Scales . . . why sure, sure, it was right over there." And he pointed across the street, and there was a little shack. And he told me, "Yeah, my name is Harry Gaddis, and we lived across the street from you." Sure enough, he was the policeman.

The house was very plain, small, and not very well constructed. It had a tremendous kitchen. Carrboro is a very poor suburb. It's mostly black, and then comes the white fringe; I guess it had been that way then, too. It was a strange community, one I didn't know very well and wasn't really acquainted with. I looked, and I was sad. And that was my odyssey. It was an anticlimax of sorts, but I was glad that I'd done that, you know, because it demystified that whole period a little. Just a little bit.

My parents never speak about that time. And, in fact, until these taping sessions, I knew next to nothing about their lives before I can remember them. I think they always wanted to protect me a little bit, and let me grow up like a normal young American girl—and, at least, not burdened by what they considered, to a great extent, their follies and mistakes. They hadn't wanted to discuss it with me before the Supreme Court decision, and then after that, it was just very ancient history. It just never really came out as it should have.

I remember living in the Bronx. My grandmother took care of me a great deal of the time, because both my parents were either working or busy with whatever they were doing. And I remember her during the year or two that we lived in the Bronx, but not much else. I wasn't going to school, and we used to take long walks down to wade in the Harlem River down about 161st Street. We lived right near Yankee Stadium, and I was a Yankee fan.

We lived in a very horrible apartment. It was very small, and my grand-mother and I shared a room. She broke her arm once because I left the bottom drawer of the dresser open, and she came in while I was asleep. I remember my room was always dark, and the apartment was always filled with noise, people noise, because there wasn't enough room to move around.

I had a lady doctor at that time, and I was very impressed. I thought that it was strange, but I was happy about it. And I remember that most of the other kids in the neighborhood were Italian and Catholic, and I thought it was pretty crazy they had to go to private school, and wear uniforms, and be Catholic. But they were my friends anyway, and we used to have fun and play in the playground when I was four or five.

I have no memory of my parents at all from that time: I remember mostly my grandmother and this girl, Diane, who was in the second grade. She used to take care of me and protect me from all the bullies. She, too, was Italian and went to Catholic school.

And about that time, my grandmother had become a Christian Scientist. Religion in my family got carried to the point of being farcical—my father coming from a Presbyterian background, my mother from a Jewish back-ground, and suddenly my grandmother's becoming a Christian Scientist. And nobody really believing in anything. It was mostly a matter of exercise if it were practiced at all. I probably told the kids in the neighborhood I was Jewish, because even though my grandmother was a Christian Scientist, she was always saying, "oi gevalt," reminding us in Yiddish that she suffered. And we also ate a lot of chopped liver.

We moved to Central Park West at 105th Street, the far upper end of Cen-tral Park West, just where it begins to deteriorate and become honest-to-God slums. This area was mostly Puerto Rican but also had a good solid black population. Though I did know the building next to us was a very strange building, I didn't understand at the time that it was a brothel.

An old man lived downstairs. He was a magician, and he used to come up to visit, and he came to my birthday party. As I've grown up and met people, my parents will occasionally say, "Oh yes, he or she was at your birthday party when you were three years old." It must have been quite an event for the younger [Communist] Party set. We had a whopping big party, and he came and pulled rabbits out of hats for us.

He was a magnificent man, and he died when we were still living there, and that was pretty sad. I'll always remember the constant exchange between him and my father and another man in the building, a fellow named Jack, whose father was a big leader in the New York Party. That was the other thing: aside from the talk and the hospitality, there was always an exchange of books.

I remember traveling around a lot with my parents at that time, '55 or '56, going to visit people, sitting in on what must have been meetings, or just Party people trying to figure out what on earth they were doing. I remember people often coming over to our apartment, having to go to bed at night, and waking up and coming out and prancing around, and there would be fifteen people sitting around the living room. And I'd want to play, but they were all very busily having a meeting of some sort.

Usually I was put to bed with a story or a little talk. But I remember it being tense and being told some simple explanation by my mother. It probably ran to the effect of, " . . . and so and so is unhappy," or "such and such is a problem," or "we're having troubles," or "you know we have to work things out, so help us out by going to bed." Although a lot of the time it was, "scram, you brat! . . . Get out of here, can't you see we're busy?"

But I remember more and more people being around, and more and more traveling. I imagine it being the Upper West Side. Also the Lower East Side, traveling around, usually getting shoved off in a corner with the other kids while all the big people were sitting and talking. And I remember friends disappearing also. I remember hearing my father make a disparaging comment about somebody and asking why and not really getting an explanation, realizing that we just didn't see them any more. Looking back on it, that was probably around the time he was leaving the Party. But it was all very much a mystery to me. I didn't know anything about it. I don't remember him being arrested earlier, and I don't remember even being exposed to the slightest hint that there was a trial going on, or that he was a subversive or bad or that he was anything strange or unusual.

Meanwhile, I started going to the Riverside School, a private kindergarten on Riverside Drive. They must have given me a scholarship. It was an all-day school, so I would be out of the house, and they could work. We used to eat lunch there, and make ourselves peanut butter and jelly sandwiches, and turn off the lights and say grace before every meal—just a nuisance, as far as I was concerned. Once, I took a bite of my peanut butter and jelly sandwich before everybody had said grace. I suddenly realized what I had done and became very nervous. I took my knife and tried to cover over the bite, when one of the teachers came along and saw it. She became furious. She took me out of the room and scolded me.

I was traumatized. I couldn't understand why this woman had bawled me out. It just didn't make sense to me. What was this ritual for? My cousins in the South would boast to me that they knew twenty-one graces, one for each meal of the seven days of the week. I just wasn't impressed at all and would make fun of them.

My parents were always among friends, supported by friends in one way or another, either to be invited away for a summer or visiting or being visited constantly. We were getting out of the city for the summers, so I never really did spend a summer in the city. These were some of the fundamental aspects of day-to-day life for our family: other people being there and being helpful, giving and taking in absolutely the most beautiful way, going away and inviting, and always considering people outside of the family.

Politics, though, was something I knew nothing about. Principles, I had heard of that; morality, I had heard about. "Don't do this because . . ." and a great list of principles would be described. But politics was something very foreign. I don't know anything about politics, although names of political figures, Eisenhower and Dulles and Nixon, were always running around the house. But I don't remember any importance being placed on the Soviet Union or Stalin or Khrushchev or anything of that sort. Other people who have been raised by left-wing families were apparently nursed on that sort of thing. You know, "Stalin" was their first word, or "revisionism," something like that. But I wasn't aware of the international scope of politics at all.

The Downtown Community school offered me a scholarship, I guess, and I went there for the first grade. Pete Seeger was the music teacher, and he'd just stand in front of us, and sure enough, 150 little kids who could hardly open their mouths to take their thumbs out were hooting and hollering. And I remember having a lot of fun.

All of first grade was a joy. My teacher knew me and knew that the day before I hadn't known how to add two and two, and she was impressed that by the next day I could. And they had specialized reading groups.

A special car used to pick us up. I remember always being excited about meeting the other kids in the morning, being excited about going to school, and being excited about coming back in the car with all those kids. And apparently I did very well.

There was a great emphasis on playing with others, on the ethic of cooperation and the principles of collective endeavor. It was so important when we were playing with blocks, for instance, to cooperate and make sure that when you put a block down you weren't interfering with Larry next to you.

Around that time I started seeing the Abernethys more. They had moved to New York probably before we had. But I don't remember their family being part of the first few years in New York, when I remember the meetings and the deliberating and the troubled looks. I remember them around the time we moved to this building near Broadway and I enrolled in the public school here. Amy, Ab and Minna's daughter, was in my grade, and Amy and I were good friends. She was in the IGC class, the Intellectually Gifted Class. Downtown Community didn't keep the same kind of records, and they weren't recognized by the public schools, so the school figured they'd try me out in the slow-learners' class.

Then I started spending more and more time with the Abernethys, and we used to go away for weekends. I guess at that time things were very hard. I never really pieced it all together. But just thinking back on it, it must have been the time of the Twentieth Congress of the Soviet Party, the time of the Hungarian uprising, then when the first trial was nearing its conclusion in 1957: probably a lot of things were going on. I didn't know where my father was, and, after a point, I think it stopped mattering to me. I don't remember being concerned at all. And all those times when he wasn't around a lot, I spent time with the Abernethys. I don't remember it seeming strange at all that I should go and stay with Amy a lot. It was kind of my following through the same policy as my parents going to the country and staying with friends of theirs.

The Abernethys got a house in Long Island in the country, and we spent a lot of time out in Hampton Bays. Amy and I spent a great deal of time together; and Ab is a nut, a very funny guy, and I just enjoyed him a lot.

We went out for weekends, for vacations, and for the summertime. I don't know, but it seemed like through most of elementary school I was living more with the Abernethys than here. I remember them much more distinctly than I remember my own parents. My grandmother was here, and we fought a lot. And so I guess going to the Abernethys was largely an escape.

Through all this time my mother was sick. She has some very rare blood disease and has been having attacks of pneumonia since she was fourteen. And from the time we moved up North, she was constantly sick. She had always been a smoker, and she must have had quite a bout because the doctor told her, "If you smoke any more, you can die," and he was serious. So the ashtrays disappeared from the house.

I remember times when I missed my parents, times when I would feel that Minna or Ab or somebody was being grossly unjust, or feeling that they were favoring Amy because she was their daughter. I remember wishing that my parents were there to arbitrate on my behalf. But, all in all, I was pretty comfortable with the Abernethys. And I preferred Ab's pancakes to my father's. It was always a battle when I came home to get my father to make them the way Ab did. My father's pancakes were light and delicate, but Ab's were gritty and greasy and thick.

Another important thing was that I never really was a city child. I wasn't aware of the city as an entity, but in elementary school I played tag and jump rope, and I was the head of the girls' gang. My friend Andy, one of the only other white kids in the school, who also comes from left-wing parents, was leader of the boys' gang. So we had what we called gang war, mostly a glorified game of tag, around the schoolyard. But I never really suffered through a summer in the city, and never really had too many friends in school, because so much of my time was spent with Amy, who wasn't a school friend but what I called a home friend. She was part of that other life.

Most of the kids in school were black, and, except for Andy and one Japanese girl, most of my school friends were black. I never felt any friction, and I even became close with a couple of people. For the most part, though, we just led very different lives. I wasn't around weekends to go running off to baseball games. I would play at school, and I would play after school. I'd see people sometimes, but most of the time I was just elsewhere.

There was one girl in the building, she was black, and there were two people in the next building, and we had a little clan, the children of the Left. It strikes me now as almost a miracle we found each other, but I guess our parents must have talked and introduced us.

I was in the slow-learners' class for the whole second year. I became the school nurse for cuts. If anybody had a cut or scratch they would come to our classroom, and I would putter around in the back and bandage them up. I don't know how this happened, but I developed my first crush because of it. I'd been keeping a close eye on Andy, and one morning before school started he'd fallen down and cut his head. I had to take care of his wounds. Oh, women's lib! Where were you when I needed you?

And pretty much that's how it was. I had a pretty good time and didn't feel particularly estranged from the other kids, although I remember that not many of them read as I did. They just didn't read, and there wasn't much encouragement.

The summer after second grade, I went down South and spent time with my father's mother, and I loved her. She was a marvelous, outstanding woman and very energetic. She'd come up North a couple of times before. And I remember always being warned beforehand by my father that she came from a different culture, that she had completely different beliefs, and not to be too surprised by them. But she never complained about my black friends.

I had a Puerto Rican friend who came over once when she was there, and she went out of her way to commend her. She said, "Oh, Gloria's a lovely girl." And I made a mental note: "Ah, she's only going out of her way, because she wouldn't ordinarily think that," because she'd been warned. She once told me, though, "Black kids are fine, but just never marry a black man because your children will be nothing." And it puzzled me, because the whole question of what color your skin was, or what language you spoke, had never been any sort of criteria for evaluating a person. My mother had always said to me, "We're all the same," so I thought we're all the same and began to stop thinking in terms of differences.

What my grandmother had said struck me as reasonable, but it didn't make sense. I mean, it's true that they were nothing—that is, not black and not white. And the argument came back to me a couple of times when I got to know Paul Robeson's grandchildren, because their mother was white and their father was black. And I remember arguing in my own mind and realizing that it didn't matter. The Robesons did exist. They weren't nothing.

Well, I spent the summer in the South and didn't like it very much, though it was fun being with my grandmother. She was a very strong-minded woman, and I was kind of intimidated by her. She was so different from people up here, but we finally got along pretty well.

My southern family was rich, and they were very gracious and very hospitable. Their houses impressed me, but I didn't feel comfortable there. My cousin Dickie-Bird used to poke me in the belly button, and they made me go to Sunday School once, and that was terrible. They used to take me into gloomy, ugly churches and say, "There's your great-grandfather hanging on the wall." And there was this great big dark painting of my great-grandfather looking like some absolutely wild character. My relatives had been the Elders, the Founders of the Presbyterian church. I remember being told this with great pride and just not being able to relate to it at all. I couldn't stand to be bored. That just made me mad.

Then there was third grade, and I had a very nice teacher. She put me into the IGC class, and we started talking about current events and doing reports on all sorts of countries. I remember coming home at suppertime, sitting and watching TV and John Daly. That was a focal point: suppertime, the news, and discussions. And not just discussions but the sharp, incisive comments my father would make. I once turned to my father, it must have been around the time of the presidential campaign, and I said, "You know, you should run for president. You'd be a great president." And I could see the significant looks that greeted my comments, and I guess a laugh. "No, I don't think that would be possible." "Why not?" I asked. "Why not?" I was sure it was possible. "Well, I don't think anybody would vote for me. . . ." Again, I couldn't understand. I was mystified. "What? How do you know how many people would vote for you? You know, it's a free country, anybody can run!"

I remember when the secretary of state, John Foster Dulles, died. He had been slandered right and left in my family, and to me he was a bad guy. So Dulles died, and I said, "That's great!" My mother was horrified, and she said, "No matter how bad a man is, never be happy anybody dies." They must have said some terrible things about Dulles because I was very surprised, and the lesson and their words just took on more significance. She still felt sorrow. She was sad he died. And I remember her adding, "He wasn't a bad man, he was just a bad secretary of state." Then, in the next breath, "And look who's replacing him, Christian Herter." And sure enough he was a bad secretary of state, too. So, apparently, it didn't make that much difference. And I guess that was really the first political lesson I had. It was a moral lesson as well.

I used to play with my parents a lot when we were here together. They lived in the living room and used to sleep on the couch; my grandmother lived in the back, and I had my room.

Sunday morning was a ritual. I'd wake up early and come running into the living room, where undoubtedly Daddy would be up reading a magazine, *The Nation* or something, and Mommy would be sleeping. Then she'd wake up, and I remember we used to talk about how we were a family, all the time, always talking about it. I guess to make sure I knew. I guess it was very hard for them, too, and they probably felt badly that they weren't spending as much time with me as they should, and as they wanted to. But I remember we used to talk about family business. The family unit was a very important thing and always emphasized.

Then it became the extended family, and the Abernethys became family also: Minna became second mother, and Ab would be second daddy, and Amy would be kind of a sister, and so there was more family.

I'm sure it was very important to them. To whatever extent it was for me, it was for them. Because the real definition of the family comes when everybody recognizes that it's such. So it was important that I understand the family-ness of us, so that it would become more real for them too. So there was family, and Sunday morning, and there were pancakes, and fairly normal business, reading the *New York Times* and reading books.

In school we were studying countries like India, and I suddenly realized that I was an idealist and became aware that I came from a different background. I noticed differences in the way I talked about what was happening in the world. We used to get this little newspaper in school, *Junior Scholastic*, and they had articles on the U-2 spy plane, fighting in Laos, and African independence. There was fighting in the Congo then, and there were lots of stories about Patrice Lumumba, the bad guy, and the good guys, and I remember challenging the teacher in class, asking, "Why is Lumumba bad?" I was ten. I insisted on considering Lumumba's opinion, on considering the rebels' position. The teacher kind of went, "Uhhhhhhhh . . ." without really responding.

By the time I was in the fifth or sixth grade, I had certain pronounced prejudices. I didn't like rich people. I guess it was partly from my family, partly from the simplified version of the world I was sometimes presented with. If I wanted a toy or I wanted money to buy candy or normal things like that, not only would I be told "yes" or "no" but with it would come a discussion. "You're not a rich girl. You're not rich like all those other people," who immediately were put in a special category all by themselves. And so I developed an image of the spoiled rich, the pampered rich, and the wasteful rich, and I decided I didn't like them. There was probably an element of resentment involved. They could have anything they wanted, you know—that's pretty good. But mostly it became a matter of principle not to be like the spoiled rich. You just don't get everything you want, so you get what's important.

When I think back on the principles my parents taught me, I think of them as a special and different approach to life, a foundation of a different ethic and a different morality. I think of my parents and their friends, the people who came out of that period with them, out of the Party and the movement either as activists or sympathizers or intellectuals, as a revolutionary group of people. Coming from all different places, somehow, collectively, they were able to develop and maintain a way of coping and dealing with the world quite differently from the accepted ways, the traditional and standard ways of America. And I don't always know if that's true or not, but thinking it has always been important to me.

For example, my father builds hi-fi sets as a part-time profession to put me through college. That was the only savings we had for years. He would build sets for friends and sell them at cost plus something like five dollars for labor. He would work for hours and days and weeks fixing people's hi-fi sets, and he wouldn't charge anything for it. My mother would be furious, and he'd say, "How can I charge so-and-so, they don't have any money?" Yet he kept saying, "I'm doing this to put you through college."

Well, the other thing that was going on starting about fourth grade was summer camp. First, in 1959, I went to the Ninety-second Street Y camp, a Jewish day camp, and it was pretty gruesome. We went swimming and did Israeli folk dances, and I enjoyed that, but we had to say prayers again. Bread prayers, which I still don't remember, "Baruch atah adonai," and I guess I must have been very confused because one year they're telling me to say grace, and a few years later it's, "Baruch atah. . . ." It was a little easier to bear this time because everybody else also seemed to think it was a farce. So whenever we got to the end, "ha-something something," whatever the last words were, "eat," and we'd dig in, and that was fine. I don't really remember very much of Camp Yomi, except that I thought my counselors were pretty square. All they talked about was their boyfriends, and I just thought that was silly.

And then I went to Camp Higley Hill, which was run by Manny and Grace Granich, whom I loved dearly. The camp was really a retreat for the kids of left-wingers, and it was marvelous. It was run-down because they didn't have the money to fix things. There were eighty kids there, and a lot of them were black. Amy went there, which is the reason I went there in the first place. And even though Pete Seeger was going to be at Woodlands, I came to Higley Hill and stayed two years until it disbanded.

It was so unstructured, my parents were horrified. They thought there were all sorts of things wrong with it: only one of the four toilets worked, there was a cow in the back field which left cow pies all over the place, and they just didn't take good enough care of us. But they did. It was a real zany free-for-all. A couple of people might be painting, and they'd wipe their brushes on the floor and say, "That looks neat," and we'd have a mural on the floor. And so it went, and the flavor of the camp developed as it went along. My first summer there was a summer of bliss and joy and freedom: crushes and softball and basketball and terrible Shirley Temple movies.

Between those two summers, the Supreme Court decision came down, and I came home from school one day, and we had a sit-down family discussion. My mother did most of the talking. I guess that's the woman's role, right? To do the talking in difficult situations. And she said, "There's something to talk about. Your daddy's going to have to go to jail." I didn't really know how to feel, because it didn't mean anything to me particularly. Jail? Jail was bad. . . . Yeah, television says jail was bad. Bad guys go to jail. But my father wasn't bad. So it never clicked, you know.

The connection of jail equals bad, Daddy going to jail, Daddy must be bad never had a chance to really sink in. Because immediately the story came, and the explanation. Again, very simple, something like: "You know your daddy has always been a very good man. He has very strong beliefs and has always tried to do the best for everybody he knows. . . . When he was much younger, he wanted to do the best for everybody he knew, so he joined the Communist Party because they were doing the best for people in the South, for Negroes and working people in the South. And the work they did was very important. Except that it's illegal to be a Communist. . . . So your daddy is going to jail."

I didn't understand what all this meant. It didn't make sense to me the same way as the girls' gang and the boys' gang did. It was a story. It had a consequence, and the consequence was going to jail. But until he went to jail, it was just a story. And it was the story of my daddy, and I was proud of him because it was posed in that way, and immediately "Communist" became good. I mean, "Communist" had never been a particularly good or bad word. It had been a classification. A Communist is a type of person, not a good person nor a bad person; a way of thinking was Communist, not a good way or a bad way, just a way. Somehow it began to be something good. I mean, it was associated with my father, good. And government was bad, because government didn't like Communists, and government didn't like Daddy. And, of course, it was oversimplistic.

Along with it came the story that he had been offered a deal—that he would not have to go to jail if he named names. He didn't want to betray his friends, even his not-friends; he didn't want to betray other people's beliefs. I didn't really understand what it meant, but it was a principle, and so it was important. Because he was going to jail for it, it was important. So he was going to jail, and I was proud.

The other thing my parents told me, which I'm sure screwed me up completely, was not to tell people. I mean, now it makes a lot of sense. They said that people who would understand already knew about it, and that most people wouldn't understand. And I shouldn't tell people about it because they might not understand. And so I pretty much didn't say a word to anybody.

People called up all that day, and a great many arrangements were being made. That same night they told me, June 5, I think, I started to make connections. My parents had known so-and-so for fifteen years, and then I began to wonder if so-and-so was in the Party. And I began to unravel it, and sure enough, all these people who had been nice friends had been in the Party, and some of them had been in jail. It suddenly began to assume the dimensions of a pretty glorious, special battle that had to be maintained. I sensed that what was happening was very important . . . and then I went back to camp. And, always, through the whole time that my father was in jail, no matter how hard things got, one of the things that kept me going was the feeling that we had a principle to maintain, and a battle to fight.

I guess I must have been the baton twirler. I was really up for it. I was ready to lead the march. Not that I understood it all, but it was our little battle, and I was very proud.

I guess I sensed that most of the people at camp were people who would understand. Suddenly that classification became very important to me: there were people who would understand and people who wouldn't. And the people who would, for the most part, were ex-Communists or Communists, people who had been in the Party or had friends in the Party, and that kind of cliquishness became almost natural to me, feeling at home among people who would understand. Even though I wasn't always conscious of it, it was something that stayed with me for a long, long time, the feeling that I had found somebody who was sympathetic to the Left. And I remember always being surprised and pleased when I found people who came from a left-wing background.

But I didn't talk about it. Susie Robeson and I became good friends that summer and used to hack around a lot; we were good tomboys together. Susie is built kind of like her grandfather—mammoth shoulders and whopping big head, very strong—and we did some building and some construction. Camp was bigger that summer and wasn't as good.

I got into a fight about Communism with a guy who always considered himself an incredible big shot. He'd go spouting ridiculousness all over the camp and bother everybody. And I still knew nothing about politics or about Communism or what it meant, except the kind of things I intuited from my parents. Once I knew they were Communists, I said, "Ah, Communism is like them, and Communism is like their friends and the things they talk about when we sit and watch the news. . . . It's a way of being with your friends, a way of thinking, and a way of responding to the newscaster John Daly." And so it was good, Communism was fine, and I was willing to defend it to the teeth. He started in saying there were all these Communists all over the place, under every bed, and "they should all be thrown in jail." An older friend, Debby, was there at the time, and she was a lot more politically sophisticated than me.

She would make these very good, rhetorical responses about how everybody's being accused of Communism these days, and asking, "What's wrong with Communism anyway?" I would sit there and listen to her, and then I'd poke my face in his and repeat everything Debby said. He turned to me and said, "I suppose your father has been accused of being a Communist." And I said, "Well, as a matter of fact, he has been. . . ." Which shut him up for the rest of the summer.

I was pleased as punch. Not only had I won that point, but the people around me, like Debby, had supported me. But I remember that confused me for a long time afterwards, because I didn't understand a thing. I had no idea that Communists were persecuted on a large scale. I had no real awareness of a McCarthy or the House Un-American Activities Committee, or even of the sit-ins that had just begun.

I hated to leave camp. I knew I wasn't going to be able to go back there. I came home. I got my school wardrobe, my notebook, and my pencils and shoes, and we celebrated my mother's birthday. I started school. On October 1, we went to New Jersey to visit friends, my father's schoolmate in college, his friend who was interested in poetry. We went there, and it was kind of a solemn occasion.

We drove down to the park on the Palisades on the Hudson and spent the afternoon picnicking and taking pictures. We still have the pictures. They're all very solemn, very sad, and the laughs, the smiles are strained. Richard took all the pictures, and I had a fairly melodramatic expression, all very silverine.

We spent the day and came home. The next morning I went to school. At noon they came here to arrest him. And it had happened. What I had been waiting for since June had happened, and it was very bad. It was very grim.

eleven

Gladys

The penitentiary years have a different quality. Of course, it was painful, but there was nothing as painful as that initial hearing, knowing that it was all over and that there was no more hope.

When he was in the penitentiary I knew I would see him once a month, and I looked forward to those visits, and wrote as often as I was permitted. And he wrote to me. It was a time of walking around in your sleep, thinking, Is this ever going to end? Visiting him was very difficult, but he was just wonderful.

He knew how painful it was for Barbara and me, and so he was always very cheerful and strong and loving. You know, you're not allowed to touch. You sit across from one another—although they don't enforce that with children, so Barbara was always around her daddy in some way. We just talked about everything.

But that was a dreadful time for me personally. I tended to withdraw. I was bitter and unhappy. I was edgy and touchy and didn't want anybody to feel sorry for me. I didn't want anybody to do me any special favors—all of my neuroses were just exacerbated, and I was paranoid as hell. I wanted to stay away from people, and then if I stayed away, I got sad if they didn't pursue me.

I was working in a Yeshiva school, and most of the people there, particularly in the English department, were people who had themselves suffered through the McCarthy period. They had been victims of the Rapp-Coudert subversive witch hunt: the time when anybody who supposedly was a member of or connected with the Party was thrown out of the New York City public school system. And they were very wonderful.

I went to work every day and enjoyed my work with the children. My close friends were constantly calling, and my family was very good to me. I just did my work and took care of my child and wrote to my husband. That was the time he started that Sunday-night forum, and I was able to get records and books for him. Just meeting the needs of somebody in prison, having a young child, and working kept me quite busy during that time. And, of course, my greatest activity was trying to get him out of jail.

We had a group of key people like Jimmy Wechsler, the editor of the *New York Post,* and Norman Thomas, the Socialist Party leader. And I would meet with them periodically to see what we could do, who we could see next, or what kind of story Wechsler wanted to do for the *Post.* I went around to see all kinds of people, begging for help for my husband. I went to see John Oakes at the *New York Times* and Gardner Cowles, who used to be the editor of *Look* magazine. That was really going into the inner sanctums of the high mucky-muck of the Establishment.

Cowles could not have been more polite. There was a very fancy inner office, all richly carpeted, with works of art on the walls. And the question that all these influential people asked me was, "How do we really know he left the Party?" So I told them, "You'll just have to take my word for it. I mean, what else can I do to explain it to you?" They wanted some kind of guarantee. I didn't like that. They should have been fighting for this man simply because the Smith Act itself was such a horrible thing. But they would never commit themselves in any way. . . . Oh, they listened. They listened very politely. The *Times* did come out with three editorials. Cowles, I don't know—I don't know what he might have done behind the scenes. Or whether he did anything at all.

I got to see Emmanuel Celler, a Democratic congressman from Brooklyn. My mother had been a friend of his sister's, so we went up to see him. His office was in the old Paramount building on Broadway, right around the corner from the *New York Times.* That was a most unpleasant meeting. He as much as said, "Well, your husband did something that was against the law, and he deserves to be punished." He was just obnoxious. Now, politicians have many faces, and I was told by other people that maybe the visit did mean something to him. But who knows?

I went to see William F. Ryan, a congressman from the West Side of Manhattan, and he also behaved like a politician, without committing himself. He, too, wanted to know if Junie really had left the Party. He was friendly, nothing like Celler, and wound up saying something like he would see what he could do. Now, for a politician to make even that much of a commitment was something.

I suppose that was my therapy, in a way. I went wherever I could and spoke to whomever I could. We had a petition sent around and had mailings—a whole organization of friends working to get him out. And, of course, the idea was to get him a pardon. The petitions were sent to famous people, people whose names we thought would make some kind of a dent, and it was quite an impressive list. The original petition was started by Reinhold Niebuhr, the philosopher, Norman Thomas, and Harold Goheen, the president of Princeton University.

I went to speak before some of the church action groups, and I saw A. J. Muste, the pacifist leader. I went wherever I could, to whatever function I could. I saw Frank Graham, a wonderful old man and a professor of Junie's from the University of North Carolina in Chapel Hill. He made no bones about the fact that he would do whatever he could . . . and then proceeded to tell me all kinds of horrendous stories about how terrible Junie had been, how he used to get to class early to put leaflets on everybody's seat. He obviously loved Junie and respected him.

I had to see Telford Taylor, Junie's lawyer, and my sister and I had to make a trip south to see McNeil Smith, Junie's North Carolina lawyer. Going back to North Carolina was pretty dreadful. It's funny that we are talking about it today, because an old friend of ours called. She had been down there most of the summer, and Junie said again, as he's said any number of times, that he never wants to go back. I don't have any of the ties that he does, and as far as I'm concerned, except for some of the wonderful people I met, my whole experience there was bad from the word "go." But he doesn't ever want to go back.

Anyway, the whole thing, the visits—it was all so amorphous. That was part of the frustration of that time: there were no real connections. There was nothing you could put your finger on and say, "Well, I saw this person, and we did this, and such and such a thing happened," because that's not the way things happen. If somebody as controversial as Junie was going to receive clemency, it all had to be done very sub rosa. And somebody had to say something to somebody else at a cocktail party. There were official channels, but just as the Paris peace talks about the war in Vietnam, there are also the secret meetings.

I think it was a very difficult time for Barbara, although she never verbalized it. Her behavior changed in subtle ways. This was a kid who was never afraid, always went to bed at night, no lights, door closed, none of that nonsense. She'd read a while and go to sleep. After a while, that wasn't the case. She insisted upon having her door open and the light on in the hall right outside her room. And she always slept so that her head was close to the door and the light and the outside. I was very concerned about her and decided I was going to take her to my old psychiatrist. I think the visit probably helped me more than anything else. You had to expect that there were going to be certain changes, particularly from a child who didn't tell you how she felt.

But as she became older and more aware, she was proud of her father and understood more the terrible injustice of it. She looked forward to the weekends we'd go visit him. And she talked about him quite freely. I know she missed him desperately. There was never a bellyache out of her; she was never whiney, even though that was a hard trip for a kid.

Just about the only catharsis I had came in the early part of December 1962. There was this whole business of his being taken down to the Washington, D.C., jail to appear before a congressional investigating committee to testify about the Party. It was just the most brazen kind of intimidation. The FBI was furious with him because he wouldn't name names. So they wanted him brought before this committee so they could ask him about people he knew. And, of course, he was going to refuse to testify, and that almost automatically meant a contempt-of-Congress citation and additional imprisonment.

We had to fight so that the government would not be permitted to call him before the committee. That's where we got help from Kenneth Keating, a Republican senator from New York, and John Lindsay, when he was a congressman. There are many people in this country who, even though we may not always agree with them politically, do believe in the traditions of this country, and Keating was one of those. He felt that this was an outrage and was, finally, the one who somehow had Junie's appearance canceled.

In the meantime, Junie had been taken to Washington and outfitted in a nice new cardboard suit. Some son of a bitch from the FBI called me. I just gave him hell, though I'm sure it just rolled off his back. He couldn't have cared less. But that was the only time I got my anger out, you know. There's this absolute frustration seeing all this happen to your husband and not having anybody's neck to grab. Well, he was the one poor soul I got. Unfortunately, he was probably some kind of underling who just wanted his $125 a week.

So I visited Junie in the D.C. jail. There were a lot of blacks down there, and when they found out who he was and why he was there and how he wasn't going to fink on anybody, the black guards were just wonderful to us. They gave him soap and razors and books he wasn't supposed to have, and he got the royal treatment.

For me, unfortunately, this was the beginning of a pneumonia which just hung on, and I eventually had to have part of a lung removed.

twelve

Barbara

We all had our jobs to do, to make up for the loss of a member of the family. Something unjust was being done to him, and we had to compensate for it, and, almost in service to Daddy, we tried to get along and not fight.

For the first two weeks, my father was held at West Street, a federal detention area in New York, and I wasn't allowed to see him. My mother saw him and would come back and tell us how she thought he was. It was much harder on her than it was on me, because I was ten and just couldn't stop things from becoming an adventure. But it was very hard on her, and I guess the tension began to wear on me. We would fight a lot—and though it was about silly things, we would fight viciously. That whole time was pretty difficult.

He was allowed to write three times a week and could write two sides of one sheet. He didn't write to me very much, but every time he wrote to my mother there would be a little note for me. We'd run to get the mail, and three times a week there would be a letter. If we didn't get a third letter, or if something was censored out, it was a horrible thing.

The summer before he went in, we were pretending for probation's sake that we were no longer in touch with anybody who knew anything about the Left in America, so they couldn't send me to a camp run by so-and-so's son-in-law or someplace like that. They sent me to another camp, a straight camp, and the kids were horrible. There was a blind girl in my bunk, and after the counselors had gone and everybody was supposed to be in bed, the evening's activity was to sneak up to her and shine a flashlight in her eyes and say, "Lynn, do you see the light?" Not just once, but many times. Some parts of the summer were really nightmarish, and then the owners fired my favorite staff member, Julius Lester, and people were quitting. He wouldn't make sandwiches, and they said he was uncooperative. Before he left, he drained the manmade lake for Visiting Day. He just pulled the plug, and all the parents came up and saw this muck. When he left, the summer was shot.

We first went to visit my father in Lewisburg Federal Penitentiary in November. It's quite a drive, and by that time my mother was teaching, so we would leave Friday afternoon right after we had both gotten out of school. It was a horrible drive: not only was it long, but it was just highway. One good thing was that they still had Burma Shave signs, and they were funny. We had to drive through the coal country in Pennsylvania, past small towns with nothing but a luncheonette with a pinball machine where everyone congregates, and slag heaps with coal dust covering everything. That always made a big impression on me because we drove through there every month. I got to know the area pretty well, and we'd stop in a couple of diners.

And I began to understand how bad a whole living situation could be. I mean, New York can be bad: I had friends, a six-person family who were living in three rooms. The mother and father and three kids would sleep in one bedroom and the dog and another kid in the other. And I thought that was pretty horrible. But that was before this. You don't have to know anything about politics; you don't have to be sophisticated to realize coal towns are just horribly depressed places. It should be country, and pretty, and the leaves should be green, but it wasn't.

My mother must have talked to me as we drove through there, and I began to see that whole lives, whole communities can be oppressed, be boring and oppressive. Why might someone be a Communist? What's to fight about? Why are you fighting? Well, that was the first thing I could see, and I could understand: I knew why she wanted to change it. And somehow Communism and the Communist Party and the coal towns of Pennsylvania began to make sense, each in terms of the other. And my parents' Communism, expressed as the desire to change these coal towns, made sense to me. Then things began to be explained: the coal was mined by people who were paid by New York businessmen. The owners never worked the mines, never saw the mines; and the workers were exploited. It became more complicated, but that was how it always came out first: lives were being wasted.

Lewisburg is a horrible one-horse town. But it was fun to stay in a hotel, except that I couldn't have been having too much fun, because I never slept. I would sit up all night and read in the bathtub so I wouldn't disturb my mother. Then, of course, I'd be very tired the next day when we had to go to the prison.

Saturday mornings, we would get up early and have a big delicious breakfast in the hotel. They had real good smoky bacon. All the waitresses wore black uniforms with white aprons and Mother Goose shoes, hearkening back to the colonial days, all lovely pink and white.

We'd get into the car and drive for about a mile out to the penitentiary. Before you get to the gates there are big fields, the prison farm where the minimum security prisoners stayed. I used to have horrible flashes from God knows what terrible movie I'd seen of prisoners running across the field, bolting over the fence, stopping the car, and killing us.

Prison was always such an eerie place, and so drab. There were the fields, a couple of trees, and a gray road. The land was gray. We drove to the prison gates and parked in a lot. First, there was the outer wall. The barbed wire and the fencing, the alarm system for the entire prison was set up by David Greenglass, Ethel Rosenberg's brother. He had ratted on her and testified against the Rosenbergs and, in effect, sent them to the electric chair. He got off with a fifteen-year sentence, and everybody in Lewisburg resented that alarm system like crazy.

A man was sitting in the tower about twenty-five feet above you, and there would be some kind of interchange like, "Hello, hello." "We'd like to come in, sir." "Yes," and the door would open wide, and you'd step into a corridor built into the wall. You'd be standing between two gates. You'd look up, and he'd ask you your name, who you came to visit, and ask if you had any weapons or narcotics. "No." "Okay." Then there was a walk of about twenty yards to a glass door, and the man inside would press a buzzer, and you could enter. The door would slam and lock behind you. You'd sign in at the desk, and the man would ask the name and the number of the man you had come to see. The number! Ewan MacColl, the British folksinger, sang: "Write me a letter, address it to my number, but say you remember my name. . . ." All my father's prison books have a number inside them.

My mother always had to check her purse. She asked special permission to take tissues because she had a bronchial condition and sinus trouble. And they would always check her tissues.

Then they would call for the prisoner, and you would have to sit and wait and wait and wait, and watch all these other mommies and daughters, and sons and brothers, and wives of prisoners sit and wait and greet their man. It's like a hotel lobby, with a lot of vinyl couches and big wooden coffee tables, and then a chair on the other side. It was always very stiff, always very awkward. There were always a lot of heads hanging down. And this prison, so they say, is particularly humane when it comes to visiting.

Daddy would come out. And there was a lot of talk about legal problems, about lawyers, the petition campaign, talk about how so-and-so was, and so-and-so. . . . For the first few months, I guess, I wasn't very aware of what was going on. I didn't particularly have anything to talk about. Occasionally I would sit and get a story, but I remember being mostly bored during the whole time, and thinking that I shouldn't be bored, that I should be very happy.

Sometimes he'd tell us horror stories about prisoners murdering each other, putting bricks in the toes of socks and slamming people over the head. It all sounded pretty gruesome, and I was worried. Then he'd tell us stories about some of the friends he was making. Once, his friend Carlos came out with the sandwiches, but they weren't allowed to recognize each other, or didn't want to, and I thought that was very strange.

Life had been relatively simple and fairly good for me up until that time. At first, my father's going to prison was an adventure. But once I had visited Lewisburg a couple of times and heard some of the stories, it just became a remarkable aberration. I didn't know where to put this. It didn't fit in my worldview. People didn't act like regular people in prison. And I figured it must be a pretty bad place.

Once, I went to the ladies' room and found a window that looked out onto a courtyard. There was nobody else in the bathroom, and I climbed up on the sink and sat in the window sill. It was a very high window, but I scrambled up into it, and I could look out and see the yard and the windows with bars on them. The windows on the front of the building didn't have bars on them because they were used as offices. I just had a very tight feeling. They were real bars, iron bars. Not just my daddy but all those other guys there, and even his friends were behind real bars. I wasn't frightened, but it was quite a horror.

And suddenly, after all those years of being a pretty happy child, and knowing other kids who were pretty happy kids, energetic and enthusiastic kids whose major concern was playing hard or reading a lot, here were people for whom life was, for every minute, painful and lived under protest—and it was quite a stunner. It was very difficult for me. That's not real life, I had thought, but it was.

thirteen
Junius

Gladys and Barbara used to come visit me in Lewisburg Federal Penitentiary. She was ten and eleven while I was there, and I'm not sure what kind of effect it had on her. It wasn't until I went to jail that she even knew I was a Communist.

The people in the neighborhood were very nice to her. And at Public School 125 she won the citizenship award. All my friends were wonderful, and every month somebody would drive them all the way to Lewisburg and back. They were wonderfully protective.

I had an indefatigable committee that raised money and carried on the most varied propaganda for my release: Norman Thomas, Harold Goheen, Reinhold Niebuhr, and a lot of others. And then, Jimmy Wechsler and Murray Kempton of the *New York Post* were writing about my case, and it got so that there was an article or column about my case just about every week. Some of my fellow inmates got the paper and would give me the clippings.

Wechsler was just relentless, and Norman Thomas went to see Bobby Kennedy, who was the U.S. attorney general at the time. Bobby Kennedy asked him to take the pressure off, and Norman Thomas says, "What do you mean, take off the pressure, what's the alternative? We take the pressure off, then what?" And Bobby Kennedy said, "Well we're doing everything we can, but. . . ." And apparently, it seems that he was having one hell of a time in the Department of Justice. J. Edgar Hoover's position was that you couldn't afford to set a precedent, that an ex-Communist had to purge himself by naming names. I wouldn't do that. Although I suppose in a way I was quite anti-Communist, I hadn't gone 180 degrees in the opposite direction. I certainly couldn't go ratting on people and saying that everything that was good is really bad.

If I had gone to the clink a few years earlier, while still in the Party, I guess I'd have felt like a political martyr, and I would have had that to grab on to. For me, now, about the only issue of principle involved in going to prison was my self-respect. After I had been in about four months, my lawyer came up and said he felt he ought to pass on some information he had gotten from Nicholas Katzenbach, the deputy attorney general. If I would simply make a statement, which they would work on with me, and name a few names, they would have me out of prison in a week. So, really, the only issue involved in my staying in or getting out was whether I had to be a stool pigeon to be an ex-Communist. J. Edgar Hoover thought I did. And Bobby Kennedy had quite a rough time and apparently put up quite a lonely fight.

Being in prison, of course, is a hazardous occupation. They don't give you insurance if you're going to be in prison. It becomes a question of survival. You feel it every day and wonder whether you're going to make it or not. It's the most bestial and dehumanizing punishment I can think of. They are really out to kill you, to crush you and break you and make you something you're not. And it's a terrifying thing to live with.

Some of the prisoners were quite good to me, really. Though some of them tried to entrap me, I suppose, so that they could rat me out to the warden. I think they were trying to get evidence that I was still in the Party or something. I found that the best method of preservation, as far as I was concerned, was simply to be consistent. I just told the truth about my political feelings to anybody who wanted to hear it. And I told the same things to everybody, friends and all.

I had it better than most people. For one thing, I kept very busy. I was teaching. Well, I wasn't exactly teaching, but I had something thrust on me known as the Literary Forum. I would tell the story of an opera and illustrate it with music in the prison library every Sunday night for two hours. Prison is such a horrible place, and everything is half-baked and done with ill grace. Most of the guys in there were pretty sloppy guys, and the prison administration was even sloppier. The first thing I saw when I walked into the prison was laundry baskets with "l-a-n-d-r-y" stenciled on them.

So I found a way of fighting back, and I'd prepare these evenings with the most enormous care. I would make sure I didn't exceed the attention span on either the music or the talking, and I'd have it worked out as near to perfection as I could. I would spend as much as an hour checking the exact spot to put the needle down on the phonograph. Everything was done professionally, you know, and this had a startling effect.

I had a growing audience. I started with about twenty-two or so, and it grew to around fifty or sixty steady people. The only problem was if I did a

French opera, the Mafia wouldn't come. But if it was Italian, all the Mafia figures would be there. I rarely if ever found anybody who had been to an opera. Most of the Mafia guys had heard their parents' records when they were kids. Well, the opera group got to be quite an institution, and it kept me terribly busy. In fact, I never had enough hours in the day.

I was fortunate to find a couple of friends. One guy had had a nervous breakdown of sorts on the outside. He and his wife had a small child and decided they would commit suicide together. So they turned on the gas, and just before they died somebody discovered them. But the child died, and he was charged with murder. By the time he reached Lewisburg, twelve years before I got there, he was absolutely off his rocker and had no business being in a prison. He should have been in a mental hospital.

Somehow, in the course of the twelve years he found himself, pulled the pieces together, and by the time I got there he was the sanest man inside the walls.

My other friend was a North Carolinian and, of all things, a political prisoner. He had fought in Korea and was then stationed in Vienna where he decided he'd go back behind the Iron Curtain to see what it was like. Well, they gave him a real rose-colored-glasses treatment there, and he thought it was marvelous. If this was such a heaven on earth, he figured the only decent thing to do was to come back and bring heaven on earth to our side of the curtain. He came back expecting to get a couple of weeks of K.P. duty, what the army called the kitchen police, maybe lose his stripes or something. He got seventeen years.

So he was in Lewisburg, and out of sheer generosity, the government had cut his seventeen years to fourteen years. He had served most of it by the time I got there and left while I was still in. We still correspond and talk on the telephone. He's a delightful character. He just wanted to see what life was all about over there. We even discovered, in the small-world department, that he almost married the younger sister of a girl I almost married, and we knew lots of people in common.

It's almost impossible, though, to relate the horror of prison life. I used to discuss this with my Carolina friend, and he said, "Don't even try to tell anybody what it's like. Nobody can understand unless they've been in prison at least a year." He said, "Just tell them stories, just tell them stories, and don't even try. I've been trying for eight years, and it can't be done." And I think he's right. It's so terrible that time softens it, and you tend to tell funny stories, and it all slides away.

The most painful thing is to see people live at such a subhuman level. You sleep in barracks with rapists and pederasts. It's an unbelievably degrading thing. But I was quite lucky, and I had quite an amusing experience. I happened to get to know quite a high-ranking Mafioso character and did him a favor. He was at Lewisburg briefly, and I put him on to a book that was helpful in his legal case, Daniel Bell's *The End of Ideology*. Bell's book has a whole section called "The Myth of the Mafia," in which he says the Mafia probably doesn't exist. This guy was so grateful that when he was leaving to go elsewhere he introduced me to all the Mafia guys. He told them, "This here is Scales. He's the guy what put me on to da book."

His lieutenant, the guy who took charge after he left, sticks a ham-hand out and says, "Anyt'ing at all, Scales, anyt'ing at all." And he checked on me periodically, watching over me like a fairy godmother or some kind of guardian angel.

Well, there was one situation I expected not to survive. There was a black guy from Washington, D.C., about the most subhuman guy I encountered, who had every intention of committing rape on me. I told him I was going to do my best to prevent it. And he said he was going to cut my throat if I didn't submit. If that were the case, I said, I'd do my best to make sure there'd be two of us dead. For a day or two, he was sort of stalking me around with a shiv, a knife, in his pocket, and then, all of a sudden, he didn't know me. I'd come into a place, and he'd go somewhere else. I found out months later that the Mafia had gotten wind of this and told him to get the hell away from me. And he apparently got the message.

The Mafia professed great admiration for me because I wouldn't rat on my buddies. Of course, ratting was one of the characteristics of many of the Mafia guys. They would run and rat to the lieutenant as fast as they could.

But they were awfully nice to me because of "da book." I told Daniel Bell all about this at a party, and he didn't think it was funny in the least. He has no sense of humor. But I'm almost glad they do exist for purely personal reasons.

On Christmas Eve 1962, President Kennedy commuted my sentence and Attorney General Kennedy saw to it that I was home for Christmas.

fourteen

Gladys

My sister, through one of her friends close to the Justice Department, got advance news that Junie was going to be released. It seemed incredible. This was the time of the newspaper strike in New York City, so Kennedy didn't get too much publicity. The official word came, and he was put on a bus, and we got him Christmas Eve. Junie's step-grandmother was with us for the holidays, our friends came over, and though I was still in rough shape with the pneumonia, that was quite a time. That was a happy Christmas.

I know because of the involvement of my sister and the people she knew that Bobby Kennedy was very moved by our story, and he was the one who recommended to John Kennedy that Junie's . . . well, he didn't get a full pardon, but his sentence was commuted.

With a full pardon he would have had all his civil rights back. Now he can't vote. I guess that's really the only thing they took, because he did get his passport, and although they tried to withhold it, he did get his driver's license. And, as he says, he'll be damned if he's going to ask them for a pardon. They're going to be the ones to ask him. But he still doesn't have his full rights as a United States citizen.

fifteen

Barbara

I was eleven years old when my father got out of jail. It was Christmas Eve, and he called up my mother from Lewisburg and said, "I'm coming home." So I had to run outside and get him Christmas presents. I think I had to borrow money from my mother. I went down to the bus, and he was home. I remember being very happy, and everybody else was there, too, and everybody was happy and hugging and kissing. We went home and had a big Christmas and then disappeared for a while.

Then, for a long time, I had difficulty readjusting to having him in the house, having him out of prison. But he handled it very well. He learned from prison, and he shared his learning. I've always appreciated that he came away from prison with stories: stories with morals, with punch lines, good stories, bad stories, and happy stories, and sad stories.

That summer, I went back with my friends who had moved on to Camp Thoreau. There I started to learn about my friends. I learned that Judy Winston's father had been in jail, and that Mike and Robbie's parents were the Rosenbergs. I learned about Susie Robeson and her grandfather, Paul. Somebody else's father was one of the Hollywood Ten, blacklisted during the 1950s. This came to me in dribs and drabs.

And throughout this time, I was dancing, folk dancing and modern. And that was really the most important thing to me through most of high school. When I left high school I finally made the decision not to dance. And, though I've never really felt quite comfortable about not dancing, I never really felt comfortable about continuing. It just seemed a very comfortable, easy, and fairly dull future. It didn't seem to me that I would feel satisfied being a dancer.

I went through high school and started reading more history. In the eleventh grade, I did a paper on the Smith Act, and politics eventually began to make sense to me—politics as something more than the personal experiences of the people I knew. But, I guess, politics never lost the fervor of personal experience: people making politics and people suffering by it.

Those few years, the prison years and the years afterward, certainly put an end to my childhood in a very startling way. I just don't meet too many people I can talk to, for whom it's somehow natural to have understood and been part of, unwillingly, the process of witch hunts and people going off to jail.

My father's going to jail really wasn't an act of heroism. He had left the Party long before. There wasn't anything glorious about it at all, except his refusal to name names to the FBI. For a long time, I wasn't allowed to tell people about it. People didn't ask where my father was, and if they did, I said he was away. It was kind of a secret, and it wasn't easy to digest for a long time. I wasn't really aware that it had bothered me for quite a while, and then I started to realize that I had many confused feelings about having grown up, about having felt myself a social freak for many years, for most of high school.

For a while, feeling different was kind of fun, because it was a crusade, our own personal family crusade. After that, though, I often found that the things I would say and the things I would do were incomprehensible to people. I'm not really sure why, but it was almost as if I was living in a different country. I had a very particular and very different position in the world, a very different reason for being there.

I remember a discussion about prisons in high school. People were saying, "Well, they should do lots of nice things in prisons. They should reform the prisons." And I said, "They shouldn't have prisons." The people said, "What? How can you say such a thing?" And I thought, "Well, it does sound crazy, doesn't it?" But, then, it just kept making sense to me. We shouldn't have prisons because they're so horrible. And I decided I was much happier taking that kind of extreme position. It just made inherently so much more sense to me than arguing over this or that reform. Because prisons are just bad.

Somehow, things would always come back to my own personal, private horror. I would always be able to say, "But people are terrible to each other," or, "People throw people in jail for no reason. Society is cruel," and things would suddenly make sense again. And when it got down to the nitty-gritty of it, that was the foundation of almost everything I believed in for a couple of years.

It's a different kind of paranoia than sitting in your house with the lights off thinking there's somebody under your bed. It's more a feeling of the ways in which people can hurt you. They aren't always apparent, but the potential for people hurting you is always there—just in the nature of people dealing with each other, and the presence of more than two people in one place at the same time.

It's something I'm trying to see my way out of somehow. It strikes me as a severely limited framework for dealing with society and dealing with people. It ties your feet before you take your first step. And the really big problem is that as a child of the Left, you're raised to trust people, to believe that people are your salvation—not necessarily even salvation, but your fate.

The world is made up of people, and along the way it's made of machines, and streets and roads and cars, and trees and grass, but essentially it's made up of people. And if you don't deal with people, then you're not really living in the real world somehow. So it's kind of a knot. But, personally, I'm ready to say, "Well, I learned my lesson. People live through hellish experiences all the time, and if there's any lesson to learn, I think it's that people shouldn't be hellish to people. And that the ways in which you oppress people and the ways you inflict pain are not always so apparent."

I find that I can't relax sometimes, that I'm always worried about me and worried about other people. And I think it's kept me inactive a lot of times in a lot of situations—times when there was political action to take and important points to make. It hasn't kept me completely inactive, although recently I've been studying in Canada and avoiding politics almost entirely. I don't think the decisions to be made are easy ones, and sometimes I think people just make them too easily and too lightly. I'm irked by the Weathermen, by people who have undertaken political actions and a year later say, "Well, we didn't always do the right things." "Irresponsible" is a bad word, but I think responsibility is a good starting place for politics, any kind of politics.

It has to do with seeing yourself as a political being, with an ethic of politics. And that's something that comes from a lot of different places, to a lot of different people; for me, it came from growing up in a left-wing family, from seeing my father go to jail and seeing him come out.

sixteen

Junius

Shortly after I got out, President Kennedy delivered a nationwide address on TV about James Meredith, the first black student to attend the University of Mississippi, and all the riots and violence that were going on down there. President Kennedy started off the speech by saying he wanted to thank all those who had fought for so many years to break down segregation in the schools, and he went on and on, and it sounded to me like he was singling out our North Carolina Communist Party. I can't quote the speech accurately, but I think he said the nation owed these people a debt of gratitude. It was quite an extraordinarily moving speech, almost to be picked out in this way.

When I came out of jail, I had a job waiting for me. Those monthly donations for my dues to the Typographers Union had preserved my means of making a living. The New York newspaper strike was on, and there was no news about my release. I got a job at the *New York Times,* and the very first day I was working, the guy I was reading proofs with said, "You know, there's a big political case about a guy named Scales. Is he any relation to you?" And he was rather flabbergasted to find out that I was the Scales he knew about. He was a right-wing guy, but it turns out he'd been contributing to my dues, too.

I had thought of trying to resume my education just before I went into the clink and had applied to Teacher's College at Columbia. I thought I'd go back and get a master's in education if I could. I thought it might be satisfying to teach at some level. I was honest with them and told them my whole background. Up until then, I was in like Flynn. But after it went to the top university brass, I got a nasty letter from the president saying that they would process my application no further until my "litigation" with the government was ended. I felt this was a pretty good indication of what would happen if I tried an academic career: get a job in a tenth-rate college and kick around from pillar to post, and put my family in thrall for years while I got my Ph.D. I decided they'd been through enough—and so I'm a union printer. Politically, I'm a peculiar brand of ex-Communist. I feel sort of radical, but I don't know. I'm amazed at, and out of tune with, most of the radical movements on American campuses, I suppose.

Leaving the Party was such a trauma—I mean, it just pulled the rug out from under us. The trauma of an internal fight like that was so strong, and the realization of the way we had been compromised and had compromised ourselves. We were all political wrecks with no place to go, and not much to do, and more in danger of ruining anything political we touched. You know, people say, "All you have to do is get active!" I can't even be politically active in my union, because all it would take is some judicious red-baiting, and I'd be a liability to any activity I was involved in.

So we found ourselves out of things and discredited politically, and rightly so. We couldn't agree more. Some of us tried to pick up academic or professional careers. A very few did who hadn't been in the field before. One friend of mine taught philosophy after a thirty-year hiatus. Another friend became a very distinguished psychologist. Some of us who had professional careers before, resumed them, but most weren't able to or didn't. I wasn't able to. I couldn't go back and pick up the loose ends of my academic career. I hadn't been at Columbia, I had been at the University of North Carolina, and if I tried to go back into the academic world, I would either have to go back and start there or start from scratch. If I started there, I'd put everybody who tried to help me in a terrible spot. Here's a convicted felon, and so on. Most people didn't have that to contend with.

So I don't know. We're a very messed up lot, and I think a lot of those who have gone into intellectual fields feel a little bit distrustful of themselves. I think they feel that anybody who could have led themselves up the garden path with so much moral irresponsibility are not very trustworthy of any intellectual pursuit. Some figure you can't go on living with it that way, and so they make a plunge, and I'm sure they're doing very creditably. I have one friend who spends most of his time studying the history of the Communist movement. He has gained tremendous erudition on the subject and gets more anti-Communist all the time. It's a very fragmented group and a very talented one, too. It's a terrible waste.

In my case, I no longer feel like a participant. I essentially feel like a specta-tor. I feel sort of burned out in that respect. Objectively, there's not a hell of a lot I could do. I mean, I certainly couldn't be useful in the South. If I lived there I'd be a liability, a memory of our past division. I'd serve no purpose. Anywhere else, my jail record is a big problem. And then again, I have the greatest reservations about trying to take any kind of leadership position.

I was pretty cocksure in my youth and during most of the time I was in the Party. And now I've got the most tremendous reservations about telling anybody what's what in politics. I don't mind talking about my own views, but trying to tell somebody, "I think you ought to do such and such" is abso-lutely out. But as to having strong feelings, God almighty, I have the sharpest reactions to the news from the South, to all political developments.

I have opinions about the current Left, and so on, and I might even pop off pretty sharply about this or that, but I'm not really sure about any of my views and wouldn't want to push them very hard. I've certainly lost a lot of self-confidence in that area.

My time is spent much more with my family, because with all of the turmoil of an eight-year political case, my family life was pretty much shot to hell. And since time is moving on, I'm involved in all kind of personal things—making a living and enjoying a country place. I don't have any illusions that that's any social accomplishment. But I do feel an obligation about having charge of our little thirty-six acres, mostly wilderness on a mountainside. I hope to keep it unspoiled, unpolluted, and beautiful and to pass it on to my daughter a better place than we found it—better for humans and for the other animals, with more and better living things on it. I have a lot more confidence in my ability as a forester, for instance, than I do as a politician.

I suppose also involved is trying to learn a certain amount of hedonistic enjoyment. It's not an easy thing for somebody oriented the way we were.

You know, we tried to keep Barbara free: we never indoctrinated her in the least, and she didn't know we were Communists until I had to go to jail and we had to tell her. We're hard on ourselves, and I think rightly so. A very dear friend of mine, George Charney, wrote this book, *A Long Journey*. I would have edited the whole thing if Gladys hadn't gotten sick, and I was only able to do the very first part of it. George deserves great credit. It's a partial failure in his eyes, and I think in the eyes of most others, but at least he tried to get something down.

When I was editing it, I kept fighting with him, saying he wasn't hard enough, he wasn't digging into it enough. He'd say that he'd gone to a meeting where so-and-so was attacked, and he was appalled. Well, why? Why were you appalled? What was going on? How did it happen? What did you do? And George, who is fifteen years older than me, would say, "I absolutely can't go that deep. I haven't got that much time." And it was true, being fifteen years older, there was just a limit to his introspection, a limit to how deep he could go—and there was not enough time to acquire the necessary perspective.

I still think the big problem with most of us, and I include myself, is that we tend to accentuate the positive and forget a lot of the rest. I don't think I said a damned thing that was negative in our first two interviews, and I was absolutely appalled. It was, and it is, just very hard to pound yourself over the head all the time.

Our past is a mixture of pain and pride and disgust—and joy in the warmth that existed. My closest friends today are the same people who were my closest friends then, and though there are many of them I don't see, if they walked in tomorrow we'd pick up where we left off. We were so close, time hardly seems to have cut any ice at all. And then, there are others I've never lost contact with in the last thirty years, and, of course, that's the most treasured possession of all. There's just nothing so valuable as old friends with whom you've shared so much.

Most of us, I hope, have learned an awful lot about intolerance. I mean, an essential part of a political outlook is dropping this demand for purity—this absolute 100 percent purity on this and that—and instead, taking people as they are and valuing them for what they are. One of my biggest regrets (and I think I have much less regret than most people I know in this area) is that of losing friends because we disagreed politically. They nearly always took the initiative, or dropped me, but I rarely made any effort to stop it. You know, you didn't feel like you wanted to push yourself on anybody. But there are many cases where you might have been able to prevent the total loss of a friendship without being pushy.

One thing about the Communist movement was that for all our humane motivation, nothing tended to dehumanize people as much as the Party bureaucracy. Some of my very dear friends, after they were in bureaucratic positions, had to learn how to be human again. Boy, people to this day tell me stories about them that in a friendly way I've confronted them with, and they say, "Oh, my God, it was worse than that," and they go into the story.

I guess the reason I talk more about the student days is that I look back on them with more happiness. We were doing concrete things. I organized students, and I organized workers, and there were very tangible results. We were genuinely taking part in the most invigorating and meaningful struggles of the times: every Party meeting had some aspect of the struggle for Negro rights on its agenda. The very fact that I say "Negro" seems so out of date now.

In fact, one of the first things I remember doing was our campaign to get the state newspapers to spell "Negro" with a capital N, and now, I suppose if they use the word "Negro" at all, there's likely to be a campaign to say "Blacks."

So a lot of it seems dated, but I think it was meaningful. As students, we organized the Negro janitors at the university. We even pulled a very successful strike. After the war, we built a Party organization in the Negro community and established an adult school. And this school became the springboard that led to our voter registration campaign, which led in turn to the election of a Negro alderman, the second Negro alderman elected in the South following Winston-Salem.

We sparked the Winston-Salem struggle to organize black workers in Thomasville and other places in eastern North Carolina and Charleston, South Carolina. This had an overwhelming effect on the area and sparked all kinds of struggles for civil rights.

I could probably have been a comfortable liberal if I could have swallowed the liberal position on Negroes in the South: Wait. Go slow. And be cautious. But, my God, it meant a gradual anesthetizing of the horrors, of the outrage you felt at being part of a community where Negroes were treated the way they were. Racism was something that tormented me from the age of about six. Remember my nurse, Aunt Lou, who was twelve years old when she was freed from slavery and who took care of me until I was seven or so. Well, once when I was a little boy, Aunt Lou gave me a hard time about something, and I called her "a mean old black nigger." My mother heard me and gave me an awful tongue lashing.

But the worst thing was the way Aunt Lou looked at me when I said it. I bawled for hours and hours and couldn't stop, and she ended up consoling me. From then on, I had an acute consciousness of racism. And when I was eighteen years old and first met Negroes as social equals, it was the most exciting thing in the world. This was one area where I couldn't buckle under, the place I parted company with the liberals.

We had wonderful liberals: Frank Graham, for example. In our branch of the Southern Conference for Human Welfare, an association of white and black liberals, we were always having confrontations on the question of going slow and being cautious. A new hospital is going to be built, and if you make a fight about having it integrated, it won't get built at all—so what do you do? The liberals would say to cool it, and maybe we'll get a black ward. Out of sheer outrage, we Communists would likely make unrealistic demands. We'd demand, for example, that the conference ask that 20 to 30 percent of the hospital staff be Negro—a wild demand in the 1940s; or that all the wards, maternity included, be integrated. And in retrospect, I'm glad I was an "extremist" on Negro rights rather than a liberal.

It was really the fight against racism, and fascism, and the struggle for trade unionism that led me to the Party. It made me believe in socialism, believe that socialism could make manual labor more meaningful. I saw fire in the trade-union movement. But I would say that it was the Negro Question that really got to my consciousness. That was the driving thing. Liberals were antifascist, and liberals were pro–trade union, but they all crawled so on the Negro Question, and that was where I just found such a big gulf. And that's why, I'm sure, I made this radical leap. The Communist Party was the one outspoken organization unequivocally for Negro rights, let the chips fall where they might. And, since I was a southerner, it made me a Communist instead of a radical liberal.

Ironically, when Rosa Parks and all of black Montgomery was walking all over the place in the midst of the bus boycott, I was there in Alabama hunting for a lawyer for my defense. So this was a new effort I never got into fully. God, this was the next step, but I was to become a professional defendant for about the next ten years. And then the trauma: trying to continue to live with such dedication, such selflessness, such intensity—and, of course, never again finding our sharp divisions of good and evil, true and false.

But it's an ever-present question and a fundamental matter of conscience. It's the question of how you're going to live. Are you going to live with injustice, are you going to accommodate to it? Are you going to let it control you and occasionally do something good when you get the chance? That's the liberal approach. And they'll be nice to some good old black man, and he'll die, and they'll go to his funeral and feel good and righteous for years to come. And, meanwhile, tell yourself: "Aren't things gradually getting better all the time?"

Or are you going to speak out against racism at every possible turn, keep hammering at it? And when I was eighteen I decided that every chance I get to ameliorate some of the suffering and misery in the South I'm going to do it, by God. It may take me thirty years, but I'm going to do it when my chance comes. I thought the chance had come.

seventeen
Gladys

At this time in our lives, it seems like I'm the one who's the activist, and whether Barbara will move in that direction remains to be seen. I don't know.

As for me, well, as so many people of my age seem to be withdrawing from life, I seem to be going in the opposite direction. I have this wild crazy drive that I simply can't repress: I'm going to try to change something through my work. I try to do it through everybody I come in contact with in schools. That's why I'm teaching this course at Bank Street, because the people who come there are people who want to change the world, too. I get a bang out of it, though sometimes when I sit down and really think about it, I think it's crazy, really, and unreal, that it's just not making that much of a difference.

But to me, it is. There's just something about not giving in to all of this, the cruelty and inhumanity and idiocy and unfairness. And the only way I can maintain my sanity is by working very hard with kids and grownups to try to make them feel that they, too, have got to work to make a better world. It sounds trite when you talk about it; but even with all the physical problems I have, I keep adding responsibility rather than pulling away.

The course I teach is called "A Seminar in Reading Problems," but the larger thing I try to bring to teachers is an understanding and appreciation of the complexity of a child's feelings about himself. I talk about the impingement of the world on a child's life and how all of this has to do with reading. You can't look at reading in some kind of isolated framework. It's complex: it's not just teaching sound or teaching words. I help teachers teach children how to read and talk and listen, how to enjoy reading and communicating and writing.

Now, at this time in his life, Junie could cheerfully go to Peaceable Hill, our country place, and stay there. I couldn't. And it's not all altruism on my part. I'm nourished by the idea that maybe I'm doing something. Once, when I came home after teaching school during the first couple of years, I told Junie that I was suddenly faced with the insight that maybe I was doing all of this for neurotic reasons. Maybe it wasn't all objectively really wanting to help kids. He helped me over that hurdle, pointing out that most behavior, particularly in today's world, is based on some kind of neurosis or other, and if your neuroses happened to be the kind that helped society, good for them.

And so I just resent every moment that I'm out of school, every moment I can't push, when I'm sick or have to go to the doctor. I guess I really respect each child that I see, and some teachers tend not to, and, in particular, black kids. Poor black kids don't get a fair shake in school. So that it's not even just a matter of teaching. It's a matter of again pursuing those same goals: seeing to it that I do whatever I can to enable people to get that fair shake, to speak out against the racism, the people who hurt children, who hold children of poverty in contempt, and who hold black people in contempt. It's just the only way I feel I can express myself in a decent way. It isn't enough for me to be a decent person. I just feel that I have to get other people to be decent. And I just burn to do everything I can.

I think the thing that brought Junie and me together, and the thing that keeps the tremendous bond of understanding between us alive, is our feeling for other people, how we react to other people, and how we really care about other people. To begin with, I find his pain unbearable, and he finds my pain unbearable. I mean pain in the face of a situation that neither of us has any control over. It starts with each other, I'm sure: there's just such a concern we share, a feeling that we have about how people feel, people we love, even people we don't love and don't know. And, then, this extends out to Barbara, and it extends to our friends. And, I guess, that's the thing that brought us into the Communist Party.

Now, I think he has it more extensively than I have. I have certain cutoff points, covering many more people. You know, I'm not as big a person as he is. Especially if people do something to me. But he's a huge person, with tremendous dimensions, tremendous understanding, and compassion. He may not always show it. I see it . . . and I don't always see it. It's probably the same thing that brought many other people together in the Party. At least the ones I knew. I'm sure there were some nuts, and the power-hungry people. I don't know what motivated some people, but the people I knew and the people I loved were the same kind of people. The world wasn't meant for them to benefit from . . . they weren't takers. They were people who cared for other people.

It couldn't have been any organization. It couldn't be the Republican Party. It couldn't be a religious organization. It would have had to be a group that really felt the way we did about people, about humanity, about the guy who was at the low end of the stick. It might have been the Socialist Party, or it might have been the Trotskyites, I don't know. . . . Maybe less so for Junie, because, again, his approach to the Party was much more cerebral than mine. I just happened to be pulled in there, you know. But it would have had to have been some kind of an activist organization, one that really tried to do something to help people. And really, of all the organizations at that time in our lives, the Communist Party was the largest and most influential and did, in many ways, the most to help our poorer people.

I know that once we left the Party, I and, I think, both of us became part of the larger community. And in no way do I mean by compromising our ideals, because we still, at least I (and I'm sure Junie does also) believe in socialism. We believe in a better life. I think I was fooled about the way the Party was going about it, and I had no idea about what was going on at the top, but I still believe essentially in the same things that brought me into the Communist Party.

I'll never forget when I first started teaching in a public school system: the thing that meant more to me than anything else was that I was part of that larger life, pursuing what I believed in, helping kids who needed help. And I think Junie feels that way, although he's really a much more alienated person than I am. And for a very good reason. I don't mean "alienated" in a bitter way, an angry way, or anything, but . . . I guess it's the difference in chemistry and the difference in experience. I'm the one who's always optimistic and much more a part of the scene than he. Society, unfortunately, has made more of an outcast of him than it has of me.

But even with this feeling, even though he is an outcast, he and I and all of the other people we knew from the Party have this added feeling now of being part of a larger community. And, although we disagree violently with many things and may shake our heads and decry many things, we're still a part of it in a way that we weren't before. We can do something about it in a different way. We're not out of the mainstream.

And yet, as I look back to my youth and to what we did, I'm not one of those ex-Communists who feels that this was all a waste of my life. Many of the good things that are a part of the American scene today are there precisely because the Communists worked damn hard for them. The reasons there are black students in the University of North Carolina now is because my husband and his friends started to fight back in the early days. He was a premature integrationist. Things are better in our society precisely because of the Communist Party, and the individual and group fights the Party waged throughout the country.

I don't think, though, that I could have gone on for my whole life feeling that I was a leper. I suppose it's part of middle age. Although, it's hard to say. Who the hell can hypothesize? But I would still join the movement, still join forces with people whom I felt had integrity and wanted to make the kind of changes I feel are necessary. The only problem is that in today's political scene, this seems to be impossible.

And although we are part of the scene, in a sense we're more outcasts than ever. Having been through so much, we almost see the hopelessness of it. Perhaps because of my particular chemistry, I do feel a tiny bit more optimistic, more a part of it than Junie and many of our friends.

I can't believe, and I don't believe, that the world is coming to an end. I don't believe that man is going to destroy himself. I just don't believe it's in the nature of the animal. He wants to survive. But the hell we are going to go through to survive. . . . Who the hell knows whether there will ever be a day when more people have more things? Though, historically, in many ways people are better off than they were in the 1200s, or the 1500s. But there are just so many things that make one feel that it's hopeless. It's time for us to pull out to some extent and let the young people do something about the world.

I suppose I'm in the same state I was in before we got the final word on Junie, on his going to prison. You just keep hoping that the best thing's going to happen. And that's what I keep hoping.

eighteen
Barbara

All through high school I was always aware how I was going back, rediscovering my own experiences, and realizing how my own experiences were vastly different from those of most people. I never doubted their validity, never questioned them. When I got to college, and found myself in Canada, where people didn't know from such things, I became almost bitter.

I wanted a vacation. I wanted a vacation from political people, from the United States, from the Vietnam War, from the construction workers who attacked the protestors, and from the student Left. It didn't make any sense to me. It all seemed much too tangled. And I just mostly hibernated and studied the German novelist Thomas Mann.

That summer, 1969, I went across the United States in a VW bus with four other people, and it was horrible—at least, the bus and four other people. It was like being a tourist, discovering a new land, and not immediately feeling at home. But I really liked America. I liked the weather-beaten faces of the sheepherders in Idaho, and I liked the middle Americans from Kansas who would go down to the lake every Sunday with a motorboat to picnic and to lead the comfortable life. And I liked the fields and the freaks you would find wandering around, peering out into space, wrapped in purple cloaks bouncing around the fields and the prairies, down in New Mexico. And we'd ask, "What are you doing here?" "Oh," and they'd pause, "we're just looking for peyote," then pick something and chuck it into their big sack.

I went back to Canada that fall, suddenly looked around and said, "What on earth am I doing here? What do I really want to do with my life? I want to be in politics, right! And there's no politics here for me. I want to learn about American history, and there's no American history here. I want to read American novels, and there's no good course in American literature here. What am I doing here?" I stuck it out a couple of months and came back to New York after Christmas. And I got a job working in a hospital in New York—University Hospital of New York University.

I thought that working in a hospital not only would be a good place to do politics but it would be a good place to learn something about the rest of the world. I stayed there six months and made a lot of enemies in the administration. A few people there had been doing some political work before I got there. I got in contact with them, and we decided to resurrect the group: two black guys, who really had a hard time of it, and Ray, an Irish guy from Cleveland.

We put out a newspaper about what was happening in the hospital and organized demonstrations in the spring around the invasion of Cambodia. I guess working with these different people, and being in New York again, helped me realize that politics keeps happening. It hadn't ended when my father got out of jail. All the things I knew then about politics still applied. People were still suffering, and people in politics were still being persecuted, and it all began to make sense in a way it hadn't before.

Up until that time, I had been able to romanticize radical politics, the student politics that was going on in the United States, and not give it proper measure. I hadn't really understood what it meant and what had motivated it. I guess that was partially because of my parents and because of what they would say: their misgivings about a lot of what they had done, and not only them but many of their friends. I had come in contact with a lot of people who would say about the New Left, "Oh no! They're making the same mistakes we did! Why don't they learn?" Which, of course, is ridiculous, because the experiences of one generation aren't always, and can't possibly be, apparent to another.

When my friend Atina was being kicked out of the University of Chicago, I wrote her a letter saying: "Atina, don't! You're going to ruin your life. Look what happened to my father. Look what happened to all those other people. Don't mess yourself up!" She was furious with me. I thought that I was the only voice of sanity. I told her, "Politics is just so confusing and so destructive, and you're not getting anywhere. Look!"

I realized, first of all, that she didn't want to hear it, and secondly, that it wasn't fair. I was repeating things that my father had learned from his experience, and not even things he had learned. I was talking about misgivings that he had about a completely different situation and from a completely different time.

In the hospital, though, I was exposed to a real world. I was seventeen, then eighteen, working there, and it was really the first experience where I was nose-to-nose with a political environment that was oppressing me, and visibly oppressing a lot of other people. Aside from putting out the newspaper, we talked about changing things in the hospital and made some simple straightforward demands about working conditions.

Doctors ate in a quiet place, and everybody else ate in a noisy place. They had a quick lunch line, and everybody else had a half-hour wait. Doctors came and went as they pleased and told the nurses what to do, hardly bothering to talk to them. Sometimes they would talk to a unit secretary because unit secretaries have to take messages, and that's what I did. So I was one notch above the menials, the orderlies, and the housekeeping crew. And if a doctor ever bothered to talk to one of them, it was only because they were standing in his way.

It goes without saying that horrible things went on in the hospital, probably nothing out of the ordinary, but to me, just horrible things. The system is stacked with black women at the bottom changing bedpans and white doctors at the top writing prescriptions and leaving orders for nurses to follow through. The whole stratification of status and role and service in the hospital was pretty depressing. If your job is to sweep the floors, you wear a purple uniform. If your job is to make beds, you wear a blue uniform. If your job is to change bedpans, you wear a green uniform. Everybody is identified by their uniform.

The people in Central Service keep everything in the hospital going. They keep the x-ray machines running, maintain the machines for breathing, scrub and sterilize the instruments, classify and file the records, and then scrub and sterilize some more. About 90 percent of the workers in Central Service are Puerto Rican. During my six months there, Ray and I got to know a Puerto Rican guy there and turned him on to being angry, saying something about the things he knew instead of just griping about them. And we got him to write an article for the newspaper.

He told a story about a Christmas party that one floor of the hospital had held. All of the Puerto Rican workers at the party were told to sit down at the big table. They sat down and were given little paper cups filled with soda. And there was a big bowl of popcorn in the middle of the table. Then all of the doctors and nurses stood around the outside of the room and sipped martinis and wine and beer. That was just the way the party was set up. And nobody even thought to say anything about it.

We talked about bread-and-butter issues like pay differentials, working hours, and days off. Some people worked ten days straight and then got two days off, even though it's in violation of the contract.

We had a special issue on Vietnam and Cambodia, and we held a teach-in. We had an antiwar demonstration. Not too many people came, mostly professionals and paraprofessionals and the people we had had contact with. We weren't into heavy politics. Mostly what we did was just to talk. I'd be reading a newspaper, smoking a cigarette in the back, and one of the nurse's aides or the housekeeping people would come in and say, "Oh, what's new?" And I'd start talking about what was new and what I thought about it.

A few of us felt free to talk about politics and weren't afraid to say something, to object, to criticize and consider another alternative. Which, incredibly enough, most people never do. The *Daily News* and the *New York Times,* and that's it—that's what's going on in the world. And it has nothing to do with you. You accept what they say . . . well, maybe you don't like the editorial policy, but what can you say?

I don't know how much we accomplished. The two nurse's aides who worked on my floor came out for the demonstrations, but most of the nurse's aides didn't. They were pretty angry women. One was Puerto Rican; the other was black.

I think it's good politics to talk about alternatives as if they were real and natural, something that's apparent. I mean, there are limitations to just sitting around and chewing the fat and talking about how things are wrong, but it seems to me that that's a place to start. And if that doesn't exist, then no political action is going to happen, nothing's going to change.

We talked about abortion and published a whole issue on women, on nurses and nurse's aides, and the kind of work they did. Some of the nurse's aides would push around trays all day long, racks of sheets and pots and pans, forty and fifty pounds of it, all day long. At the end of the day they'd be sore and stiff and without a hell of a lot of energy to do much of anything. Yet they went home and they cooked, and they took care of their families.

I didn't like working in the hospital very much. I came late a lot, and I made a lot of enemies in the administration. I was caught passing around a petition among the unit secretaries in support of the union and a possible strike vote. I was bawled out and reported. That must have been the beginning of the end. I finally left the hospital, partially because the strike didn't happen. Ray left for Ireland to fight for Irish independence with Bernadette Devlin. I was tired of it and was planning to go back to Canada to school.

I registered and ran into a couple of old professors, one who was kind of the Marxist-in-residence there. We were talking, sitting there out on the grass, and suddenly from out of nowhere every political person that McGill has ever spawned managed to work their way into a circle around us. McGill, the school of the Canadian ruling class, was having one of its first political conversations.

Sometimes I feel kind of like a cop-out because I'm packed away comfortably in Canada, and I'm not here in the United States, out in the streets. But I don't think I have to. It just seems to make innate sense to me that our lives are political whether we want them to be or not, that my life is political whether I want it to be or not. It's fairly simple except that it isn't simple, and there are always more sides to it than you think there are.

Occasionally, I began to think my parents were crazy, just totally off the wall, mad as the carbon series, the universe itself. Walking around the house naked, only for me to find out later that parents don't walk around the house naked. I thought, "My parents must really be strange," feeling all sorts of strange feelings, embarrassed and ashamed and confused. It was perfectly natural at home, but here I am, and other people are saying, "People just don't do that sort of thing." Being puzzled, and having to come to terms with things in ways which weren't easy; having to understand things for myself.

If I wanted to go somewhere or do something, I would always say, "But Mommy and Daddy, so-and-so is doing it. Why can't I?" And I would always get the answer, "You're not so-and-so. You are you! We live our way; they live their way. You listen to us!" And maybe sometimes they were authoritarian. But growing up for me was never a matter of doing something just because everybody else was.

Occasionally, I was able to say to myself, "My parents are just crazy. All this stuff they're telling you is just making it difficult to do anything. They're only saying it because they're crazy." And I'd get bitter.

So I decided my parents were crazy, and I made all sorts of excuses for them. I still do. It's something I really haven't been able to conquer completely yet. I always say, "Well, they suffered a lot. They had a hard time. They don't really know what they're talking about." Which sometimes I think is true. Sometimes I think they're not experiencing the sixties and seventies in any sort of fresh way. They're experiencing it—well, it began in the fifties and sixties and so far the seventies—through a great deal of bitterness, through the filter of the really hard times they had. This isn't always something I can understand without experiencing it.

In part, I feel almost trapped. In a way, I feel as if working in the hospital and putting out the newspaper, doing that sort of stuff, is a very poor attempt at trying to recapture and experience for myself what it was that my parents have done. And the only way I can understand, so far as I can see, is to do it. But it's not the same, and it can't be the same.

I've felt for a long time that a lot of my initiative wasn't my own: that it is, in part, an attempt to catch up with my parents, to figure out what their lives were all about. And that makes me feel bitter sometimes.

I resent their bitterness. I resent being taught to be bitter . . . I mean, I wasn't taught to be bitter, but somehow it was just there. I know they couldn't help it. I know it was just there, and I know they had a lot of hard times, but it certainly makes growing up a lot harder.

A lot of ex-Party people are bitter and angry and really think they were failures. Some people think that every minute they spent in the Party was a waste of time. And I would imagine that the bitterness and the vehemence that some of them have about their past, their own Communism and their own radicalism, has done a great deal to confuse their children.

I've heard from a lot of the people I've run into, who are kind of vintage red-diaper babies, that they, too, had a hard time in many of the same ways. Some didn't want to get involved in politics; it just seemed like one big nightmare they wanted to avoid completely. Some have gone off into the woods, into country houses, never to return. Some felt they weren't allowed to live their own lives. Some felt they had been taught to be bitter against the world, to be scornful of people. They felt they had been taught to approach the world from a great big backlog of hurts—unable to approach the world fresh—and with the bitterness that comes of trying to change the world and being stopped in your tracks.

My mother is constantly saying, "I'm so sorry we passed on such a terrible world to you, but you've got to do something with it. I'm really sorry, but there it is. Now it's your turn." But I don't think my mother thinks that her life has been a failure. She's got herself in a pretty good situation. She's teaching, advising, and setting policy. She's doing important work, and she's influencing the workings of an entire school district. And she's saying important things about education to a lot of people.

A whole lot of former Party people have been able to get into professions. Many of my parents' friends are now university professors: some are psychologists, a couple teach English, a couple teach music, some history. And they're in a position to talk to people.

I'd like to learn more about the Party, learn more about what my parents did and why. But I don't think they were failures. I think they have a lot to give us. To some extent, they never got to teach us, teach me, our generation.

I guess what makes me saddest is that my father isn't doing anything. It makes me very sad that he's kind of tucked away in the middle of the night at the *New York Times* reading proof. And I wish there was some way that the world could make room for him—just say, "Here! Sit! Talk . . . tell us." I guess it can't.

I think my father thinks that he was a failure. And this is what early on influenced me to write those letters to Atina. I think my father thinks that he's in some way thrown away part of his life, screwed it up. Not that he didn't do something worthwhile in the first forty years, but that he left himself with no place to go at this point, except to keep working at the *Times* until he retires. I think he's sorry that he's not teaching, that he doesn't have a degree, that he might have been able to do a lot more.

There's no way of knowing. I think he's just pretty sorry that his life didn't turn out differently. I don't think he's particularly bitter against the Party . . . for having existed. He's bitter, I think, about a lot of people taking it into their heads that they were really changing the world when hardly anybody knew they were around. I think he's bitter about people thinking they were more than they were.

I sense in my father a great deal of regret that, for him at least, the world turned out the way it did; that things just didn't work out the way he wanted them to. That he fought the good fight and lost.

And he's realizing now that there are a lot of different ways to fight to change the world, to do your bit. I guess he keeps worrying about me, worrying, as I sometimes worry, that I'll make the same mistakes he made. So he tried to do a lot of thinking about what somebody can do.

But, you know, I think they've provided me, and everybody I know from left-wing backgrounds has gotten from their parents, some special kind of self-awareness, the sense that you're always a political being. In that sense, they definitely weren't failures.

They weren't the first, but they talked and acted and tried to live as political people—living, as best they could, with the constant awareness of other people. And whether their politics succeeded or not, that kind of principle is something we can learn about, and learn from. The spirit of political people, the spirit of cooperation, the ethic of sharing isn't really that easy to live by. My parents did their bit and struggled in their own way.

Now we have new groups, and we have the Black Panthers and the women's movement and people's parks and alternative high schools. And all these people are trying to live by that ethic. They sense it's an important thing to try and do.

And that's something I've learned from my parents' generation. And it always amazes me when people find it for themselves, when I meet political people whose parents aren't leftists. I'm always happy. Maybe this means it isn't just a strange quirk on the part of my parents and their crazy friends but that these are really important principles. And I think they are. I'm even happier to meet people who haven't learned it from their parents, because it's fresher and it comes out in whole different ways.

By looking at what they did in that way, it's not a failure at all. Unfortunately, sometimes people don't see it that way. And it makes me sad to see people who have been in the movement withdraw and become bitter. Because I think they're denying the best lessons they could ever teach.

I feel very uncomfortable talking about ideology or calling politics by a name—not because I think there are no more labels or that they don't count, that it's the end of ideology, but because I don't think it says anything. And I guess that's what it all adds up to: from the hospital and over the course of the last year in Montreal, from the Quebecois, the people who struggle for socialist Quebec, the people working with the Panthers, young people in Berkeley, my friends Cat and Atina in New York. Politics isn't a party or a name; it isn't ideology or a slogan. It's the way you live every moment of your life.

Barbara Scales

There is a flood story in the Greco-Roman tradition, a story told by Ovid in his magnificent work of the ongoing making and transformation of the universe, *Metamorphoses*.

This is a story that has always reminded me of my parents. It tells of a flood brought about by the gods to banish "monstrous mankind" from the earth. At the end of the flooding, as the waters recede around Mount Parnassus, Deucalion and Pyrrha moor their skiff:

> There lived no better nor more upright man,
> No wife more reverential than his own.[1]

When the waters recede, revealing a desolate and barren wasteland without any other life, the two old people understand that they can not survive alone and that a new society, a new world, is required to sustain them and for there to be any human future.

They go to the Temple of Themis and pray for a restoration of humanity. They ask for the gods to be swayed by pity and love, by the sight of the misery on earth, and plead for a second birth of mankind. Themis provides an enigmatic demand:

> "Go from my temple now,
> With your heads covered and your robes unbound;
> Behind you, toss the bones of your great mother!" (527–29)

The couple puzzle over the command of the goddess until Deucalion hits upon an interpretation:

"The righteous oracles can't counsel evil.
So If I am not very much mistaken,
Our 'great mother' is the earth itself;
I reckon that the 'bones' the goddess meant
Are merely stones in the body of the earth:
It's stones we're meant to throw behind our backs!" (541–46)

The couple descends from the mount from the temple and toss stones over their shoulders. These stones metamorphose into a new mankind:

As they descend,
They veil their heads and loosen up their robes,
And cast the stones behind them as the goddess
Bade them to do—and as they did, these stones
(you needn't take this part on faith,
For it's supported by an old tradition)—
These stones at once begin to lose their hardness
And their rigidity; slowly they soften;
Once softened, they begin to take on shapes.
Then presently, when they'd increased in size
And grown more merciful in character,
They bore a certain incomplete resemblance
To the human form, much like those images
Created by a sculptor when he begins
Roughly modeling his marble figures.
That part in them which was both moist and earthy
Was used for the creation of their flesh,
While what was solid and incapable
Of bending turned to bone; what had been veins
Continued on, still having the same name.
By heaven's will, in very little time,
Stones that the man threw took the form of men,
While those thrown from the woman's hand repaired
The loss of women: the hardness of our race
And great capacity for heavy labor
Give evidence of our origins. (552–77)

Other forms of life returned to earth—the domesticated and the monstrous. In one version of the story, Deucalion and Pyrrha die together, and where they are buried, two trees spring forth and wind their trunks each around the other, growing together to this day.

■ ■ ■

One interpretation of any myth is that it is a representation, on a large and fantasized canvas, of our lives.

In some sense, humanity faced many "floods," many disasters during the lives of Junius and Gladys. Both were deeply affected in their early years by the ending of the economic boom of the 1920s with the Great Depression—its hunger, loss, and all that was encompassed in "the lean years." They both stood against the brutality of the Nazi takeover of Europe, Junius serving in the armed forces and Gladys in the war industries. Despite the ultimate defeat of fascist and Nazi forces in Europe, millions of dead were left behind.

After their early and ardent support of the Soviet experiment, they suffered the shock of realizing the horrors of Stalin's Soviet Union. Only a modest token of these horrors was revealed to the ardent defenders of the Communist experiment during the Twentieth Party Congress in 1957.

Junius and Gladys spent the rest of their lives discovering writings and hearing firsthand accounts of what life had been in the Soviet Union before, during, and after Stalin. Horrified by the Soviet invasion of Hungary and confronted with irrefutable evidence that Stalin, far from being the hero of a glorious socialist society, was the architect of the planned and heartless destruction of his people, Junius and Gladys, like many others around the globe, picked up the pieces of their beliefs and dreams for humanity and started to throw them over their shoulders, not knowing what would become of it all.

My parents, however, had an additional disaster awaiting them: eight nightmarish years of preparing for, living through, and awaiting the results of the courtroom drama of *Scales v. the United States,* followed by the incarceration of Junius Scales. Tested to the limit but without breaking, Junius served his time in prison until my mother, Gladys, and a band of principled individuals that included Eleanor Roosevelt, Reinhold Niebuhr, Norman Thomas, James Wechsler, and many others managed to persuade Attorney General Robert Kennedy and then President John F. Kennedy of the injustice and inappropriateness of Junius's imprisonment.

After fifteen months of imprisonment—with pained correspondence between my parents and heartwrenching visits that my mother and I made within those walls—on Christmas Eve 1962 the gates opened and then shut behind him.

In the family and among a circle of friends, we referred to Gladys, admiringly, as Fidelio, a reference to the heroine of Beethoven's only opera, the eponymous tale of a brave woman who, at great personal risk and with singleness of purpose, sets out to liberate her husband, a victim of political oppression, from prison. When they were reunited, my mother was thirty-nine years old, my father was forty-two, and I was eleven. As a family, we had never known "normal."

What was left after youthful passion and certitude had led them down a path that had proven to be disastrous? Their country would still face many seismic disasters: the deeper involvement in a terrible war, the revolts in the inner cities across the nation, the assassination of the two Kennedy brothers who had heard their pleas and then of Martin Luther King, who had embodied so much of what they had still dared hope for.

Junius explored some options but felt that his presence would taint any public campaign. He focused on supporting his family. Gladys came into her own in that period, devoting her energies to teaching and to restoring some semblance of family life. I flourished in those years, attending Hunter High School, the Martha Graham School of Dance, and finding my own political engagement at Hunter in protest demonstrations and in electoral campaigns.

I had moved on, in 1968, to studies at McGill University in Montreal. At my parents' urging, I moved to a different country to allow me to understand something about the nature of the individual in another society. This was a journey from which I would not return, much to my parents' chagrin.

The interviews that make up this book came at the end of that period of difficult family reintegration and my departure for Montreal. My mother would have ten years to live; my father survived her by twenty-two years. What happened to them and to me in the years after these interviews is left for me to recount here.

■ ■ ■

Three great threads formed the warp of Junius and Gladys's lives from 1971 to their ends. Built into the very nature of their selves was a sense of the importance of sharing their understanding of life, their lives, and the world as they knew it through conversation, teaching, and writing. Those friends and acquaintances with whom they would share this understanding embody the second thread: friendship as a value. The boldest strand in the fabric of their lives was their sense of mission to make the world a better place for people in the future.

I had understood the last point all of my conscious life. When I was about eight or nine years old, I was walking with my mother near the elevated subway on Broadway as a train rumbled overhead. I held her gloved hand, and when the rumbling had stopped, I announced, in a rather solemn tone, that I understood that the reason we live is to make the world a better place for those who come after. My mother accepted my declaration with approval.

Then we moved along to catch the subway, to anoint life with meaning, and to go shopping for new shoes. That insight, although an epiphany, was nothing unusual for me: it was in the air that I breathed, the conversations I overheard, and the actions of both of my parents.

What I understand now is that, for Junius and Gladys, "those who come after" meant the sons and daughters of all of their friends, and it very pointedly meant me. It also meant people none of us would ever meet, never dream of, in parts of the earth we had never heard of. Their job and ours was to make human society a better place: cleaner, healthier, more fair, and with its wealth shared more fully. As parents, their job was to allow me to become a person with the tools to make the world a better place.

Junius and Gladys exchanged visits regularly, two or three times each week, and phone calls daily, with friends who were like family. I thought of it as an underground network of friends weaving a safety net in a city of millions. Time and money were always budgeted not only for our own needs but also for our friends, for spending time, for welcoming.

Conversation, teaching, and writing were very much a part of who they were. Their interlocutors included not only old friends but new acquaintances, students, young scholars, and whoever might knock at the door, including a sympathetic social relationship with local Jehovah's Witnesses in the Hudson Valley, who literally did knock at the door.

One very special relationship of Junius's was with a very bright but seriously mentally disabled young man, a student of a dear friend who responded to nothing so well as to classical music. Jason found a learned and sympathetic ear in Junius. For over ten years, Jason called daily and sometimes several times a day to talk about music, his beloved little sister, and about his other passion, baseball. At Junius's memorial service, Jason startled everyone, breaking up the pace of sober encomiums by rushing to the front of the church hall to urgently recount detailed and heartfelt stories of their conversations and declaring that he would miss Junius forever.

■ ■ ■

The setting in which their evolution took place was a world of art and ideas and equally a world of nature. Gladys and Junius had an unquenchable thirst for insights into what is human, revealed with the most refined skill and sensitivity in literature, painting, music, dance, and theater. This meant a constant presence of recorded music in the household, a constant turnover of literary works on the coffee table and bedside tables, subscriptions to the opera and theater seasons, and many concert series.

They pursued intellectual activities together, my father providing an ear as my mother worked out her ideas about childhood language development, proofreading and editing her master's thesis on reading-skill acquisition in the young child.

Mother Nature became central to my parents' lives when, in 1969, they bought their country home in the Shawangunk Mountains on the western edge of the Hudson Valley, just south of the Catskills. Peaceable Hill was a neglected and long-abandoned parcel of land with two dwellings in a state of collapse and a garage. My parents took possession of one of the dwellings, the garage, and the land in the summer of 1969 and turned it into a haven from the tumult of the last thirty years: a place to listen to recordings, to read, to welcome friends, and also a world to build anew.

My father acquired an intimate knowledge of the thirty-seven forested hillside acres. He gave shape to the land. I still enjoy the hundred spruce trees we planted one summer, many years ago. As we cleared trails and repaired the gravel road, he led the way in learning the trees, the plants, the "critters," and their spore. He fed the birds and left a salt lick and feed for the deer in the harshest months of winter. He climbed the trees to prune limbs that blocked the view. He created makeshift benches, which doubled as rest stops on the way up the hill and as lookouts onto the Hudson Valley and the mountains beyond. Junius repaired the old gazebo at the top of one sloping field so my mother could lie in her hammock, dividing her attention between reading and the view of the countryside. Their ashes are buried by that gazebo.

■ ■ ■

The ashes remind me of more hard details of these years. Around 1970, just after the purchase of Peaceable Hill and just before these interviews, my mother's health took a dramatic turn. She was diagnosed with lymphoma. Gladys was treated with the best available care as a research patient at Sloan-Kettering Memorial Institute and at Mount Sinai Hospital. She went into remission for a few years, but, despite first-rate medical care and her ferocious appetite for life, she eventually succumbed to her illness. Over the course of ten years, her body became smaller and more frail. There was less for my arms to wrap around with each visit home. Both the disease and the medications took a toll on her face with its ever-beautiful gaze and on her vitality.

In the period from 1971 to 1981, she channeled most of her energies into her teaching. She speaks ardently about her work in these interviews. That informed commitment left her colleagues sincerely admiring of her.

An African American school principal in her district, whom I remember as Judy, grew to admire Gladys's work and to love her, despite a healthy mistrust of the ability of white people to understand the inner lives of young black students. Judy left her school position to become an undersecretary in the Federal Department of Health Education and Welfare during the Carter administration. She knew my mother had not long to live when she arranged for her to be awarded an honor as national Educator of the Year. It was in the summer of 1980 that a fragile Gladys, weighing not much more than a hundred pounds, flew down to Texas to receive this award.

The sweet irony was not lost on the circle of close friends: the woman who had not been able to teach in New York City's public schools due to their "loyalty oath," whose husband had been and was still a convicted felon for supposed crimes against the state, named Educator of the Year in the United States of America.

Her innovative development of reading programs and the training of volunteer, community-based assistants to work with the kids who had difficulty with language acquisition worked on many levels: community closeness, educational efficacy, and solid theoretical underpinnings. The result was that the gates of a better life were opened to hundreds of kids whose needs had brought them to her program.

So great was her commitment that even as her health failed, she insisted on going into the schools where she worked and tending to her kids. When she broke her hip and her legs would no longer support her, she used a walker and then a wheelchair. As the cancer overtook her body and her weight diminished to below a hundred pounds, Junius carried her to the waiting car of her colleague, Doris, who drove her to school. In order not to draw attention to her difficulty, she arrived early at her desk so that students would not see the evidence of her growing disability.

She worked until the last days of February 1981. One week later, weighing approximately eighty pounds, she died in her sleep in the early morning hours of March 6. She had spent fifty-seven years in almost constant battle with some demon or other.

For my father, there was unspeakable sorrow. Despite her ill health, she had seemed to be endlessly resilient. For a phalanx of friends and colleagues, the battle for her life was over. There was little to do but to share stories.

Over four hundred people came to a memorial service at the Community Church of New York. The speeches made in her honor by family, friends, her doctor, and her colleagues were unstinting in their praise of her courage, her energy, her wit, her sense of humor, her love of life, her grace, and her gift of bringing people together in her wise embrace. For me, her loss is still raw and impossible. A caring and imaginative presence still lives in my dreams.

Gladys's death changed the landscape enormously: the many friends who were held together by her very existence seemed to drift apart. Junius, a man of sixty at the moment of her death, sought another partner with whom to share his life. Despite warm and devoted relationships with two other women of remarkable qualities in the ensuing twenty-two years, there would be no one to replace the already legendary Gladys.

■ ■ ■

During the 1970s, throughout my mother's illness, Junius's first concern was for her health and her work. He worked crazy hours at the *New York Times,* 2:00 to 9:30 AM, the "lobster" shift. He arose from his sleep every afternoon when Gladys came home and spent the dinner hour and the evening with her. They would often attend concerts and continued visits with friends. They were alone in the apartment as I was living and studying in Montreal. His life was about bringing in a steady income, supporting his family, and seeing opportunities to find more meaningful employment dissolve.

My father began to realize, with some despair, that there would be no other professional doors open to him. He was determined to come to terms with many of the questions that Mickey Friedman asked in these interviews and many more that gnawed at him and which emerged again and again in conversations with friends. The question was, How to tackle the enormity and the raw wound of his experience?

At that time, without his knowledge, something was brewing.

In 1976, Lou Lipsitz, a professor of political science and a poet at the University of North Carolina in Chapel Hill, was approached by the North Carolina Humanities Council to write a play about Junius's second trial of 1956–57. *The Limits of Dissent* is based directly on the trial transcript. Produced by students from the Winston-Salem School of the Arts, the play toured the state in 1977, playing in twenty-nine courthouses with "juries" made up of members of the audience. Junius, Richard Nickson, and I went, incognito, to North Carolina to see the play at the Raleigh courthouse.

Here is what Lipsitz recalled about the development of the play in an interview in 2001, when the play was reprised and toured again throughout the state:

In 1976, Lipsitz said he had written to Scales about the play, and Scales had told him not to do it because the incident had brought pain to so many people. But Lipsitz said he thought Scales was wrong, that the play should be written because it would help to heal what had happened.

Scales wound up coming to see a performance of the play in 1977 in Raleigh. "It changed his life," Lipsitz said. "He came out of seclusion, wrote an autobiography, published by the University of Georgia Press."[2]

I don't know that any single event triggered the dramatic change in his life in that period, but this was an important moment—a theatrical rehearing of his trial that led to a first step toward reconciliation. In twenty-eight of the courthouses, the juries voted him not guilty; in one, it was a hung jury.

Junius previously had believed that his life and story were toxic and inappropriate for public attention. Friedman's interviews, Lou's play, and the dogged attention of Mark Pinsky, a young North Carolina journalist, helped him to realize that people cared about the issues he had struggled with and that he did have a story to tell. After the interview with Pinsky, he had a personal visibility in North Carolina for the first time in many years. It would not be the last time.

I longed for my papa to emerge from his seclusion. I was proud of him and knew that he had intelligence and talent that were wasting through official disdain and neglect. I wanted him to find a vehicle for his talents. It was mind-numbingly senseless for me to witness the disjunction between the great qualities I knew in this man and the misery he suffered. He believed himself to be outcast from, and without purpose in, the society for which he had sacrificed so much.

For Junius, there were some false starts: an offer to work at one of New York's largest bookstores setting up a record section, which he declined because he felt he needed to stay with a more stable and better-paying job to provide for his family; an invitation to write a book in a series of biographies for adolescent readers on the great African American soprano Leontyne Price, which he felt obliged to turn down as it came at a time when my mother's health was precarious and he was her primary caregiver.

There was no movement for him to be part of, no meaningful employment, no public engagement. As a convicted felon, he could not even vote. There was, however, the act of reflection, the consideration of the problems he had once hoped to help solve, the lessons he had learned, and the telling of his story.

Friends and former colleagues had written about their lives in the Communist Party. Junius felt that these were not an adequate telling of either the good or the bad of the Party experience and its impact. Lou Lipsitz's theatrical adaptation of his trial may have been the tipping point that led him, with the unswerving support of his dearest friends, including Richard and Lia Nickson and Bea and Bernie Friedland, to undertake the telling of his own story. With his lifelong friend Richard agreeing to be co-author, he embarked.

Questions emerged: to write it in the first person (more natural) or the third person (better suited for critical analysis of the life under discussion)? When should the story end: after the trial, after prison, up to the moment? And, of course, the struggle with the content, the meaning of those years: Was it all lost? What was learned? What could be passed on?

In 1982–83, after my mother's death and while the book was under way, Helen Whitney, a producer and writer for ABC's *Close-Up* series, prepared a two-hour documentary called "American Inquisition" on the anti-Communist hysteria in the 1950s with four stories to tell. The section on Junius was filmed over the fall and winter of 1982–83. We did interviews at home. We traveled to Lewisburg to film on the prison grounds and spent many days with Helen and her fine crew. His story was to be the closing episode, the crown of the work.

I related this to a friend, Karen Rosenberg, who was the TV reviewer for the *Boston Phoenix.* She called me early one morning in June 1983 to tell me that she had received the review copy of the program, that it was only one hour, and that there was nothing about my father. Indeed, on June 23, 1983, "American Inquisition" was aired as a one-hour broadcast.

The major sponsor for the series, the soon-to-be-defunct Eastern Airlines, had insisted on pulling the second half of the program, the part concerning my father, because the featured principal was not sufficiently repentant of his Communist ideas and allegiances. Another false start, another dashed hope for a platform to tell his story.

The corporate sponsor controlled access to the airwaves, but they couldn't control what Junius did sitting at his old typewriter. The book proceeded. His memoirs, painfully reconstructing the facts and the inner workings of his life from birth to his release from prison, took most of ten years to write, to rewrite many times, and then to edit, with the steadfast collaboration of Richard Nickson. The University of Georgia Press released *Cause at Heart: A Former Communist Remembers* in March 1987.

Junius toured North Carolina shortly thereafter, speaking at universities across the state. He was more concerned with what his incarceration revealed about the fault lines in the application of the Constitution, which he had enlisted to defend in 1941 and fought for all of his life, than for the many terrifying moments of discomfort and anguish he personally had suffered.

Thirty years of struggling with the demons of his allegiance with the Communist Party had paid off in a clear-eyed statement:

I joined the Communist Party in 1939. I found the poverty and racism I saw around me absolutely intolerable. The Party's program was for full economic, social, and political equality for blacks; it advocated the organization of unions. And it said people should live together in peace and brotherhood. I agreed and joined them.

We did some good things—maybe because we had such good people, black and white.

We helped organize unions—interracial unions.

We protested and publicized some of the worst injustice to blacks.

We opposed fascism.

Later, we opposed the cold war and worked for peace.

As a white southerner, I stood with blacks against racism two decades before the civil rights struggles of the sixties.

Of those things I am proud.

But there was a price to pay:

Along the way I became a closed-minded ideologue.

I became a total apologist for the Soviet Union—a country devoid of basic freedoms.

My tortured ideology became partly destructive of the very things that were constructive.

I became arrogant, narrow, and sectarian in my outlook and almost quit thinking for myself.

My disillusionment was complete eighteen years after I joined, when Khrushchev revealed to the world that Stalin was an unprincipled tyrant and mass-murderer; and when Soviet troops marched into Hungary and shot down Hungarian workers in the streets of Budapest.

My father told me before he died in 1940 that he respected my ideals of human brotherhood and freedom but that all his instincts and experience told him that I was picking the wrong group to realize them. He was right.

But still, with all the wrong turns and missteps I made, those ideals of human brotherhood that led me into the Communist Party and out of the Communist Party are the same ones that I will advocate as long as I live.

I've written (with my oldest friend) a book about my experiences, which I hope some of you may read. I believe it will give you something to think about.

After this brave avowal, he turned to his audience and appealed to their calling as students:

> College is a place where one should ask the hardest question—of oneself and of everyone you come across.
> I'm ready for yours.

My father was encouraged by historian friends to attend the meetings of the Organization of American Historians, the Southern History Association, and the American History Association.

He squeezed money from his modest pension to pay for flights, shared rooms with friends, and, to his surprise and delight, he found that historians young and old were coming to him to hear his story and ask his opinion on matters within his purview. He was not only a witness to a significant moment in history, he had been a key figure in that moment. Scholars treated him with respect, admiration, and healthy curiosity. At last, I thought, he and his story mattered.

Reviews of the book were generally favorable, but in the *New York Review of Books,* Murray Kempton wrote scathingly not of the book but of Junius for having been a Communist. Ex-Communists were merely another sort of Communist for Kempton. Larry King interviewed him, unsympathetically, on his radio program. Based on slow sales and less than 100 percent support from reviewers, the University of Georgia decided not to reprint, nor to bring out a paperback edition at that time. The first run sold out, and the book became almost impossible to find.

■ ■ ■

In March 1996, a Scales of repute died in North Carolina. When it came through on the wire service, a North Carolina newspaper, thinking it might be Junius Scales, called up local papers in the Hudson Valley looking for information. They found Oliver Mackson, a young journalist, on duty at the *Times Herald-Record* in Middletown, New York. The *Times* obituary department asked whether he had heard that Junius Scales was dead. Mackson deadpanned that he had heard that Calvin Coolidge was dead (a reference to Dorothy Parker's quip when told that Coolidge was dead: "How can you tell?") but was puzzled as to why he should care about Scales.

Mackson looked up Junius Scales in the phone directory, called, and asked whether he were dead. Junius's response was in line with Mark Twain's comment about "rumors of my death being greatly exaggerated" and explained that he was feeling rather well.

The two men clearly had complementary wit and launched into a long and warm conversation. The journalist followed up with a visit and an extended interview. On March 24, two days before his seventy-sixth birthday, the *Herald-Record* ran a full-page front-page photo with a full-page story on page 2. A friendship formed, and Junius's cloak of privacy in the Hudson Valley was removed.

Sometime later, when Mackson's union was on strike at the *Times-Herald,* he brought some of his colleagues to visit Junius. Some of them felt uncomfortable about picketing. Without addressing their particular situation, Mackson asked my father to discuss questions about working men and women, the importance of the right to strike, and the struggle to acquire this right. Mackson relates that all of his colleagues were proudly out on the picket line the next day.

On July 4, 2000, Mackson wrote a feature about the meaning of Independence Day, interviewing Junius for the occasion and telling his story to underscore the importance of dissent, freedom of expression and ideas, as part of what the holiday should celebrate.

In 1998, Junius was diagnosed with Alzheimer's Disease, which was later revised. The diagnosis jolted him into choosing to move permanently to Peaceable Hill, to make me a signatory to his bank account, and to give me the keys to his car. It also meant that he was more dependent on me for his activities. I would come at least once a month to spend a few days with him and often more.

During this time I got to know some of his regular activities. By signing his checks for him, I learned about the more than two dozen organizations to which he sent small monthly checks out of his fixed income: the ACLU, Amnesty International, the Nation Foundation, the NAACP, several gay and lesbian rights organizations, the Mexican Lettuce Pickers, the Lewisburg Prison Project, and many others. He also contributed to political candidates across the country and regularly supported whoever ran against Jesse Helms in North Carolina.

He corresponded, in long and thoughtful letters, with many friends, young and old. The sheer physical weight of his correspondence was impressive. He gave serious consideration to each letter and each response. He also read manuscripts for historians who were writing about material in which he had some expertise.

Hours were spent on the phone with friends near and far. After his faux-Alzheimer's diagnosis, Sidney Rittenberg, a friend from college and Party days who had survived many years in detention in China, called him every single day, from wherever he might be—in North Carolina, Washington state, or the Beijing Airport, where he was often found as he continued to do business in China. He called to do his part to keep Junius mentally agile and to exchange jokes, reminiscences, and news—but mostly he called because he wanted Junius to know how great was his love.

Papa died on August 5, 2002, at the age of eighty-two. I had moved into the hospital room with him and stayed with him talking, playing recorded music for him, massaging his limbs, and welcoming visitors for three days while he was disappearing into a coma. On the fourth day at about twelve-thirty in the afternoon, I heard his breathing change, and I knew these were to be the last breaths. He died in my arms. What a journey it had been. What a great loss. What a great human being.

■ ■ ■

Although he had been largely out of public life for forty years, and his book had been published and had disappeared fifteen years earlier, there was no mistaking the interest that marked the last years of his life and his death.

Two North Carolina homes associated with Junius Scales were in the news in 2001. The mansion where he grew up was up for sale for $3.5 million. Articles in the real estate section referred to it as the "Scales mansion," even though it hadn't been in the Scales family for seventy years, and mentioned prominently that it was the home where Junius Scales had grown up.

Months later, the house where my parents lived when I was born, the shack in Carrboro, was declared a landmark with an ACLU plaque marking the house where Junius Irving Scales had lived while he was organizing for the Communist Party and being hunted by the FBI. Lou Lipsitz's play toured again in North Carolina that same year.

When Junius died, the *New York Times,* the *Los Angeles Times,* the *Globe and Mail,* the Associated Press, the major North Carolina papers, the *Times Herald-Record,* and many others across the continent carried original obituaries, and even more picked up the AP story. National Public Radio did a piece on him in their magazine show, and CNN had it on their crawl ticker. I was relieved of the agony of calling more than a circle of friends, because everybody in the United States and Canada seemed to have heard about his death. Memorial services were held in North Carolina and in New York.

Three years after Papa's death, *Cause at Heart* was reissued. At the urging of Vernon Burton, the University of Georgia Press brought it out in paperback in 2005. The new edition includes an impressive introduction by Burton and James R. Barrett. They provide more information on the period of the

South in which Junius had grown up, underscoring the institutional and structural injustice as well as the important strikes and grassroots activity that would have given leavening to young Junius's sense of wrongs needing to be righted.

The introduction also spells out the link between the Alien and Sedition Act, the Smith Act, and the recently minted Patriot Act. The limiting of democracy in the face of fears of attacks from outsiders places the United States in the delicate position of the cartoonist Walt Kelly's Pogo Possum's assessment: "We have met the enemy, and he is us." It is no coincidence that this was one of Junius's favorite quotations. He had, indeed, found himself fingered as the enemy by the very society he had worked to improve.

Was all of this posthumous attention a matter of a guilty conscience on the part of a nation? Belated respect? Junius cared about the world he lived in, and his story resonates, many years after the events. His family, from his youth, had always shared him with his engagement with history.

Now, having lived his life as fully as he was able, his story belongs to future generations. A life ends, and history begins.

■ ■ ■

For my parents, I was the future. It is appropriate that their story ends, or perhaps continues, with me. They are both gone—their lives, their dreams, their struggles, and pain, over. Junius and Gladys are with me, the roots of my own rich and complicated life.

My parents' backgrounds could hardly have been more different from one another: their families, their stations in life, their religious backgrounds, their customs and attitudes.

When Junius and Gladys met, at the ages of thirty and twenty-seven, respectively, a little the worse for wear and in the midst of their own battles, they fell deeply in love. It was a love that bore fruit. They maintained a steadfast support for each other through thick and a great deal of thin. Throughout their lives they affirmed their love for each other, for their friends, their shared commitment to justice, to fairness, their undying vision of a global community, and to me, my peers, and the future.

I paid attention, and I learned.

I spent the 1970s, after completing my B.A. at McGill in 1973, doing some research work, working at a gay/lesbian and feminist bookstore, teaching dance and theater, being assistant director at a McGill residence, and completing a master's thesis on Hegel's aesthetics and the question, What does it mean to say that art belongs to its time? I knew that I wanted to be part of the art of my time. One must know the world before one is able to change it. I wanted to know and to change my world in ways that only art can afford.

In 1981, weeks after my mother died, I started a small artist-management business, Latitude 45 Arts, which is now incorporated and has offices in three countries. I focus on artistic creation, particularly on music and music-based projects. I work in a global marketplace, representing artists from and doing business in Latin America, Asia, Europe, Africa, and North America.

My work in the arts allows me to navigate along the threads that I discovered in my parents' lives: the role of great art in forming and shaping community, in bringing people together across the imagined identity boundaries of nation, race, religion, or gender. I have found a calling in life that takes me across the globe, exchanging ideas, discussing art and life with people in parts of the world I had thought to be inaccessible and wondering, always, what can I do to make the world a better place.

My devotion to the arts also comes from knowing that my parents spent many of their happiest moments together attending performances and concerts and exploring the wealth of music festivals. My own childhood was enriched with an ongoing attendance at public performances, including Leonard Bernstein's Young People's Concerts, the Metropolitan Opera, New York's great dance companies, and the Guthrie Theater's New York season.

My father saw me start and develop my business. He attended, with interest, concerts of my clients in the New York area.

He also lived long enough to know my daughter, Nadja. She is named for Nadezhda Mandelstam, a favorite author of my mother's, whose gripping account of Soviet terror and the arrest and death in confinement of her husband, the poet Osip Mandelstam, she read with great interest and emotion. Gladys entered empathically into the circle of writers and artists in the Soviet Union of the 1930s and 1940s through Mandelstam's books *Hope against Hope* and *Hope Abandoned.* Nadezhda means "hope."

Nadja, who never met her grandmother, was eleven when her grandpa died. They had time to form a close bond and to discuss the meaning of friendship in the relationship between Shrek and Donkey. Junius had come to Montreal to usher her into the world when she was born; Nadja came to New York to be present in his last conscious hours, to talk about friendship and to say goodbye.

■ ■ ■

The fruit hasn't fallen far from the tree. It is, in some sense, the tree of Junius and Gladys, like the double-trunked tree of Deucalion and Pyrrha. Is the world repopulated with those who are equipped to make a better world thanks to the patient and troubled efforts of my parents? Although they have not trained the leading scientists, businessmen, or professionals of my generation, there is much for all of us to gain from the stories of Junius and Gladys Scales.

Making the world a better place for all is a neverending and many-faceted challenge. My mother was an educator; my father a political activist and political prisoner turned writer. My own path takes me through the performing arts—with its acts of creation, of renewal, and of transformation.

All life stories end in death; but in all great stories, death is not the ending. The Brechtian conceit that the play succeeds not through catharsis but rather in bringing the audience into the streets ready to change the world provides a clue as to how to end this story.

The world is made, conserved, or changed by our many hands. We are not just hapless bystanders, observing the work of powers hiding behind screens, like so many Wizards of Oz, pulling levers and making smoke.

If the story of Junius and Gladys teaches us anything, it is that despite the floods and disasters of epic proportions, natural and manmade, there is a resiliency in the power of human creativity, in the strength of community, and in critical intelligence rooted in abiding love.

May we all put this book down, take our courage in our hands, and use whatever tools we have to make the world a better place.

A HISTORICAL ESSAY ■

Gail Williams O'Brien

In the oral history you have just read, you got to know Junius Irving Scales, his wife Gladys, and their daughter Barbara as people with hopes and dreams, successes and struggles. The goal of this essay is to sketch out the larger American and southern context in which their lives unfolded and to which they contributed.

Junius Scales was born on March 19, 1920, and he cemented his relationship with the American Communist Party (CPUSA) in the summer of 1939 in Greensboro, North Carolina. Located in the northern North Carolina piedmont, Greensboro considered itself a progressive city, and in some ways it was. With only the Cape Fear River flowing directly into the Atlantic Ocean and entry into that body of water made treacherous by a large deposit of sediment known as Frying Pan Shoals, North Carolina was settled in the eighteenth century largely by internal migrations from other colonies. While these settlers represented a variety of socioeconomic and religious backgrounds, most were seeking a small plot of land to farm. By the mid-nineteenth century, large land- and slave-owners were present in all parts of the state, though on the eve of the Civil War, North Carolina remained the poorest state in the Confederacy. Given the marketing difficulties, the piedmont elite engaged in economic endeavors beyond agriculture. These included railroad building, mining, and industry. Indeed, with thirty-nine cotton mills and nine woolen mills, virtually all of which were located in the piedmont, North Carolina was the only state to effect an arrangement with the Confederate government to supply its own troops with uniforms.

With a start toward industrialization before the Civil War, North Carolina became the South's most industrialized state by 1900, and most of the industry was located in the piedmont, with much of it concentrated in the Greensboro vicinity: textiles in Greensboro itself; furniture in nearby High Point; and tobacco in Winston-Salem, Reidsville, and Durham. While the southern tobacco industry reigned supreme in the nation from its rise in the last third of the nineteenth century, the Textile Belt, stretching from the northern North Carolina piedmont into South Carolina, Georgia, and Alabama, surpassed New England as the nation's premier manufacturer of cotton cloth by the 1920s. Thus, in comparison to poor rural areas that predominated in the South long after the Civil War, Greensboro viewed itself as a center of progress.

Perhaps foreseeing the potential in Greensboro, Junius Scales's grandfather, also named Junius Irving Scales, and his great uncle, Alfred Moore Scales, moved from Richmond County in the southern piedmont to Greensboro after the Civil War. Both men were attorneys and members of the southern antebellum elite. Junius Irving had moved from North Carolina with numerous slaves to the Yazoo River Valley in Mississippi in 1858 and acquired much land. When Mississippi seceded from the Union in 1860, he joined the Thirtieth Mississippi Infantry Regiment and quickly became a colonel. Captured at the battle of Chickamauga in September 1863, he spent the remainder of the war in a federal prison. He returned to North Carolina initially to farm and then to practice law with his brother, serving as a state senator and managing his brother's political campaigns until his early death in 1880 at the age of forty-eight.

Junius's great uncle Alfred Moore Scales, a Confederate brigadier general, was a member of Congress before and after the war (1857–59; 1875–84) and governor of North Carolina from 1885 to 1889. Both Raleigh, the capital of North Carolina, and Rockingham, the county seat of Richmond County, possess Scales Streets. Junius's family's place among the North Carolina elite was also secured by his grandmother, Junius Irving's wife, and his great aunt, Alfred Moore's wife. These women descended from Richard Henderson, a royal judge in North Carolina before the Revolution, and Richard's son, Leonard Henderson, the first chief justice of the North Carolina supreme court.

Although only ten at the time of his father's death, Junius's own father, named for his uncle, Alfred Moore Scales, went on to become a lawyer, state senator, real estate developer, and insurance executive in Greensboro. After the death of his first wife in 1912, he married two years later Mary Leigh Pell of Richmond, Virginia. Though his father was adversely affected by the steep decline in the housing market that preceded the Great Depression in 1929, Junius grew up in a thirty-six-room mansion in Hamilton Lakes, a subdivision developed by his father and named for his paternal grandmother, Euphemia Hamilton Henderson Scales.

Thus, despite the transportation difficulties that plagued North Carolina throughout much of its early history, the relative poverty of the state as a whole, and the disparate origins of its settlers, a social and economic elite emerged early and persisted. Intermarriages linked elite families in the east and piedmont and on occasion, as with Junius's father, in Richmond and Petersburg, Virginia. Junius's family was deeply ensconced in this elite.

Although members of North Carolina's elite often divided between Democrats in the southeastern part of the state and Whigs in the northeastern corner, piedmont, and mountains prior to the Civil War, almost all came together in the Democratic Party when faced during Reconstruction with a Republican Party composed primarily of African Americans and less affluent whites. After losing the election of 1868, Democrats regained control of the state legislature in 1870 and the governorship in 1876. Yet Republicans remained a threat, garnering 40 to 45 percent of the vote in every gubernatorial election until they joined with Populists and won the governor's race in 1896. Already, by "fusing," the Populists and Republicans had gained control of the legislature in 1894; thus, their victory in 1896 gave them control of all three branches of state government. Nowhere in the nation were Populists, in partnership with the minority party, so successful.

To thwart this effective Fusionist challenge, Democrats launched a highly racist campaign in 1898 that resulted not only in Democrats seizing control of the state legislature but also in a horrendous attack on African Americans in Wilmington, the port city in southeastern North Carolina where large slaveholders had predominated prior to the Civil War and Republicans prevailed in local elections more recently. Continuing a campaign of racist slander in Democratically controlled newspapers, intimidation, violence, and corruption at the polls, Democrats not only won the gubernatorial election of 1900 but also managed to add to the state constitution an amendment that disfranchised almost all black voters and most poor whites. As in other southern states, laws segregating blacks and whites in public places soon followed. Greensboro proved no exception, though the city prided itself as much on its progressive attitude toward African Americans as on its industrial economy. In fact, this attitude of paternalism and civility at best would lead the historian William Chafe to label the city's racial attitudes "a progressive mystique." For Junius, however, who had known African Americans only as servants, eating with black students when he attended a student-labor conference in his junior year in college raised new, exciting possibilities, possibilities that would motivate him to work for racial integration on a basis of complete equality.

Like racial civility, industrialization in the Greensboro area had a grim underside, for it was built on cheap labor. This resulted not from individualistic traditions, as conventional wisdom would have it, or from lack of trying to effect change on the part of workers. As early as the fall of 1900, a fierce battle raged in Alamance County, Greensboro's neighbor to the east, as workers walked out of cotton mills and a sympathy strike ensued among other workers. Strikes also roiled the textile industry as World War I ended, the sharp demand for textiles experienced during the war slowed, and mill management attempted to recoup losses by firing workers and drastically reducing the wages of those who remained. Unable to roll back wages as readily as they had planned, many small mills closed, while others, with J. Spencer Love's Burlington Mills in Alamance County leading the way, turned to time-efficiency experts and new technology to speed up production and cut workers and wages—or, in mill management's terms, "costs." These changes meant not only that workers had to work at a relentless pace, the "speedup," but also that those employees who remained had to tend to more machines, the "stretch-out," and these conditions prevailed in both struggling cotton mills and the new synthetic, full-fashion hosiery plants, a part of the textile industry that boomed as women hiked their skirts and the twenties roared.

As early as 1927, a major union-organization effort and strike occurred in Henderson, North Carolina, and two years later a strike in a German-owned mill in Elizabethton in eastern Tennessee leapt across the Blue Ridge Mountains into Marion in western North Carolina. Although six of the striking workers in Marion were killed, it was a walkout at the Loray mill in Gastonia in the southwestern piedmont that grabbed headlines, because some of the organizers there, like the native North Carolinian Kelly Y. "Red" Hendricks, were members of the CPUSA.

The organizing efforts and confrontations in 1929 were only the prelude to the largest single strike in American history, a walkout by four hundred thousand workers in the Textile Belt in the fall of 1934. As the Great Depression worsened, reaching into the middle and sometimes the upper classes—affecting both Junius and Gladys—executives in hard-hit industries like textiles worked with Washington officials to create a set of codes under the National Industrial Recovery Act (NIRA), enacted in 1933. While the NIRA relaxed antitrust restrictions, letting trade associations like the Cotton Textile Institute set production limits and prices, it created the National Recovery Administration to work with manufacturers to establish minimum-wage and maximum-hour codes in an effort to keep employment and wages up and thereby stimulate consumption. Billed by President Franklin Delano Roosevelt in his fireside chats as a "cooperative movement" among government, employers, and employees to save the nation from economic disaster, the NIRA also contained Section 7a, which guaranteed the right of workers to organize.

After a brief recovery in 1933, the overstocked textile mills began finding ways to manipulate the codes to their advantage, and letters regarding "code chiseling" poured into the president. Rather than being forwarded to the National Labor Board, as happened with most industrial complaints, however, those from textile workers were sent to the Cotton Textile National Industrial Relations Board, which shared them with agents of the Cotton Textile Institute and asked the complainant's employer to look into them. Not surprisingly, out of 3,920 complaints, only ninety-six investigations occurred, and only one was settled in favor of a worker.

Hard hit by "code chiseling" and frustrated by the lack of attention to their grievances, but still believing that this was a cooperative endeavor and the government would mediate disputes in organizing campaigns, textile workers began joining an American Federation of Labor (AFL) union, the United Textile Workers (UTW), in large numbers. To the dismay of government officials and management alike, union membership soared from an estimated forty thousand in September 1933 to 270,000 by August 1934. When the textile board authorized another 25 percent reduction in production hours in June 1934—and employment and wages were reduced accordingly—workers walked out in northern Alabama. Then, led by southern militants at the national UTW meeting in New York, the union authorized a general strike to begin on September 1. Within a week, "flying squadrons" of striking workers sped in their automobiles from one mill to another across the Textile Belt, and the entire industry was shut down as four hundred thousand workers vacated the mills.

Support for workers varied from one community to another, as did violence. In a city where there were large numbers of other industrial workers, such as Durham, North Carolina, support for the union could be strong, but in most southern communities, the conservative elite dominated, as it had since disfranchisement at the turn of the century. In less than a week after the strike began, textile executives had appealed to state governors, and fourteen thousand troops were on duty in North and South Carolina alone, guarding mill property—and nonstriking workers who were willing to cross the picket lines. The worst strike violence erupted at Chiquola mill in Honea Path, South Carolina, where union and non-union workers were allegedly divided about half and half. Almost everyone who was not in the union was deputized, and striking workers, according to their descendants' accounts, were fired on from the mill windows. Seven striking workers were killed.

Although ten thousand people arrived in Honea Path to mourn these deaths, no one was ever charged with the shootings, and the UTW officially ended the strike there, as elsewhere, on September 22, only three weeks after it had begun. Not only had striking workers faced guns and bayonets, but also owners with huge backlogs of goods ceased or slowed manufacturing until unemployed workers, and their union, could hold out no longer. For a variety of reasons, including his dependence on the votes of southern congressmen for future New Deal programs and the voluntary nature of the NIRA, Roosevelt kept his distance from the entire affair, appointing New Hampshire Governor John G. Winant to head a committee to look into the situation but making no effort to see that the Winant commission's recommendations were followed. In the wake of the failed strike, union men and women and their families were fired, put out of their mill homes, and "blacklisted" throughout the textile mill region.

Following the Wagner Act in 1935, which legitimated unions and created a National Labor Relations Board (NLRB) to mediate union efforts and labor disputes, the rise of the Congress of Industrial Organizations (CIO) as industrial unions split from the AFL in the mid-1930s, and the growing demand for textiles that accompanied World War II, a few mills were unionized in the South, but most organizing efforts proved extraordinarily difficult if not impossible. This was the world into which Junius stepped to begin mill work and organizing efforts in the fall of 1940, after completing the CPUSA summer school and becoming a "professional revolutionary." The textile mill world he would encounter in 1945 after four years' service in the American military was quite different in many respects from the one he experienced in 1940, though employers were no friendlier toward labor organizations than they had been before the war.

One of the most successful, if fleeting, union efforts in North Carolina occurred in the 1940s at the R. J. Reynolds tobacco plant in Winston-Salem, one of the three communities that, along with Greensboro and High Point, form the present-day Piedmont Triad. Union success at Reynolds emerged from the larger context of New Deal legislation and World War II, along with the commitment of leftist leadership in the CIO and CPUSA and of black workers, especially women who worked in the stemmeries division stripping tobacco leaves from tobacco stems. A union contract between Reynolds and Local 22 of the CIO's Food, Tobacco, Agriculture, and Allied Workers (FTA) Union, was successfully negotiated in the summer of 1944 and renewed in 1945 and 1946.

Like other unions around the country, Local 22 ran into problems as employers and political conservatives, Democrat and Republican, regained momentum following the war. In 1947, contract negotiations stalled when Local 22 sought increased wages and Reynolds's managers refused. A strike, called for May 1, ensued for thirty-eight days before a settlement was reached. During the strike, the *Winston-Salem Journal* constantly bemoaned Communists in the union and warned of the likelihood of riots. That summer, the House Committee on Un-American Activities (HUAC) held a hearing that focused on Communist involvement in Local 22.

Dogged by factual accusations of Communists among its local and national leaders, the FTA not only had to deal with hostile employers and congressional representatives but also with a widening rift within the CIO itself. Increasingly, anti-Communist leaders within the CIO challenged left-led unions like the FTA, and they sent a rival union, the United Transport Service Employees (UTSE) to challenge Local 22 at the Reynolds plant. Meanwhile, Reynolds stepped up its campaign to reduce the size of the African American workforce through the mechanization of operations like the stemmeries and the recruitment of more white employees from surrounding areas. The company also made overt appeals to white workers to abandon the FTA, which the Communists themselves worsened with a vigorous attack against "white chauvinism" within their own ranks. Additionally, the FTA contributed to red-baiting by openly supporting Communist workers' movements around the world. Yet, despite all of these handicaps and the rival UTSE, the FTA still won a plurality of the votes in an NLRB election in March 1950. It lost a runoff election only because the NLRB decided to count the ballots of low-level white supervisors. With this narrow loss, Local 22 disappeared from the Winston-Salem scene, as happened with most of the left-led unions in the South and across the nation.

Following the strike by Local 22 in the spring of 1947 and the HUAC hearing that summer, Junius decided to reveal publicly that he was a member of the CPUSA. He hoped that the respect that he and his family commanded in the Chapel Hill vicinity and around the state would demonstrate that Communists were not the demonic threat that the growing anti-Communist movement asserted. Unfortunately, his hope did not materialize.

When Scales joined the CPUSA on his nineteenth birthday, March 19, 1939, it was on an upward trajectory in terms of membership and influence. When he left in 1957, at the age of thirty-seven, it was falling apart. The successes and failures of the CPUSA stemmed in part from the nature of the Marxist-Leninist doctrine to which it adhered. They also resulted from the relationship between the CPUSA and Soviet Communists and from the actions and responses of anti-Communists in the United States to the Party during the middle decades of the twentieth century.

A significant problem encountered by the American Communist Party was that the United States was quite different from the worlds in which Marxism and Leninism were created. In *The Manifesto of the Communist Party* (1848), Marx and Engels contemplated the evolution of British and European society from a feudal to an industrial state. As Marx saw it, over time wealth would become increasingly concentrated in the hands of fewer and fewer capitalists, while growing numbers of workers would become more and more destitute. Eventually, a workers' revolution would bring a classless and equitable society. How and when this revolution would take place, and what rule by workers would look like, were left unclear.

Vladimir Lenin modified this doctrine in light of conditions in early twentieth-century Russia in his 1902 work, *What Is to Be Done?* Given that Russia at this time was largely a peasant society, Lenin envisioned a small group of highly disciplined, highly centralized "professional revolutionaries" who would provide political leadership to the underdeveloped working class. Additionally, given the repressive measures with which the Russian tsar met any political challenge, this vanguard party would seize power through a highly secretive, underground operation.

Most Americans who were born and reared in the United States, including industrial workers, did not buy into Marx's vision, let alone Lenin's alterations. Having never experienced feudalism and the persistence of an aristocracy based on bloodlines, most did not think in terms of social stratification or "class." Appeals for "class solidarity" had little resonance with workers divided by race, ethnicity, and gender as well as skill level. Workers around the country, like those in the textile industry in 1934, were more than willing to join labor unions and to strike if necessary, but they sought a larger piece of the economic pie, not its destruction. Nor did the secular approach of Marx and Lenin sit well with the religious traditions of many American workers.

For these reasons, the CPUSA, established in 1919, was not nearly as large and significant as its counterparts in Europe. Not surprisingly, the majority of members in the CPUSA at the time it was founded and for many years thereafter were immigrants, especially from southern and eastern Europe.

Given the disconnect between Marxist-Leninist doctrine and circumstances in the United States, the CPUSA veered back and forth between two extremes from the time it was founded in 1919. In the late 1920s, early 1930s, last half of the 1940s, and first half of the 1950s, it adhered rigidly to Communist dogma, preaching class solidarity and revolution, creating its own labor unions, and trying to effect a revolutionary alternative to the Democratic and Republican Parties. When in this mode, the Party remained, or increasingly grew, small and isolated. In much of the 1920s and from the mid-1930s through the mid-1940s, it downplayed its doctrinal views, softened its language, and joined with left-liberals in union efforts and partisan affairs. During this time, the Party's membership and influence increased. As Theodore Draper noted, the extremes of political orthodoxy or "sectarianism," on the one hand, and mass influence or "opportunism," on the other hand, were not irreconcilable; individuals could assume one stance or the other, depending on time and circumstances, and often, Draper added, these tendencies warred for supremacy within the same person.[1]

Although factions representing both of these positions were present at the first meeting of American Communists, and open arguments ensued, Soviet Communists largely determined the direction the CPUSA would take. They did this for many years through the Communist International (Comintern), which Lenin founded in 1919 and Stalin dismantled in 1943 as a goodwill gesture toward British and American allies during World War II. In 1947, Soviet Communists formed the Communist Information Bureau (Cominform), but this organization coordinated European Communist parties; American Communists never participated. Instead, when the Party made its final sectarian turn in 1945, it did so by discerning the Soviet Party line indirectly through a variety of sources.

In the wake of World War I, many Communists thought that capitalism was on its last legs and the workers' revolution was imminent in advanced industrial countries. By 1920, however, Lenin had decided this was not a likely scenario, and in a pamphlet entitled *Left-Wing Communism: An Infantile Disorder,* he explained that the Soviet Union needed a period of stabilization and that Communist movements in the West should cease sectarianism. With Lenin's stroke and subsequent death in January 1924, power struggles within the Kremlin ensued, and by 1928, Joseph Stalin found it to his advantage to purge moderates and declare a "Third Period" of revolutionary orthodoxy. The majority of American Communists balked; a minority accepted the turn. An American delegation consisting of both groups was subsequently summoned to Moscow. There, on May 6, 1929, Stalin laid out the principle by which world Communism would operate. It would be wrong "'to base the activities of the Communist Party'" on the specific features of American capitalism, or those of any other nation. Instead, the basis for Communist activities must be "'the general features of capitalism which are the same for all countries,'" and it would be Soviet Communists, acting in their own interests, who would decide what those features were at any given time.[2]

If being a member of a worldwide movement whose main direction was determined in Moscow created problems for American Communists, it also provided them with an enormous sense of pride and purpose. Small and weak in comparison to its European counterparts, the CPUSA appreciated the funding and advice the Soviets provided, especially as factional disputes roiled the Party in the 1920s. Above all, American Communists were pleased and honored to be part of a worldwide movement led by the only Communist revolutionaries who had at that time succeeded—and they had done so in a country that was a major player on the world stage.

In retrospect, it may be difficult to understand how anyone could admire a regime headed by a brutal dictator like Joseph Stalin, but what we know about Stalin today was not always clear at the time, and even when it was, it was often downplayed. Thousands of American writers, scholars, journalists, and some government officials, as well as radicals, traveled annually to see the efforts being made by Stalin and his central planners to modernize the Soviet Union. Most praised these efforts and minimized their horrendous effects on Russian peasants. Eight million died in 1932–33 as agriculture was placed under political control or collectivized and grain that would have been used for food and seed was removed from the countryside to feed industrial workers and to export for cash to purchase machinery. American visitors to the Soviet Union glossed over this horrible occurrence largely because they were convinced that modernization was highly desirable and that Russian peasants were hopelessly backward. These views had developed over a long period of time; neither materialized in the wake of the Russian Revolution.

In the late 1930s and 1940s, Stalin unleashed a reign of terror on his alleged enemies, many of whom had been his compatriots in the revolution. In high-profile show trials, "conspirators" confessed to alleged crimes against the government that were so fantastic that "most contemporary observers— communist and non-communist alike—simply could not believe they were *not* true."³ Not only were top leaders openly tried, forced to make false confessions, convicted, and later shot, but also the Russian secret police, the NKVD, eliminated hundreds of thousands of earlier revolutionaries, now deemed Stalin's enemies, and sent millions more to "gulags," forced labor camps in Siberia, where many died from overwork and malnutrition.

While the show trials were designed to be public, the widespread atrocities against millions of other Soviet citizens were not well known. Many rank-and-file Communists may have been unaware of them. Others may have thought, as Junius did when he heard something negative about Stalin, that it was just American propaganda. Without question, most American Communists were focused on the dangers of *fascism* in the 1930s and early 1940s. When Francisco Franco led an insurrection against the republican government of Spain from 1936–39 and German and Italian Fascists rushed to support him, Communists hurried to assist the democratic loyalists. Two-thousand, eight hundred Americans joined the international Abraham Lincoln Brigade, three-fourths of them Communists, and they suffered enormous losses. Over half were killed.

Feeling increasingly threatened by the rising tide of German Nazism, the Comintern started backing away from the rigidity of Third Period Communism when Hitler came to power in 1933. Indeed, Hitler succeeded in part because the powerful Communist Party in Germany refused to work with moderate Social Democrats, and both were destroyed. Aware, too, that the long-predicted revolution was not occurring as the Depression deepened, the Comintern formally reversed its position in 1935, leaving behind Third Period Communism and creating a Popular Front of liberals and leftists against fascism.

Energetic, committed, and highly disciplined CPUSA members had already begun trying to assist poor people as the Depression worsened. The Comintern's formal adoption of the Popular Front coincided with the Second New Deal and Roosevelt's more favorable turn toward unions. Thus, when John L. Lewis led the United Mine Workers out of the AFL in the mid-1930s to form the CIO, he welcomed experienced Communist labor organizers. By the end of World War II, CPUSA organizers and their allies would control unions representing 20 percent of the membership in the CIO, including nine hundred thousand United Electrical Workers. Many people who did not formally join the Party worked in "front" organizations like the American League against War and Fascism.

The bold stance of the Comintern and CPUSA against fascism attracted what would become the Party's "most important constituency: urban, up-

wardly mobile, second-generation American Jews."[4] Given that the CPUSA's
headquarters was in New York and that Party membership there was always
larger than in any other city, it is not surprising that as Gladys sought friendship and a commitment to a larger cause as a teenager, she would find both
in the Young Communist League (YCL). As the Party downplayed sectarianism and worked within the New Deal framework, membership shot up from
about thirty thousand just before the Comintern's declaration of the Popular
Front to eighty-two thousand at the end of 1938, three months before Junius
joined. As early as the summer of 1936, native-born Americans surpassed
immigrants as a majority within the Party.

While Junius learned about radical politics at Abernethy's bookstore in
downtown Chapel Hill and about the CPUSA from northern Jewish students,
Party chapters had been created on campus in the wake of the 1929 Gastonia
strike. The native North Carolinian Paul Crouch recalled, in a statement he
made in the early 1950s after he left the Party, that a question regarding the
status of Communism in the South was raised at the Comintern early in 1928,
the year the Third Period was proclaimed. After returning to the United States
from that meeting, Crouch toured the South and suggested Charlotte, North
Carolina, as the headquarters for the Party in the area. He also recommended
Fred Erwin Beal, a textile worker and labor organizer in New Bedford, Massachusetts, as the most suitable person for organizing in the Charlotte vicinity. Beal, who went to Charlotte in late 1928 or early 1929, selected Gastonia
as the best place to begin. A strike commenced there on April 1, 1929.

In the course of the Gastonia strike, the Party came in contact with liberals
and leftists at the University of North Carolina at Chapel Hill, and by 1930,
a CPUSA unit had been established on campus. In 1934, Crouch, who was
then head of the state Communist Party in Utah, was sent back to his home
state as district organizer, while his wife Sylvia became district organizer for
the YCL. Shortly after they returned to North Carolina, Paul relocated the
district headquarters from Charlotte to Greensboro. In 1937, Paul was succeeded by Bart Logan as Carolina district organizer, and Bart's wife Belle
became the head of the YCL.

In the summer of 1939, Bart showed up at Abernethy's bookstore and
procured Junius's assistance in mimeographing and distributing leaflets in a
CIO (Textile Workers Union) organizing effort under way in the Greensboro
vicinity. While working with Bart, Junius got to know some of the striking
workers, and he was very impressed with the growing confidence and self-
esteem that their participation in the union produced. Already he had been
engaged in interracial activities through his involvement in a student-labor

conference. "'It's working people and Negroes that make the Party tick,'" Bart explained to Junius at their first meeting, and they became the source of Junius's commitment.[5]

In August 1939, just before Germany invaded Poland, the CPUSA was blindsided by the German-Soviet Non-Aggression Pact. In September, top American leaders decided that the war between Germany and the Allied powers was an imperialist war, and the Party should remain neutral. A short time later, the American Party was told to abandon the New Deal. Not surprisingly, membership in the CPUSA and in associations that the Party had helped organize dropped immediately. Only in the CIO, where John L. Lewis shared their antiwar stance, was the Party relatively unscathed.

In June 1941, a little less than two years after the Non-Aggression Pact, Germany invaded Russia. Once again the pendulum swung, and the CPUSA became superpatriotic, backing the Allied powers, which now included the Soviet Union, and supporting the war effort in every way possible once the United States entered in the wake of the attack on Pearl Harbor in December 1941. An estimated 20 percent of the CPUSA members served with the American armed forces in World War II, Junius among them. Once the American Party rejoined the war effort, membership and influence again rose. Wartime conditions and the Party's support were major factors in the success of Local 22 at the Reynolds plant. Still, many liberals gained an underlying distrust of the CPUSA from this experience, and most would not leap forward to demand protection of the civil liberties of CPUSA members once anti-Communism intensified.

Given the gap between Marxist-Leninist doctrine and American realities, most Americans had always been dubious about Communism, and certain aspects of the CPUSA heightened their suspicions once World War II ended and the cold war unfolded. First, the subservience of the CPUSA to the Soviet Union and the constant swings back and forth from political orthodoxy to mass influence made Party members appear untrustworthy. Their situation was not helped by another turn to sectarianism in 1945, when Earl Browder was strongly denounced as a "Marxist revisionist" and replaced by William Foster. This move upset Junius so much that he hitchhiked to New York shortly after returning from military service to talk about his concerns. Though he was never really pleased with the shift toward orthodoxy, a two-hour verbal pounding by the *Daily Worker* editor John Gates persuaded him that his "big bourgeoisie/landed aristocracy background" had falsely led him into revisionism.[6] The membership and influence of the CPUSA did not immediately shrivel, but both had declined considerably by the end of 1948 as a result of Communist opposition to the Marshall Plan and the Party's support for Henry Wallace and the Progressive Party over Harry S. Truman, which incurred the wrath of centrists in the CIO like Phillip Murray.

These abrupt flip-flops could not possibly have been accomplished if the CPUSA had operated democratically; it did not. The insistence by Soviet Communists that all national parties adhere to the Soviet Party line produced a very authoritarian structure. The euphemistic term "democratic central-ism" in fact meant that instructions came from top leaders in New York to lower-level functionaries who presented them to Party members. Lively discussions might ensue at the state and local levels, and apparently did so in North Carolina, but top leaders neither sought nor expected suggestions from the grassroots.

Finally, one of the CPUSA characteristics that was most harmful was its secretiveness. Party members often kept their political affiliation quiet as they toiled in labor unions or participated in other organizations, even during the Popular Front decade from 1935–45.[7] In response to the Red Scare in 1919–20, Communists went underground. Because top leaders like Foster believed that fascists were about to take over in the United States following World War II, the CPUSA implemented an underground plan again in 1951, when the U.S. Supreme Court upheld the convictions of eleven high-level Communist leaders in the first Smith Act trial. At this point, Junius was forced to leave Gladys and his infant daughter Barbara behind, becoming "operational but unavailable" as he traveled circuitous routes from city to city under a system of aliases, conducting furtive meetings with Communist groups in southern states under his jurisdiction as district organizer. This underground opera-tion took an immense toll on everyone who participated, and most who were involved, like Junius, left the party in the mid-1950s, along with thousands of others, in the wake of revelations by Khrushchev about Stalin's crimes and the suppression of the Hungarian revolution by the Soviet Union.

Interestingly, no Communist Party in any other democratic country prac-ticed secrecy to the extent that the American Party did, and it undoubtedly contributed to, as well as resulted from, the intensity of McCarthyism. The main weapon of congressional committees—most significantly, the HUAC and the Senate Internal Security Subcommittee of the Judiciary Committee—was *exposure*. Being called before one of these committees and refusing to "name names" could bring a contempt citation and jail term. Taking the Fifth Amend-ment on the grounds that you might incriminate yourself avoided a jail sen-tence but not public derision. Either could result in ostracism from friends and neighbors and the loss of a job, an apartment, and even an insurance policy.

Adherence to the existing Soviet line, a nondemocratic structure, and secrecy did not cause the repression experienced by the CPUSA and those who
had been affiliated closely or remotely with Communism, but these features
did help its enemies demonize them. Although Senator Joseph McCarthy
garnered public attention from 1950 to 1954, concern about Communists and
mounting opposition to them dated from the Second New Deal in the late
1930s. Employers always worried about radical elements in American society
whenever organizing efforts and strike-waves occurred, and the late 1930s
proved no different. Conservatives like former President Herbert Hoover also
worried about the rise of "big government." Concern about fascists as well
as Communists resulted in the creation of the HUAC in 1938, and in 1940
the Smith Act was passed, making it illegal to participate in a conspiracy to
overthrow the American government with force and violence and to be a
member of an organization that advocated such a conspiracy. By 1940, the
German-Soviet Non-Aggression Pact was in effect, and liberals as well as
conservatives had grown highly suspicious of the CPUSA.

In 1946, Republicans recaptured control of Congress for the first time since
the Depression, and a combination of Republican and southern Democratic
conservatives passed the Taft-Hartley Act, making the closed shop illegal. The
act also required union officials to sign statements saying that they were not
members of the CPUSA. Worried about increasing attacks from conservative
opponents, President Truman instituted a loyalty-security program in 1947
for all federal government employees. While this program had little impact
on Communists, most of whom were not federal employees, it became a major source of anguish for the hundreds of thousands of Americans who had
passed briefly through the Party, one of its front organizations, or an association thought to have been Communist-dominated in the 1930s and 1940s.

Two of the three instruments that would be used to publicize the Communist threat and hound people who had, for however brief a period, been
associated with Communists or alleged Communist organizations were now
in place: congressional investigating committees and the loyalty program.
Two years later, the third instrument was crafted: criminal prosecutions. In
1949, the U.S. Department of Justice prosecuted the CPUSA general secretary Eugene Dennis and ten other high-level leaders under the Smith Act.
(William Foster was not prosecuted because of health-related issues.) All
were found guilty, and in 1951, in a six-to-two decision, the Supreme Court
upheld their convictions.

In the wake of this decision, the Justice Department moved against lower-
level Party officials. Ultimately, almost 150 people throughout the nation were

indicted on Smith Act charges, though all did not go to jail. All but a handful of those prosecuted under the Smith Act were accused of violating the first part of the act—participating in a conspiracy to overthrow the American government through force and violence. Only one person in the country was prosecuted *and imprisoned* for simply being a member of the CPUSA: Junius Irving Scales.

The Federal Bureau of Investigation (FBI) was "the bureaucratic heart of the McCarthy era."[8] It passed along information to congressional investigating committees as the FBI director J. Edgar Hoover deemed appropriate, shaped and executed the loyalty-security program, and provided materials and informants for the Smith Act cases. It leaked information to the press and shared it with state and local officials and with private employers. Under the Responsibilities Program, which the bureau operated from February 1951 to March 1955, it alerted "governors and other 'appropriate authorities'" regarding eight hundred people who were "alleged subversives, more than half of them public school and college teachers."[9] In 1950, the FBI had twelve thousand people in its Security Index; by 1954, this number had grown to twenty-six thousand, and by 1960, the index contained 430,000 files on persons and organizations that were allegedly subversive.

Ironically, the FBI shared two characteristics with the CPUSA: it was highly authoritarian and operated in secrecy. According to McCarthy, "'The FBI is J. Edgar Hoover,'" and even high-level employees who occasionally disagreed with the director squelched their concerns and did as he ordered.[10] The FBI operated within the law and outside it, obtaining information illegally through means such as unauthorized breakins and wiretaps. Without authorization, the bureau had begun compiling lists of alleged dangerous persons in 1939, the year Junius joined the CPUSA. In 1943, Attorney General Frances Biddle ordered Hoover to cease this operation, but the FBI director simply renamed and continued the program until he received congressional approval for it in 1950. Not surprisingly, Junius and Gladys experienced FBI surveillance and harassment, and Junius lost job and educational opportunities at the agency's behest. Especially Junius's mother was enraged by the intrusion of the bureau in their lives.

While the FBI had some accomplishments in the realm of espionage, paradoxically, they contributed to its failures and excesses. In 1950, the FBI agent Robert J. Lamphere broke what was probably the most significant espionage case in U.S. history when he identified Klaus Fuchs, a German-born scientist who had fled to Great Britain in 1933, as the likely head of a spy ring operating in Britain, the United States, and Canada between 1941 and 1943. The information Fuchs passed to Soviet authorities accelerated their nuclear program, but Lamphere's brilliant detective work helped prevent further leaks. Lamphere also pieced together information from Fuchs that led to the arrest of Julius and Ethel Rosenberg in 1950 and their execution in 1953. (Although Ethel was probably not involved in espionage, and the information Julius passed to the Soviet Union was of minor importance, he had orchestrated a number of spies, one of whom was apparently Al Sarant, the "brilliant young engineer" whom Gladys dated when she was working in a defense plant during World War II.) Earlier, in 1945, the FBI had learned that espionage was being conducted by some local Communists in American, British, and Canadian defense plants.

All of these discoveries comported well with what Hoover had long believed, and his deeply held assumption that all spying derived from American Communists led him and his agency to overlook Soviet spies who were recruited on the basis of "money, not principle," once Russian Communists discerned that American Communist spies were being arrested.[11] Additionally, the obsession of Hoover and the FBI with the American Left led them to overlook certain issues that needed the attention of the bureau in the 1950s, such as organized crime. Most significantly, the lengthy pursuit of Communists violated the civil liberties of many people during the surge of McCarthyism in the late 1940s and early 1950s and long afterwards, when the CPUSA had become a small, isolated, powerless sect. Ironically, as the Party was disintegrating in the mid-1950s, the FBI launched its Counterintelligence Program, which would result in the harassment not only of Communists but of many other radicals in the 1960s and early 1970s, including black nationalists, antiwar protestors, Students for a Democratic Society, and other members of the New Left who were prominent when Barbara was "coming of age."

The excesses of the bureau resulted not only from espionage successes and Hoover's personal belief system but also from the advantages these alleged countersubversive activities brought to the FBI. Humiliated in the wake of the National Security Act of 1947, which created the Central Intelligence Agency (CIA), stripped the FBI of its oversight of Latin America, and attempted to place general supervision of American intelligence in the hands of the CIA, Hoover clearly understood that the intensification of McCarthyism helped the bureau recoup. Under the loyalty-security program, the FBI investigated two million federal employees, conducting twenty thousand full investigations. Thus, despite the agency's diminished authority resulting from the 1947 Security Act, the number of FBI agents increased from 3,559 in 1946 to 6,451 in 1952. Unfortunately, by refusing to participate in an intelligence structure headed by the CIA as mandated in the 1947 Security Act, Hoover also contributed to the decentralization of American intelligence that would continue to hamstring American operations through September 11, 2001.[12]

Though authoritarian, secretive, and quite formidable, Hoover did not act in a vacuum. His early participation in the Red Scare of 1919–20 was under the auspices of Attorney General A. Mitchell Palmer, and he shared with Franklin D. Roosevelt a firm belief in a strong executive. Truman, not Hoover, instituted the loyalty-security program, and Congress, not the FBI, set up powerful, public investigating committees. Hoover also had strong public support, which he carefully nurtured, just as he did his support in Congress and with others who shared his views, such as high-level officials in conservative organizations like the American Legion.

A larger concern than the FBI per se might well be the enormous role played by all three branches of the federal government, and by many ordinary Americans, in responding to fear and in generating it. Without question, the times were disconcerting, as Russia exploded an atomic bomb and China became Communist in 1949, while the cold war turned hot in Korea from 1950 to 1953. Not surprisingly, the hysteria at high levels fell on fertile soil at the state and local levels, and all three reinforced each other. Still, no Western country outside the United States experienced anything equivalent to McCarthyism. Why did it occur only in this nation? In pondering the answer to this question, it might help us to ask who benefited and who lost. Why the contrast between the United States and other Western nations?

And perhaps as we ponder how we, and our government, should respond to the "terrorist threat" in the wake of 9/11, it would be useful to remember Roosevelt's advice in the midst of the Great Depression: "All we have to fear is fear itself." This does not mean that we should treat national security casually, but a panicked response in which we forsake our democratic principles and civil liberties is clearly not the solution, for what does it profit a nation if in seeking security, it sacrifices its own soul? "Politics," Barbara learned from her parents, "isn't a party or a name; it isn't ideology or a slogan. It's the way you live every moment of your life." It's about critical "self-awareness" and about "the constant awareness of [and concern for all] other people" within our nation and around the world. Democratic principles and civil liberties are not genetic; to flourish, they must be carefully and thoughtfully nourished, individually and collectively.

SOURCES

Chafe, William H. *Civilities and Civil Rights: Greensboro, North Carolina, and the Black Struggle for Freedom.* New York: Oxford University Press, 1980.

Crouch, Paul. "Brief History of the Communist Movement in North and South Carolina." North Carolina Historical Collection, University of North Carolina at Chapel Hill, post-June 1951.

Draper, Theodore. *American Communism and Soviet Russia, the Formative Period.* New York: Viking Press, 1960.

Hall, Jacquelyn Dowd, et al. *Like a Family: The Making of a Southern Cotton Mill World.* Chapel Hill: University of North Carolina Press, 1987.

Hall, Jacquelyn Dowd, Robert Korstad, and James LeLoudis. "Cotton Mill People: Work, Community, and Protest in the Textile South, 1880–1940." *American Historical Review* 91.2 (April 1986): 245–86.

Haskell, Thomas. "Modernization on Trial." *Modern Intellectual History* 2.2 (August 2005): 235–63.

Jeffreys-Jones, Rhodri. *The FBI: A History.* New Haven: Yale University Press, 2007.

Klehr, Harvey, and John Earl Haynes. *The American Communist Movement: Storming Heaven Itself.* New York: Twayne Publishers, 1992.

Korstad, Robert Rodgers. *Civil Rights Unionism: Tobacco Workers and the Struggle for Democracy in the Mid-Twentieth-Century South.* Chapel Hill: University of North Carolina Press, 2003.

Korstad, Robert Rodgers, and Nelson Lichtenstein. "Opportunities Found and Lost: Labor, Radicals, and the Early Civil Rights Movement." *Journal of American History* 75.3 (December 1988): 786–811.

Potter, Karen. "British McCarthyism." In *North American Spies.* Ed. Rhodri Jeffreys-Jones and Andrew Lownie. Edinburgh: Edinburgh University Press, 1991. 143–57.

Scales, Junius Irving, and Richard Nickson. *Cause at Heart: A Former Communist Remembers.* Athens: University of Georgia Press, 1987.

Schrecker, Ellen. *The Age of McCarthyism: A Brief History with Documents.* 2d ed. Boston: Bedford/St. Martin's Press, 2002.

———. *Many Are the Crimes: McCarthyism in America.* Princeton, N.J.: Princeton University Press, 1999.

Starobin, Joseph R. *American Communism in Crisis, 1943–1957.* Cambridge, Mass.: Harvard University Press, 1972.

Stoney, George, et al. "The Uprising of '34." Videorecording. New York: First Run/Icarus Films, 1995.

PREFACE

1. *Scales v. United States,* 367 U.S. 203 (1961). "In this instance it is an organization which engages in criminal activity, and we can perceive no reason why one who actively and knowingly works in the ranks of that organization, intending to contribute to the success of those specifically illegal activities, should be any more immune from prosecution than he to whom the organization has assigned the task of carrying out the substantive criminal act." For the oral reargument of *Scales v. United States* before the Supreme Court, see <http://www.oyez.org/oyez/resource/case/1069/reargument.mp3>.

2. Theodore Draper, *The Roots of American Communism* (New York: Viking Press, 1957) and *American Communism and Soviet Russia, the Formative Period* (New York: Viking Press, 1960); Irving Howe and Lewis Coser, *The American Communist Party: A Critical History (1919–1957)* (Boston: Beacon Press, 1957); David Shannon, *The Decline of American Communism* (New York: Harcourt, Brace, and Co., 1959); Nathan Glazer, *The Social Basis of American Communism* (New York: Harcourt, Brace, and World, 1961); George Charney, *A Long Journey* (Chicago: Quadrangle Books, 1968); Joseph Starobin, *American Communism in Crisis* (Cambridge, Mass.: Harvard University Press, 1972); Al Richmond, *A Long View from the Left* (Boston: Houghton-Mifflin, 1973).

3. Junius Irving Scales and Richard Nickson, *Cause at Heart: A Former Communist Remembers* (Athens: University of Georgia Press, 1987).

4. "President Discusses War on Terror at National Endowment for Democracy," October 6, 2005, July 1, 2008 <http://www.whitehouse.gov/news/releases/2005/10/print/20051006–3.html>.

5. "Uniting and Strengthening America by Providing Appropriate Tools Required

to Intercept and Obstruct Terrorism (USA PATRIOT ACT) Act of 2001," October 24, 2001, July 1, 2008 <epic.org/privacy/terrorism/hr3162.html.> The act's definition of "domestic terrorism" is so broad that anyone arrested while protesting government policy might be investigated and prosecuted under this definition. _215 of the act allows the FBI to seize "any tangible thing"—books, papers, documents, computer files, records from bookstores and libraries—and it forbids anybody to "disclose to any other person . . . that the Federal Bureau of Investigation has sought or obtained tangible things under this section." Your friends, neighbors, local police, and librarians cannot tell you that you are being investigated or that your records have been taken.

The act permits the government to search your home with no one present and to delay notifying you of the search indefinitely (J213) and amends the Foreign Intelligence Surveillance Act by eliminating the need for the FBI to show "probable cause" before conducting secret searches and surveillance (J218). It also allows law-enforcement agencies to give the CIA sensitive information gathered during investigations without a court order, including wiretaps and Internet surveillance (J203).

6. The public library of Iowa City posted the following notice for its borrowers:

> ATTENTION: Under Section 215 of the USA PATRIOT ACT (Public Law 107–56), records of all books and materials you borrow from this library, and of Internet sites you visit on library computers, may be obtained by federal agents. This law prohibits librarians from informing you if federal agents have obtained records. (Iowa City Public Library, May 28, 2008 <http://www.icpl .org/policies/patriot-act.php>.)

See Joan Airoldi's account of the FBI's demand for a list of all those who had borrowed a biography of Osama bin Laden from the library at Whatcom, Washington. Joan Airoldi, "Librarian's Brush with FBI Shapes Her View of the USA PATRIOT Act," *USA Today,* May 17, 2005, May 29, 2008 <http://pen.org/viewmedia.php/prmMID/755/ prmID/918>.

7. "President Bush signed a secret order in 2002 authorizing the National Security Agency to eavesdrop on U.S. citizens and foreign nationals in the United States, despite previous legal prohibitions against such domestic spying, sources with knowledge of the program said last night." Dan Eggen, "Bush Authorized Domestic Spying," *Washington Post,* December 16, 2005, May 29, 2008 <http://www.washingtonpost .com/wp-dyn/content/article/2005/12/16/AR2005121600021.html>.

The *New York Times* reported that "[t]he volume of information harvested from telecommunication data and voice networks, without court-approved warrants, is much larger than the White House has acknowledged, the officials said. . . . Some officials describe the program as a large data-mining operation." "Spy Agency Mined Vast Data Trove, Officials Report," *New York Times,* December 24, 2005, May 28, 2008 <http://nytimes.com/2005/12/24/politics/24spy.html>.

8. "Counterterrorism agents at the Federal Bureau of Investigation have conducted numerous surveillance and intelligence-gathering operations that involved, at least indirectly, groups active in causes as diverse as the environment, animal cruelty and poverty relief," the *New York Times* reported in December 2005. Eric Lichtblau, "FBI Watched Activist Groups, New Files Show," *New York Times,* December 20, 2005, May 29, 2008 <http://www.nytimes.com/2005/12/20/politics/20fbi.html>.

9. David E. Kaplan, "Nuclear Monitoring of Muslims Done without Search Warrants," *U.S. News and World Report,* December 22, 2005, May 29, 2008, <http://www.usnews.com/usnews/news/articles/nest/051222nest.htm>.

10. *Scales v. United States,* 367 U.S. 203 (1961).

CHAPTER 2

1. On August 23, 1927, Nicola Sacco and Bartolomeo Vanzetti were executed after being convicted of robbing a paymaster and guard at a South Braintree, Massachussets, shoe factory in 1920. Many on the Left believed they were innocent victims of a growing hysteria against anarchists. For more information, see Robert D'Attilio, "Sacco-Vanzetti Case," July 18, 2007, July 1, 2008 <http://www.writing.upenn.edu/~afilreis/88/sacvan.html>, and Court TV's "The Trial of Sacco and Vanzetti," 1998, July 1, 2008 <http://www.courttv.com/archive/greatesttrials/sacco.vanzetti/trial.html>.

2. Nine black teenagers in Scottsboro, Alabama, were falsely accused of the gang rape of two young white women. When the NAACP decided the case was too politically explosive, the Communist Party aggressively defended the Scottsboro Boys. Their trials, convictions, and appeals galvanized the nation.

CHAPTER 3

1. Readers likely know of Bull Connor from the days of the 1963 civil rights demonstrations in Birmingham, Alabama, when he used dogs and water hoses against peaceful marchers.

2. The 1929 strike of the Loray mill in Gastonia, North Carolina, by textile workers was countered by state troopers and ended in violence. When the police attacked the union headquarters, Chief Aderholt was killed.

3. The Molotov-Ribbentrop Pact, or the Nazi-Soviet Non-Agression Pact, was signed by Stalin and Hitler on August 23, 1939. Article 1 of the pact stipulated, "Both High Contracting Parties obligate themselves to desist from any act of violence, any aggressive action, and any attack on each other, either individually or jointly with other Powers." Part of the agreement was secret and recognized "spheres of influence" for both parties, in effect calling for the division of Poland and the border states. On September 1, 1939, Germany invaded Poland. Whatever guarantee of safety Stalin hoped to achieve was shown to be illusory on June 22, 1941, when Germany invaded the Soviet Union.

CHAPTER 5

1. Winston Churchill, "The Sinews of Peace," March 5, 1946: "From Stettin in the Baltic to Trieste in the Adriatic, an iron curtain has descended across the continent." See <http://hpol.org/churchill/> for the complete text of this speech.

2. Clara Zetkin, "Lenin on the Woman Question" (1925), February 29, 2004, July 1, 2008 <http://www.marxists.org/archive/zetkin/1925/lenin/zetkin2.htm>. Zetkin, recounting her conversations with the Russian Communist leader, claimed that Lenin credited women for playing a large role in the Communist victory: "In Petrograd, here in Moscow, and in other cities and industrial centres, proletarian women showed up splendidly during the revolution. We would not have won without them, or hardly." See also V. I. Lenin, *The Emancipation of Women: From the Writings of V. I. Lenin* (New York: International Publishers, 1970).

AFTERWORD

1. Ovid, *Metamorphoses,* trans. Charles Martin (New York: W. W. Norton, 2004), ll. 445-46. All subsequent line numbers will be given parenthetically in the text.

2. Susan Brioli, "*Limits of Dissent* Brings Back Trial of Junius Scales," *Chapel Hill Herald,* May 18, 2001.

HISTORICAL ESSAY

1. Theodore Draper, *American Communism and Soviet Russia, the Formative Period* (New York: Viking Press, 1960), 23.

2. Qtd. in ibid., 409.

3. Ellen Schrecker, *Many Are the Crimes: McCarthyism in America* (Princeton, N.J.: Princeton University Press, 1999), 21.

4. Ibid., 14.

5. Junius Scales and Richard Nickson, *Cause at Heart: A Former Communist Remembers* (Athens: University of Georgia Press, 1987), 69.

6. Ibid., 151.

7. This was the case especially in single-industry towns like Flint, Michigan, or Kannapolis, North Carolina; in a city like New York, the CPUSA operated more openly.

8. Schrecker, *Many Are the Crimes,* 203.

9. Ibid., 212.

10. Qtd. in ibid., 204.

11. Rhodri Jeffreys-Jones, *The FBI: A History* (New Haven, Conn.: Yale University Press, 2007), 154.

12. On FBI-CIA rivalry, see ibid., 142-48; on the search for Communists as a form of job creation, see 160.

■ ■ ■

Mickey Friedman is a filmmaker and writer. He has produced seven films for Blue Hill Films, including *Songs from the Heart: Edith Wharton, Good Things to Life: GE, PCBs, and Our Town,* and *World on Fire: Spc. John Flynn's War in Iraq.* Friedman is also the author of plays about Emily Dickinson and W. E. B. DuBois. He blogs about the climate crisis at http://penguinsunited.com.

Gail Williams O'Brien is professor emerita of history at North Carolina State University. She is the author most recently of *The Color of the Law: Race, Violence, and Justice in the Post–World War II South.*

The University of Illinois Press
is a founding member of the
Association of American University Presses.

Composed in 10.5/13 Adobe Minion Pro
with Berthold City display
by Jim Proefrock
at the University of Illinois Press
Designed by Kelly Gray
Manufactured by Cushing-Malloy, Inc.

University of Illinois Press
1325 South Oak Street
Champaign, IL 61820-6903
www.press.uillinois.edu

A RED FAMILY